Where the Other Half Lives

Where the Other Half Lives

Lower Income Housing in a Neoliberal World

Edited by
SARAH GLYNN

PLUTO PRESS
www.plutobooks.com

First published 2009 by Pluto Press
345 Archway Road, London N6 5AA and
175 Fifth Avenue, New York, NY 10010

www.plutobooks.com

Distributed in the United States of America exclusively by
Palgrave Macmillan, a division of St. Martin's Press LLC,
175 Fifth Avenue, New York, NY 10010

British Library Cataloguing in Publication Data
A catalogue record for this book is available from the British Library

ISBN   978 0 7453 2858 4   Hardback
ISBN   978 0 7453 2857 7   Paperback

Library of Congress Cataloging in Publication Data applied for

This book is printed on paper suitable for recycling and made from
fully managed and sustained forest sources. Logging, pulping and
manufacturing processes are expected to conform to the environmental
standards of the country of origin. The paper may contain up to
70 per cent post-consumer waste.

10   9   8   7   6   5   4   3   2   1

Designed and produced for Pluto Press by
Chase Publishing Services Ltd, Sidmouth, England
Typeset from disk by Stanford DTP Services, Northampton, England
Printed and bound in the European Union by
CPI Antony Rowe, Chippenham and Eastbourne

CONTENTS

LIST OF FIGURES

PREFACE AND ACKNOWLEDGEMENTS

Our title harks back over a hundred years to a book that helped draw attention to the miserable housing conditions of 1890s New York. Jacob Riis's *How the Other Half Lives*[1] was very much a book of its time, and while I hope that this volume may also help shine a light on more neglected areas of housing and society, it does not share Riis's safe, market-based conclusions.[2] In fact, its core message is a repudiation of the revival of a form of political economy that sees everything through the lens of business interests and is bringing about a return to historic levels of inequality.

The idea of putting together an edited collection of studies examining the impact of neoliberalism in different countries germinated in a double session I co-organised, with Michael Punch, at the Institute of British Geographers Conference in the summer of 2006. We called our sessions 'Housing in Crisis'. Today, this phrase screams out of every newspaper, but discussion, like policy, tends to focus on those who are better off, and their ability to get on (or not fall off) the housing ladder. If mention is made of what William Booth, founder of the Salvation Army, called the 'submerged tenth'[3] of the population, this is generally rather vague, and often takes the form of regarding them as a problem, external to the rest of society. The purpose of this book is to begin to restore the analytical balance and turn the spotlight on those who have suffered most from the flip side of neoliberal economics, and who, if not quite another half, certainly make up more than a tenth of modern western society.

My own journey into housing studies owes its origin to an accident of circumstances. In 2004, Dundee's public housing was threatened, first with proposed privatisation, and then, immediately afterwards, with a large-scale programme of demolition: I became involved with tenants, helping to uncover what was happening and campaign against the imposition of decisions that most of those effected did not want. When, in 2005, I was appointed to a lectureship at Edinburgh University, I had the opportunity to investigate more fully the network of forces – local, national and international – that were impacting on what I could see happening around me. I was able to use the understanding I was gaining from my academic research to help dissect what was going on in Dundee, and I was able to use the insights gained from working alongside local tenants to help throw light on more theoretical understandings and dissect the official policy discourses. So my first thanks must go to all my friends in the tenants' movement and other housing campaigns – in the Scottish Tenants' Organisation, Glasgow Save Our Homes, Edinburgh Against Stock Transfer, and here in Dundee – and also down in Liverpool. Thank you for all you have taught me. And thank you to Edinburgh University for enabling me to develop my understanding.

I would like to thank all the contributors who have enabled this project to have the truly international dimension appropriate to a discussion of international economic and social forces. Thank you for contributing your work and ideas, and for your faith in this project. Thank you, too, to all those who took the photographs that make it possible for readers to visualise some of the places and people discussed. (Every effort has been made to contact the photographers to ask for permission to use their work, though in one case we have had no response. Copyright for all photographs remains with the photographer.)

I am, as always, grateful to all those who have read and commented on various parts of the text – to Peter Ambrose, Tom Slater, Simon Glynn, and especially my parents, Ian and Jenifer Glynn. Thank you for your suggestions and encouragement. And thank you to my copy-editor, Jeanne Brady, and to David Castle at Pluto Press for their help, patience and good humour, which have allowed me to survive the inevitable crises and frustrations of pulling together a project of this kind. Finally, I want to thank Tony Cox, who takes most of the credit (or blame) for getting me involved in housing activism, and who, through years of discussion, has helped me develop the understandings and ideas expounded in this book.

Postscript

Housing has rarely been so politically important, but it is a difficult time to write about it as events are changing so quickly. As we were going to press, Leeds City Council announced that the global financial meltdown had necessitated the removal of all private residential development from the regeneration scheme described in Chapter 4, and that they will only be building public housing. Such events, and the confusion that surrounds them, only emphasise the necessity of analysing what has been happening. Leeds City Council still regard this change of plan as a temporary setback and, more broadly, there is enormous resistance to understanding the current crisis in capitalism as a systemic failure, rather than the product of a few greedy bankers. We hope that this book can play a part in explaining what has gone wrong.

We have also just heard that Elizabeth Pascoe, whose fight against the demolition and redevelopment of homes in Liverpool is followed in several of the chapters, has lost her second High Court appeal against the compulsory purchase of her house. Her battle to save her neighbourhood has cost her four years of her life and £40,000 – paid for by taking lodgers. On emerging from the court she emailed fellow campaigners:

> As 'the wider public' know, despite the 'stakeholders' rhetoric'[,] the support I have had has been almost universal both in this city and across the nation ... As I see it the battle is like housework. We don't ever 'get anywhere' but my goodness it is so much worse if we don't try... I have no contingency plan, it was a fight 'to the death' as far as I was concerned. It has to be up to others now, younger than I, to fight for 'the future', against the insanity of mindless consumerism, obviously damaging the planet and society, not just our built heritage, and the sort of hype that tells us what is being done is progress. My conscience is clear. I tried. I fear greatly for what our grandchildren will inherit. Hopefully sense will prevail before it is too late.

The Council's reaction in the *Liverpool Daily Post* not only repeats their old rhetoric, but also shows no acknowledgement of the changed economic climate.

Neoliberalism will not die quietly. Even the growing number of abandoned development sites is only the visible fraction of a much larger wasteland of financial contracts that will take a long time to unravel. And, crucially, at the same time as welcoming the opportunities that are opening up for alternative approaches, we are only too aware of how much needs to be done to rebuild the left so that it can make use of those opportunities. We are also aware of the frightening growth of authoritarian power and forms of social control that are being put into place by those determined to protect the current neoliberal world order.

We cannot predict where we will be a year from now, but we can be sure of the urgency of theoretically-grounded political action.

Sarah Glynn
Dundee
March 2009

Notes

1. Riis, Jacob (1890) *How the Other Half Lives: Studies Among the Tenements of New York* (New York: Charles Scribners and Sons) The book can be viewed on line at <http://www.yale.edu/amstud/inforev/riis/title.html>, or, in a later edition with striking photographs, <http://www.authentichistory.com/postcivilwar/riis/contents.html>.
2. Riis's solution comprises the usual nineteenth-century mix of sanitary law and 5 per cent philanthropy (in the form of model dwellings and Octavia Hill-style improvements, as described in my Chapter 1), though he does allude to the possibility of subsidies and rent regulation. We obviously do not share his racial prejudices either.
3. This is the title of Chapter 2 of Booth's *In Darkest England and the Way Out* (1890) <http://sailor.gutenberg.org/etext96/detwo10.txt>.

INTRODUCTION

Sarah Glynn

For millions of households across the world, the nature of their home is changing as the political orthodoxy of neoliberalism puts into effect some of the most financially significant and socially pervasive mechanisms of deregulation and privatisation. Despite the magnitude of these changes, and an almost endemic sense of housing crisis, at the time that this book was first conceived, housing rarely made newspaper headlines. When it did, the main concern was the seemingly inexorable rise in house prices. Over two years later, a lot has happened, but key underlying concerns remain. Indeed, the almost universal commitment of our ruling elites to the policies of neoliberalism seems, if anything, to have become further entrenched. Just as they have done when administering 'structural adjustment' to developing countries, the promoters of these policies argue that if the neoliberal medicine is failing, the dose is not high enough. Even when they seem to be looking at more Keynesian approaches, these become distorted by a neoliberal lens that confuses the health of finance capital with the health of society. And, whether the housing market is heading skywards or crashing through the floor, those who suffer most as a consequence of these policies continue to be the people at the bottom of the housing pile – the people who are the focus of this book.

To argue that we are going through a housing revolution may no longer seem remarkable, but although what have become known as the 'subprime crisis' and the consequent 'credit crunch' have demonstrated the significant role of housing in the wider economy, there has so far been little attempt to understand what is happening to housing as part of the wider critical debate on neoliberalism.

1

Work in housing studies tends to focus on policy detail, and have only limited engagement with broader economic forces. Studies of neoliberal globalisation tend to avoid the complexities of housing policy. There have been exceptions, notably in work on gentrification, but even here it has been argued that critical perspectives are in decline, and studies of the impacts of gentrifying developments on those they displace are notable by their absence.[1]

The aim of this book, then, is to put housing into the heart of critical economic and political debate. In doing so, we hope to make a distinct contribution to the theoretical literature in comparative housing studies, and also to reach people who might not normally look at the academic housing studies literature – housing activists and others who want to know what exactly neoliberalism is and how it is affecting us all.

That homes are for living in should go without saying – and access to adequate housing is internationally recognised as a human right.[2] However, this basic function is increasingly being put a poor second to that of generating profit. For developers, this has always been the case, but the investment function of housing is directly or indirectly dominating the lives of the majority of households in a way it has not done since before the First World War. This is a situation that has been deliberately encouraged by nearly three decades of government obsession with homeownership, and exacerbated by the liberalisation of mortgage lending, which has enabled house prices to rise out of all proportion to incomes. At the same time as more and more people are being pushed into house purchase and debt, social housing stocks built up over decades are being destroyed in the zealous pursuit of privatisation, and to make way for more profitable development.

The long housing boom proved a very efficient mechanism for enlarging existing disparities of wealth. Falling house prices can affect all investors who have misjudged the market, but those for whom financial loss most often translates into tragedy are those with no financial reserves – such as families encouraged into unmanageable debt, or households evicted because their landlord needs to sell up – and they are being forced to compete in an increasingly deregulated rental market.

While government policies have generated a situation of endemic housing crisis, government responses have been conceived within a narrow market-centred framework and have served to fuel further marketisation. With social housing limited to those in most need, the poverty of its tenants has been used as a reason for further demolitions; the problems facing those desperate to get on the housing ladder due to lack of other options have been used to justify subsidies that put even more money into an overheated system; and now that boom has turned to bust, attitudes and policies remain fundamentally unchanged. Regardless of growing job insecurities, new schemes are being promoted to encourage more people into forms of homeownership for the sake of the housing market (even while earlier schemes remain empty and unsold), and housing associations are being seen as tools for bailing out private developers, despite serious questions over the quality or suitability of speculative housing stock for social housing.

These are just some examples. There are plenty more in the pages that follow, which have been designed to give both an authentic picture and a theoretical understanding of what is happening to housing under the neoliberal hegemony. By setting detailed multinational case studies into an extended analytical framework, we hope to weave together an analysis on three different levels. We hope to link the experiences of tenants and residents, the changes in housing policy that produce those experiences, and the global political and economic forces that drive those policy changes. Everyday experiences will be put into socio-political context, and political forces will be illuminated through their material consequences. This provides the essential foundation for the fight-back that we begin to address in the latter part of the book.

In order to understand what is happening today, with the dismantling of the Keynesian welfare state, it makes sense to begin by looking at the nature of what is being lost. The book starts with a brief overview of developments in twentieth-century housing policy, and of the forces that impelled them into being. It next examines, at a general level, how current developments in housing fit into the neoliberal project for the restoration of elite power (as theorised by writers such as Duménil and Lévy[3]), and how policies that favour the rich have come to be so widely regarded as the way of the world. Then, before going on to the more detailed case studies, it looks at one of the primary mechanisms used to implement neoliberal policy: large-scale, state-sponsored gentrification, often presented as regeneration.

The case studies have been chosen to illustrate a wide range of national housing systems and housing situations, and so show how pervasive the forces of neoliberalism have become. Each chapter includes enough policy background to place the study in context,

Figure I.1 This and the other drawings in this book were done by me for use in various housing campaigns – Sarah Glynn.

but we do not pretend that this book can give a comprehensive picture of either the different ways that housing has been affected or different national policies. Sea changes in housing patterns are taking place throughout the world – and often, as in China, with even more devastating affects than those described here – but we have chosen not to attempt any sort of encyclopaedic survey or to get bogged down in different development histories. Instead, the book concentrates on a representative group of older industrialised countries from north-west Europe and the Anglophone nations. These share many basic characteristics, and, significantly, are frequently used as models of neoliberalism,[4] making them of universal relevance.

Finally, the book will move beyond an analysis of the impacts of neoliberalism to examine the possibilities for resistance and argue for a more equitable future.

Notes

1. Slater, Tom (2006) 'The Eviction of Critical Perspectives from Gentrification Research', *International Journal of Urban and Regional Research* 30(4): 737–57.
2. Office of the High Commissioner for Human Rights, Fact Sheet 21 'The Human Right to Adequate Housing' <http://www.unhchr.ch/html/menu6/2/fs21.htm>.
3. Duménil, Gérard and Dominique Lévy (2005) 'The Neoliberal (Counter-) Revolution', in Alfredo Saad-Filho and Deborah Johnston (eds) *Neoliberalism: A Critical Reader* (London: Pluto Press).
4. Especially in Russia and the eastern European countries that have made the transformation to capitalism in the last two decades.

Part I

Background: When 'There is No Such Thing as Society'[*]

* Margaret Thatcher, Interview with *Woman's Own* magazine, 23 September 1987 <http://www.margaretthatcher.org/speeches/displaydocument. asp?docid=106689> [accessed 26 November 2008].

Part I

Background: When There Is No
Such Thing as Sorcery

1

IF PUBLIC HOUSING DIDN'T EXIST, WE'D HAVE TO INVENT IT

Sarah Glynn

A housing crisis is not a natural phenomenon. Housing systems are man-made, and can be remade. The argument in this book is that current developments in housing must be understood as part of a long-planned and deliberate imposition of neoliberal economic systems that are spreading – albeit unevenly and with local variations – across the globe. Neoliberalism, as the name implies, is based on a return to the ideas of free-market liberalism that predominated before the development of the welfare state and the Keynesian mixed economy. The history of this earlier period provides a stark warning for those who would rely on neoliberal economics to provide adequate housing. In fact, the same social-democratic welfare systems that are currently under attack by the forces of marketisation have their origins in attempts to rescue the casualties of that previous period of free-market capitalism.

Before starting to look at what is happening as those systems are dismantled, it is important to understand why and how they developed in the first place. Significantly, even states, such as the US, that have always placed strong emphasis on free-market values, found it necessary for government to intervene to some extent in the housing market so as to provide a safety net of a minimal amount of subsidised rented housing. The nature and form of housing market intervention differs widely from country to country. All that can be done here in this brief introduction is give some idea of the kind of systems that emerged – and that are now facing different forms of marketisation and privatisation.

But first this chapter will look at why they emerged, and it will do this by focusing on the historical example with which the editor is most familiar.

British housing policy cannot claim to be any sort of norm or model, though the forces that created it are similar to those found elsewhere. But Britain was in the vanguard of industrial urbanisation, and Thatcherite and post-Thatcherite Britain has become a vanguard of neoliberalism, so it is not inappropriate to concentrate some attention on the developments in British housing that happened in between. Crucial to those developments were debates about state intervention in the market and a reluctance to interfere in private property. Similar debates were occurring across the industrialised nations and provide ominous prefigurations of arguments today.

Nineteenth-century Capitalist Paternalism

By the mid nineteenth century, the overcrowding and squalor of Britain's rapidly expanding industrial towns and cities was being recorded in numerous concerned reports and sensational newspaper articles. But under *laissez-faire* capitalism, it was not believed to be right or necessary by the ruling classes to intervene in the housing market. Until after the First World War, nine out of ten households rented their home from private landlords. It was not thought to be the role of government to unbalance the relationship between landlord and tenant, while charity was believed to encourage dependency and fecklessness.

Poverty was generally seen as part of the natural order of society, but there were limits to what was regarded as acceptable, both morally and practically. Victorian society made an important distinction between the deserving and undeserving poor, with ideas and practices that appear to be seeing a revival in policies such as the US system of Workfare and its derivatives.[1] It was believed that those who were better off had a duty to help those who were unable to help themselves – such as the sick and aged – and to keep them from total destitution. And those who, through no fault of their own, had fallen on hard times should be given help to help themselves and be shown the correct path by their well-heeled moral superiors. But many, especially among the very poorest, were believed to be responsible for their own fates and little better than criminals. An important step in the argument for better housing was to stop blaming slum housing on those who lived in it.

At a practical level, though, slum housing affected everyone. There was a fear that close proximity to the lowest layers would pull down the 'deserving poor', and that slums provided a haven and hiding place for criminals. Importantly, diseases that thrived in the slums did not respect the slum's borders. Improved housing would help maintain a healthier, more efficient work-force. It would also help to keep calm potential sources of unrest. The destruction of working-class housing in Paris was regarded as contributing to the 1848 revolutions,[2] and that same year Lord Shaftesbury claimed, after a meeting of the housing association that he co-founded, 'this is the way to stifle Chartism'.[3]

While the mass of housing provision was left to the market, a few pioneering groups attempted to temper market forces through the agency of housing associations, or the establishment of model villages. These were, however, still commercial ventures that were expected to bring in a certain degree of profit. Model villages, which included homes for sale as well as for rent, were the product of the benign despotism of certain leading industrialists. The villages were an attempt to realise a paternalistic vision of an ideal, and highly controlled, social order: a vision of a community of healthy, happy workers based around their employment. Housing associations were generally funded by wealthy shareholders and aimed to demonstrate by example that it was possible to build good-quality homes for working-class tenants and still bring in a comfortable 4 or 5 per cent return on the initial investment.[4]

Both model villages and housing associations were aimed at better-off workers, and this approach was defended by the argument that improvements would filter down as the workers vacated their old homes. The idea of benefits filtering down is one that has often been used by proponents of the free market ('trickle-down economics'), but with little evidence of success. Despite a growing population, better homes were left unlet where people simply could not afford the rent, and it has been estimated that in 1914 15 per cent of households were sharing with others and unable to afford their own home, while 4 per cent of homes were empty.[5]

Octavia Hill used piecemeal improvements to provide better homes for a poorer layer and avoid the wholesale displacements of slum clearance, but physical standards were lower and the level of paternalistic control considerably higher. She herself described her method as a 'tremendous despotism' and referred to ruling over her tenants.[6] Together with a team of women workers trained in her methods, she worked for some of the more philanthropic owners of existing slum property to manage and improve it and yet still bring in a 5 per cent profit. This was done through personal involvement with the tenants, to 'rouse habits of industry and effort'.[7] Those who responded were rewarded with improvements to their homes, while others whose behaviour fell short of the required standards, or who did not pay the rent, were evicted. Hill was highly and vocally critical of the idea of state subsidy and her elevation of the doctrine of self-help has found echoes in current criticisms of the welfare state. It is also possible to draw parallels between Victorian ideas about the civilising influence of middle-class example, which influenced Hill and also the contemporary settlement movement, and arguments now being put forward in support of mixed-income communities (of which more in Chapter 3). Although the fame of Hill's enterprises was international, their actual influence was very limited and took no account of the scale of the housing problem. As A.S. Wohl concluded:

> ... her contribution was, after all, a negative one. Traditional philanthropic capitalism and individualistic efforts had to be proved inadequate and wanting before late Victorians could comfortably accept the necessity for state or municipal socialism, and the need for the council flat.[8]

The Health of the Nation

Nineteenth-century housing legislation was largely prompted by concerns over public health, and in 1875, local authorities were given the power to demolish whole areas deemed unfit for human habitation. Reconstruction was usually carried out by the housing associations, but was far from adequate; and with compensation to owners based on rent receipts, the worst, rack-renting landlords were rewarded at huge public expense. Moreover, for every slum cleared, overcrowding increased in the surrounding areas. The Public Health Act of the same year gave rise to new local by-laws on the design and layout of new buildings – but extra building costs were reflected in higher rents. Ten years later, the Royal Commission on the Housing of the Working Classes, set up in response to appalling conditions in London, reached the important conclusion that the problem was the acute shortage of affordable housing: slum dwellers could not generally be blamed for the conditions in which they lived, and the state had a duty to intervene to overcome what was seen as a temporary housing shortage.

Besides the immediately practical drivers for reform already noted, developments at this time need to be understood in the context of a growing labour movement. Workers were gaining a new political weight, which was also reflected in an extension of the election franchise, and politicians were being forced to listen to their concerns. The Paris Commune of 1871 (like the later Bolshevik revolution) was seen as a warning of the alternative.[9]

Although there are earlier examples of local authority housing, the 1890 Housing Act is seen as a milestone in British housing legislation, as it made it easier for the authorities to build and manage housing themselves, resulting in around 28,000 'council houses' by 1914. These were still expected to make a profit – if only a small one – after servicing the heavy debt on the borrowed funds used for their construction. So, once again they could not house the poorest people (including most of those displaced by slum clearance) and relied on filtering down. There was, however, scope for local authorities to subsidise their homes using their own income, which was raised through the rates – a local property tax. This was found increasingly necessary, accounting for a quarter of the running costs of British local authority houses by 1916–17.[10]

Interfering with the Sanctity of the Market

While some degree of interference in the market had become accepted as unavoidable, the reluctance with which this was done was made clear by Lord Salisbury, under whose prime ministership the 1890 Act was passed. He thought that the local authorities should be given the chance to try and build cheaper dwellings than the housing associations, but that for them to get involved in the 'general provision of cottages' would only be justified where 'some exceptional obstacle has arrested the action of private enterprise'. He was also very wary of 'rents which did not represent the real cost' of building, which he felt would drive everyone else out of the market.[11]

The history of the gradual acceptance of the need for government intervention, and eventually, after the First World War, of government subsidy, is worth revisiting because so many of the old arguments against interfering in the market have never really gone away and are being revived today. It is a history that is highly politicised because it has impacts for the future of state-subsidised housing. Debate centres on the significance of the special circumstances of the war, and there are also arguments, which will be taken up in Chapter 13, about the role played by campaigns organised by tenants and progressive politicians and by the fear among the political elites of more radical political demands. The crucial question is whether poor housing was inevitable under a capitalist economy, so that state subsidy was a necessity if people were ever to have decent homes.

By 1914, the acute shortage of affordable housing for those on low incomes, and the poor quality of much of the housing that did exist, had long been acknowledged. Private investment was not producing the necessary homes, and councils who built under the 1890 Act were increasingly having to subsidise them themselves out of the rates.

Campaigns for state intervention were supported by socialist groups, but many Conservatives also welcomed proposals that would take a burden off the rates, and there was also support by some Liberals, although they generally preferred to concentrate on land reform. Arguments for government to take a role in improving housing did not have to depend on appeals to morality. There were good economic and political reasons for promoting a healthy work-force and a fit source of military recruits, and everyone benefited from a healthier city.

But the political elites were also responding to pressure from below, and this will be examined in greater detail in Chapter 13. The power of tenant protests lay not just in their immediate impact, but also in the fact that they were supported by an increasingly powerful labour movement, and it was hoped that by meeting some working-class demands through limited reforms within the existing system, support for a more revolutionary approach would be weakened. Such arguments were hugely strengthened by the Bolshevik revolution in 1917 and by the unrest that followed the war. In the wake of the 1915 rent strikes, the Industrial Unrest Commission of 1917 argued that poor housing was an important source of tension, and the Royal Commission on the Housing of the Industrial Population of Scotland, completed that same year, concluded: 'Before the war, the demand for better housing had become articulate; to-day, after three years of war, it is too insistent to be safely disregarded any longer.' In fact, the influential Scottish Royal Commission regarded housing conditions as a 'legitimate cause of social unrest', and even – rather patronisingly, as though admiring an example of self-help – recorded their 'satisfaction' that workers were refusing to tolerate those conditions.[12]

We cannot of course know if or when state-funded housing would have been introduced without the First World War, but many already thought it was necessary and there was considerable support in important places. The war is generally thought to have provided a catalyst, reinforcing all the conditions that had made this seem the solution before, and providing examples of state intervention. Although the Scottish Royal Commission was completed in 1917, it had been set up in 1912 and was careful to show the weight of pre-war evidence for the 'inability of private enterprise to provide houses for the working class'. 'Doubtless the climax came with the war'; they argued, 'the failure, however, had become manifest long before the war'.[13]

For the four war years, almost nothing had been built and maintenance had been minimal. Government needed to promise the 5 million returning soldiers and the similar numbers who had worked in the wartime factories that their sacrifices were not in vain. They knew the importance of promising to provide decent housing, and only the day after armistice Lloyd George called an election with the promise to provide 'habitations fit for the heroes who have won the war'[14] – which became shortened to the rather more snappy sound-bite 'homes fit for heroes'.

From 1917, housing had been at the centre of plans for post-war social policy, and there had been increasing realisation of the need for government involvement. The government responded to the Industrial Unrest Commission with an, admittedly vague, promise of financial assistance for local authority house building,[15] and the Scottish Royal Commission, quoted above, concluded that

> ... the disorganisation flowing from the war makes an immediate revival of uncontrolled commercial enterprise on an adequate scale impossible. There is, in our view, only one alternative: the State itself, through the Local Authorities, is alone in a position to assume responsibility.[16]

They argued that the position should be reviewed again seven years after the end of the war, but that the scale of the problem allowed no alternatives. Although a minority report disputed giving local authorities a major role, this became official British Ministry of Reconstruction policy.

During the war two key events moved the government closer to a concerted policy of intervention in housing. One was the government-funded building of homes for war workers. Wartime conditions developed ideas and practices of central planning and government involvement more generally, and, given the ongoing debates, it was not surprising to find the government taking an active part in house building when the demands of war made this necessary and urgent.

The resulting housing estates provided physical evidence of the possibilities for state-financed housing, but the other, more important, event was the rent control legislation introduced as an *ad hoc* measure in response to the massive rent strikes of 1915 (examined in more detail in Chapter 13). This legislation constituted a fundamental attack on the *laissez-faire* housing market and proved to have lasting significance. The emergency Act froze all rents of properties below a certain value to their pre-war levels. It was supposed to be lifted six months after the end of the war, but this would have been politically impossible as rents would have rocketed to take advantage of the shortages, and rent control of various sorts continued to be renewed.

The existence of rent control, and the impossibility of removing it, was, and still is, frequently blamed for the failure of the private market to build more houses after the war. The contention is that with rents so low it was not worth private investors investing in new homes, but that until there were more homes, it was necessary to keep rent control to prevent profiteering. Consequently, it was argued, state funding was needed to build up the housing stocks. Rent control is thus seen to lead to the necessity of state-funded housing, allowing some to suggest that without any state interference private markets could have provided the homes required. However, it was not that simple.[17] Markets were failing to provide needed homes before the war, and afterwards, high building costs and an expectation that prices would fall did not favour post-war investment in housing. Besides which, rent control was itself an important part of housing policy that had been campaigned for well before the war.

State-subsidised Working-class Housing

The result of all this was the 1919 Housing Act, which, crucially, brought in government subsidy and made it compulsory for local authorities to assess their housing needs and make plans for the necessary new dwellings. There was an emphasis on quality: the new homes had to conform to minimum standards and there were model plans produced by the Ministry of Health. Although there was central state funding and local government control, money had to be borrowed and materials and labour bought on the private markets. (See Figure 1.1.)

Figure 1.1   The Logie Estate, Dundee, the first state-funded council housing in Scotland (*photo: Sarah Glynn*).

The understanding was that the need for state funding was temporary; the Act would provide for half a million homes, after which it would be possible to return to market forces (including uncontrolled rents). But the housing problem was not so easily solved. Costs were also higher and construction slower than anticipated, and with the threat of revolution receding, the programme was wound down in 1921. The Conservative government that replaced the post-war coalition continued to subsidise housing, but their 1923 Housing Act gave priority to private developers, who received help for nearly six times as many houses as did the local authorities. It was left to the first Labour government, which took power for nine months in 1924, to instigate a major programme of council-house building. The minister in charge, Health Minister John Wheatley, had played a significant role in the Glasgow rent strikes and was a strong supporter of municipal socialism.

Councils were now succeeding in building good-value, good-quality houses, but they were not benefiting those most in need. Rents were still high and tenants – who had to show that they could afford to pay – were predominantly from the relatively financially comfortable, skilled working class. The division of working-class interests has long been recognised, with much debate centred on the idea (first articulated by Engels in 1885) of a privileged labour aristocracy able to negotiate for themselves a comfortable place within capitalism.[18] The craft-based unions had learnt to live with the system rather than try and change it, and proposals from the unions to the 1885 Royal Commission specified different grades of working-class housing, including more homeownership.[19] In labour politics, such attitudes began to be cut across with the organisation of the unskilled in the New Unionism of the late 1880s, but housing activists were generally from the skilled section of the class and were focused on its interests. In arguing for state-subsidised housing in 1915, the Workmen's National Housing Council insisted that schemes should not be built 'down to the poverty standard of the ill-paid and unorganised classes', but be generously laid out and supplied with modern services.[20] Once again, the poorest would have to rely on filtering down – though if such superior houses had been made available to them this would not only have required much higher subsidies but would also have been seen as grossly unfair by those the poor had overtaken.

In 1930, the second Labour government brought in an additional scheme to rehouse people living in the slums. Local authorities were required to produce a five-year plan for slum clearance and the rehousing of those displaced, and government subsidies were made available based on the numbers rehoused. This two-tier system introduced an element of class segregation and stigmatisation into council housing. For slum-clearance housing, emphasis was on the quantity of homes built rather than their quality, and competing claims for quality or quantity under a restricted budget were to characterise council housing history. In 1933, under the 'National' (coalition) Government, earlier types of subsidy were ended, and for the rest of the inter-war period the only council housing built was in slum-clearance schemes. There was also pressure to make that housing smaller and cheaper. At the same time, the lack of new 'general needs' housing forced those who were better off, and experiencing a rise in real wages, to turn instead to the private developers. Pro-business policies had nurtured a fast-growing house-building industry, and while rent control had made it no longer worthwhile to build for rent, growing numbers of households were taking out mortgages from the rapidly expanding building societies to buy their own home.

The Keynesian Welfare State

By the time war broke out again in 1939, which put almost all building plans on hold, local authorities had built 1 million homes, which made up about 10 per cent of the total British housing stock. But for those interested in council-house provision, the most significant developments took place in the first phase of post-Second World War reconstruction, when Aneurin (or Nye) Bevan, Minister of Health in the newly elected Labour government, offered a glimpse of a socialist vision of housing as a universal public service (like the health service). Briefly, it seemed that this vision might become a reality.

The Second World War left Britain with an even greater housing crisis than the First. And, as before, plans for reconstruction started well before the end of the war, and an important concern among politicians of all parties was to provide sufficient improvements to prevent discontent that might threaten the existing political system.

The labour movement had grown in strength during the 1930s, and certain sections saw in the Soviet Union a model for an alternative form of society. It was in the interests of the political establishment to show that improvements could be achieved within the existing capitalist system. There was a widespread belief that the society that emerged after the war should be a better and fairer one. The 1941 New Year issue of the *Picture Post* both demonstrated and contributed to that view.[21] Arguing that a new planned Britain was an essential war aim, it commissioned important thinkers to address issues such as 'work for all', social security and a state medical service. Houses would be designed for the needs of the housewife (who it was assumed would not work), and Maxwell Fry envisaged a wholesale utopian (and what would now be considered rather brutal) replanning of Britain's towns and cities. The following year, the Beveridge Report, which laid the basis for the welfare state, was compiled for the wartime coalition government, and some of the first steps towards that welfare state were carried out before the post-war election. The evolution of coalition policy was always a contested process, but could not ignore the huge public appetite for reform.[22] In 1945, Labour was elected with a large majority indicating a general move to the political left – and the new Parliament also included two Communist MPs. In addition, the threat of more revolutionary demands was not far away, and British troops had themselves helped crush revolution in Greece. Against this background, and with the experience of six years of wartime central planning, there was cross-party consensus on the need for government intervention to mitigate the worst inequalities of capitalism, though the extent of that intervention and how long it would last remained to be debated.

The Labour government did not challenge the primacy of capitalism, but believed in a Keynesian economic programme in which government intervention could be used to redistribute resources and make the system more equal (and consequently more efficient). In the new welfare state, government would use its powers to levy taxes in order to fund basic services such as health care, education, unemployment benefit and pensions for everyone as they needed them. In other words, these were universal services. Some of these services already existed in a less developed form, but in areas such as education the changes were comprehensive, and the overall scale of what was happening across so many different areas brought fundamental change to British society.

There was no single clear vision for the position of housing in all this. For those on the left, and most notably Nye Bevan, the minister responsible, housing too was regarded in some ways as something that should approach a universal service. Bevan's plans for post-war reconstruction concentrated on good-quality homes built by the local authorities that would be rented by people in different walks of life and of different ages in mixed communities. Famously, his 1949 Housing Act removed the description of public housing as 'for the working classes'. However, rents were still too high for those worst off, and, importantly, a thoroughgoing nationalisation of housing was never attempted – either for new building or existing homes.[23]

What Bevan did do was arrange that the local authorities built four-fifths of the country's required new homes. In this period of shortages and rationing, private developers wanting to build houses for sale had to get a permit from their local authority, and these were strictly limited. Bevan argued that mass-built public housing enabled overall planning, so homes could be constructed more efficiently and meet actual needs; and that, unlike any form of housing association, local authorities were democratically responsible to their tenants. He also raised subsidies significantly, arranged for low-cost government loans, and fought to ensure that standards were not compromised. Cuts in standards he regarded as short-sighted, cowardly and cruel. 'After all,' he explained, 'people will have to live in and among these houses for many years.'[24]

The high standards of the homes produced at this time are still recognised, but the post-war Labour government was not able to produce the number of houses needed – which the Conservative opposition lost no opportunity to point out. The scale of the housing problem was immense – as highlighted by the mass squats that took place in 1946 – and demand was increasing with record numbers of marriages and births. Initially, the constraints restricting building were mainly beyond government control, but up until the financial crisis of 1947, Bevan's policy had shown itself capable of expanding to produce the houses needed.[25] In that year, slower than expected economic recovery produced a balance-of-payments crisis that was exacerbated by the falling real value of American loans. Cuts had to be made, and in the ensuing Cabinet battle, investment in housing lost out to the demands of foreign policy and defence. The building programme was forced to slow down. Bevan himself resigned from government in 1951 (over health service charges) and his replacement made the first cuts to standards too, even before Labour was voted out of office.

The Conservatives had campaigned on the housing crisis and the new Housing Minister, Harold Macmillan, saw his first task as beating Labour at the numbers game – subsidies were raised, standards were lowered and restrictions on private developers were eased. But once his stated goal had been reached, government could, in the words of the 1953 White Paper, 'promote, by all possible means, the building of houses for owner-occupation'.[26] Anthony Eden, then deputy leader of the Conservatives, had raised the vision of a 'nation-wide property-owning democracy'[27] in 1946, and although public housing was still regarded as necessary, private development was seen as the main source of new homes.

Housing had not been recognised as a fundamental and integral part of the welfare-state system of universal service. Instead it was regarded, in Cole and Furbey's words, as 'an expedient service, intermittently making good the shortcomings of the private market'.[28] Peter Malpass has argued that this contingent understanding of state intervention in housing has been there since the introduction of state subsidies: that council housing always played a supporting role to the private sector by supplying the needs that were not met by the market, securing the health of the construction industry, and withdrawing from more mainstream roles when they became more profitable (as in the retreat from general-needs housing in the 1930s and 1950s).[29] According to this argument, welfare-state rhetoric became retro-fitted onto the existing pattern as a sort of 'ideological overlay'. This provides an important reminder of the continuities of capitalism, but it risks obscuring the major ideological debates that lay behind policy compromises, and belittling the very significant variations in outcome produced by the resulting differences in emphasis.

Malpass goes on to be extremely critical of recent changes in housing policy, but arguments that stress continuity can be taken up by those deliberately seeking to depoliticise the policy debate. Depoliticisation as symptom and tool of neoliberalism has a long pedigree. A report on council housing produced in 1976 by the decidedly left-wing Community Development Project warned against the then new conventional wisdom that housing policy should be an administrative issue removed from politics. They contrasted 'the political struggle of the working class to establish a socialised form of housing which recognised the right of everyone to a decent house at a reasonable cost' with a political right who 'have always tried to contain development of council housing by narrowly defining the purposes for which it is to be provided, and creating an alternative to it more closely related to their interests'.[30]

Ideological struggle is not, of course, simply represented by party differences, and when it comes to housing, some of the biggest debates have taken place *within* the Labour Party. More radical proposals that never made it into policy include the public ownership of the construction industry (supported by the 1944 party conference) and the municipalisation of the private rented sector (proposed in 1949 and later adopted as party policy for a period while they were in opposition). Even during the period of welfare-state consensus, Conservative governments attempted to reduce distinctions between public and private housing. They tried to tie council housing closer to the market by forcing up rents and making councils borrow on the open market (which burdened them with unmanageable interest payments). The Labour governments of the 1960s and 1970s did not deliberately set out to make council housing a less attractive option; however, it was allowed to lose out to budget pressures. On top of this, a significant proportion of the electorate, including a large part of the better-off working class, had taken advantage of the Conservatives pro-private ownership policies. It had become politically expedient for the Labour leadership to adopt policies that favoured owner-occupiers.

For almost three decades, as council housing increased its share of the British housing stock – peaking at just under a third in 1979 – it was being progressively confirmed by governments of both parties as a residual tenure for those who could not afford to own their own home. There were significantly different levels of emphasis and investment, but both Conservative and Labour governments came to regard owner-occupation as somehow 'normal' and 'natural'.[31]

Naturalising Homeownership

There is, of course, nothing inherently 'natural' about homeownership. Well-off Swedes, Germans, Swiss and New Yorkers still seem to exist very comfortably in rented housing; and surveys that show large preferences for ownership need to be treated with caution. They may well indicate a genuine preference, but there are simply too many different variables that can be understood to be included in the concept of ownership. Is what is important ownership *per se*, or are people more concerned with security of tenure, freedom to personalise their home, avoiding high rents, not missing out on the financial gains to be made from rising house prices, social status, or any combination of these? Would views be different if rented housing was generally of better quality and value and with greater security of tenure? Jim Kemeny has argued that in Sweden, before homeownership was allowed to become financially advantageous, middle- and upper-income households showed little more propensity for ownership than did manual workers;[32] while Forrest and colleagues point out that

> ... in the not so distant past in Britain discussion of housing tenure was relatively unimportant. Moreover, many of the dimensions of housing which are now inextricably associated with home ownership (e.g. independence, privacy, freedom, a garden) were seen [in the 1940s] as quite separate and no more an inherent feature of owning than of renting.[33]

People opt for homeownership because so many factors have been stacked in its favour. At the same time as council housing has been allowed – or even actively encouraged – to become less attractive through financial attrition, owner-occupation has been actively promoted with significant financial incentives (to the benefit of a whole range of commercial and professional interests concerned with all aspects of property development). Incentives for ownership have included mortgage interest tax relief, government aid to building societies, exemption from capital gains tax on house sales, and improvement grants. Aspiration to ownership is not an independent factor but a result of policy decisions. (And ownership is no guarantee of good housing conditions, especially for those with no money for repair and maintenance.) Homeownership appears normal because it has become the tenure of the majority of the population, with renting being disproportionately concentrated among lower income groups; however there is no such bias in favour of owning business premises, although the desire to do this might seem equally natural.

By 1979 and the election of Margaret Thatcher, the majority of British housing was divided into two main tenures – privately owned homes and council housing – with council housing increasingly stigmatised. Even before the 1980s, and its thoroughgoing 'residualisation' as poor housing for poor people, council housing was regarded as a residual tenancy for those who could not afford to own their own home. But there was nothing inevitable about this, and there is no intrinsic reason why public housing should not be a tenure of choice.

Opportunities Won and Wasted

Even despite restricted investment and the many problems of poorly designed and run-down estates that were already so evident in the 1970s, most council houses provided good homes. Discussion of council housing in the media and in research focused on the 'problem estate'. But, as Alison Ravetz reminds us:

> In 1980 only some 5 per cent of the total were recognized as 'problem estates', and it must be assumed that throughout most of its history the bulk of council housing functioned as the housing managers would have it, to give tenants 'the quiet enjoyment of their own homes.'[34]

Certain estates had a bad name, but many people were glad to be council tenants. For the majority of working-class people – especially in Scotland with over half its homes in the public sector – it was being a council tenant that was normal; which of course did not mean that tenants did not protest about the way the system was run.[35]

Council housing has suffered from three connected problems. It was often poorly designed (with an over-reliance on inadequately tested systems building) and built to a cut-price budget, it was generally poorly managed by a distant and unwieldy bureaucracy, and it was increasingly regarded as intrinsically less desirable. There are, of course, examples of good design. These are often more low key than the iconic 'failures', though Newcastle's Byker Estate, an innovative design developed with tenant involvement, is a city landmark.[36] There are also successful examples of tenant involvement in local management, notably in the now disbanded 'tenant management co-ops' that operated under Glasgow City Council before it got rid of its housing stock.[37] However, even where there is good design and the possibility of more sensitive management, this does not necessarily solve the problem of desirability. Britain was and continues to be a very class-divided society, and whenever public housing has focused on those regarded as the least successful members of society it has become stigmatised. This was a problem whenever funding concentrated on slum clearance or other special needs, and the problem has increased as the amount of council housing has been reduced. Even the Byker Estate has had its difficulties.

Problems with council housing centre round supply and subsidy levels. There was never enough good council housing for everyone wanting it. What there was had to be rationed, and people were forced to turn to other options. If housing was allocated on the basis of need, then it naturally came to be associated with those who were needy – often those on the lowest incomes. Where different methods of allocation were used, or rents were too high, then those with the greatest need lost out.

The solution is to build more good-quality, well-subsidised public housing, so that all who want it can use it. As we have seen, briefly, under Nye Bevan, a vision was put forward of housing as something approaching a universal service. A universal service, like the health service, is meant to be readily available to everyone. This could only have been achieved through a massive government commitment to direct investment in good-quality public housing on a scale that few of those in power besides Bevan ever contemplated. It was not just the cost of this that governments did not like, but the subversion of an important commodity market in what was, after all, still a capitalist system; and, again, the priorities and profits of a powerful coalition of private property and business interests were put first.

Council housing was always integrated with the private sector. Although it was promoted and allocated by local authorities – and although a proportion of earlier council housing was built by direct labour organisations and periodic use has been made of the Public Works Loans Board – the majority of council houses were financed through private-sector loans and built by private contractors.[38] Indeed, they were seen as making an important contribution to the development of the private house-building industry.[39]

For housing to have become a truly universal service, not only would all new housing have had to be publicly owned, but government would have had to nationalise – or in this case municipalise – the existing stock.[40] However, even without being truly universal, council housing did become the mainstream working-class tenure, providing the basis for decent living standards for millions of families. If council-housing standards had been allowed to rise with other living standards, instead of being constantly cut back, and if this had been matched by more sensitive and inclusive management, it could have retained wide popularity and contributed more towards more equal living conditions. This need not have implied greater public expenditure on housing, just a different prioritising of funds.[41]

National Variations

The main forces in this history will be familiar to those who have looked at housing histories elsewhere, but what is unusual is the allocation of the leading role to the local authorities. The reasons for this lie in the nature of the British labour movement, the development of British local government, the failures of British landlordism, and the limits of the early housing associations.

The important characteristic of the British labour movement in this context was its emphasis on parliamentary socialism. There was a strong belief, most notably expressed through the Labour Party, that real improvements for the working class could be achieved by reforms enacted in Parliament, and locally through the municipalities. This was in contrast to many European socialists, who were more wary of state involvement and set up separate organisations, including organisations for providing working-class housing.

British local government had developed along with industrialisation and was already involved with many areas of planning, building control and service provision, and to some extent with housing. Local authorities had long been seen as an important force for social improvement by progressive forces – through what has been described as 'gas and water socialism' – and, as it was put at the time: 'They already possess the knowledge of what is required and most of them have the organisation and technical staff necessary for planning and supervising the work.'[42]

In some countries, significant subsidies for new building were given to private landlords, but the British urban-landlord class – largely made up of small investors who owned just one or two properties – was both unpopular and lacking in effective organisation.[43]

Early British housing associations were very limited geographically, and associations rooted in individual philanthropy and private investment would have been unlikely to gain support from the labour movement as the main source of working-class housing.[44] In countries where housing associations have played a more significant historical role, the associations were founded by more broad-based community groups. In the last three decades, housing associations, run as non-profit companies but with increasingly commercialised structures, have become more significant in Britain as they have been used to break down municipal control and introduce private organisation into 'social' housing. Before that time, though, their role was only subsidiary, with small, often more community-based, organisations being encouraged in the 1960s and 1970s for the promotion of inner-city regeneration and the provision of housing for the elderly and disabled.

When we look at what is commonly known as the social rented sector, consisting of subsidised housing run on a not-for-profit basis, the dominance of municipal housing is, as noted, unusual. There are other examples of local-authority sectors on a small scale, but in most other northern European countries the majority of social rented housing has been provided through various forms of independent non-profit organisation roughly akin to British housing associations. These might have been set up by local authorities (as in Sweden and to a significant extent in Germany and France), by employers (in France and Germany) or other organisations including trade unions and churches (in Germany). Outwith the UK and Ireland, local authority involvement was always more remote, such as through membership of the executive board, but could extend to housing allocations (in Germany and the Netherlands), and could include a relatively high level of regulation and control (as in the Netherlands, where limited state subsidies were brought in as early as 1901). In some countries (France and Germany), private owners have been subsidised to rent their properties at 'social rents'. There are also various types of co-op, which may function similarly to housing associations or, like most of those that make up an important form of tenure in Sweden, be co-ownership schemes, where shares change hands for significant sums. Swedish co-operative housing has always been beyond the reach of all but the better-off working-class families, but until the late 1960s, prices were regulated to prevent sellers from making a profit.

In New Zealand, public rented housing was built and managed by the state, while in federal Australia this was done by the individual states, with the federal government providing the greater part of the subsidy. The limited US public housing was funded by the federal government but owned and run by local public housing authorities overseen by boards of commissioners. Canada has public housing owned and managed by the federal state and also housing managed by churches, community groups, non-profit corporations and municipal administrators. Some of the federal housing is under co-operative tenant management.

There have also been important national differences in where social housing has been focused and how it has been perceived. We have already looked at some of the tensions between providing high-quality homes that people would aspire to, and catering for the needs of the poorest. In many places, and especially with homeownership increasingly promoted as a more desirable option, social housing has become associated with housing for those with no other choice. However, even today there are differences of emphasis reflecting historically different approaches. In the United States social housing has always been regarded as a residual safety net, whereas in countries such as the Netherlands or Sweden, it has played an important role in the housing histories of many middle-class as well as working-class families.

In all countries, housing policy is incredibly complicated and confusing because it has evolved piecemeal through successive bits of government legislation, responding to different stimuli with different, and sometimes even contradictory, aims and results. Everywhere, too, subsidy is by no means confined to housing in public or non-profit sectors. There have been and still are many subsidies and tax concessions for owner-occupiers and private landlords. Although all subsidies mitigate the effects of the market, they are by no means all redistributive or progressive. Bruce Headey has pointed out that although 'one of the *stated* objectives of all Western governments has been to subsidise the housing of low income families', most 'have wound up subsidising all sections of the community [and] have actually been more generous to upper income home-owners than to lower income tenants'.[45] Beneficiaries of these subsidies and tax breaks have included property developers and private landlords.

This chapter has concentrated on the evolution of bricks-and-mortar, or supply-side, subsidies: subsidies that support construction through grants or preferential loans. Governments also intervene in the market through personal, or demand-side, subsidies such as housing allowances, or benefits and tax relief. Often, as with the example of mortgage interest tax relief, this is to the benefit of wealthier owner-occupiers, while housing benefit in a system dependent on private renting can be seen to feed into landlords' profits. A shift to demand-side subsidy is often used as part of a marketisation strategy, however, a comprehensive system of housing allowances can form part of a progressive housing policy where profit is restricted, as demonstrated by the Social Democrats in Sweden, where some 40 per cent of households became eligible for subsidy.

The Swedish model, though not without its own inbuilt inequalities (such as between tenants in old and new housing stock) proved exceptionally successful in generating good-quality affordable accommodation.[46] For a quarter of a century, from 1942 to 1967, this was achieved through a combination of low-cost house-building loans, and rent regulation that severely restricted the profit that could be made by private landlords. The loans were differentially subsidised and especially rewarded cost-rental non-profit (mainly municipal) building corporations, and the construction of apartment blocks. Co-ops also received more than private developers of single-family homes, and the number of loans of different kinds was regulated. The year 1968 saw the end of this subsidy system and a phasing out of the rent regulations; but private-sector rents were tied to those in the public sector, which were negotiated nationally with the tenants' union, and increased allowances compensated for higher average rents. In 1974, new mortgage subsidies and property taxes were introduced to attempt to reduce the differential benefits between tenures, but they avoided penalising ownership and the impact was limited. Tenants would have benefited in the long term, but meanwhile owner-occupation was growing, and in 1976, for the first time in 44 years, the Social Democrats were voted out of office. The growth of ownership, and its accompanying regressive wealth distribution, was encouraged by the system of mortgage interest tax relief, which the Social Democrats had not abolished, and which was made more significant by high taxes and high interest rates.[47] The year 1974 did, however, see a progressive step of a different kind, with significant developments in the system of municipal land purchase, aimed at preventing speculation in land designated for housing.

A crucial ingredient of Swedish success was the level of investment in housing and in associated facilities that was possible under a high-tax, high-welfare regime that refused to idealise market relations. The essential characteristics of Swedish housing policy in these years can be summed up as: high government spending, high-quality homes and amenities in all neighbourhoods, the aim of equality between households and tenures, increasing security and autonomy for tenants, discouragement of speculation and its inevitable booms and slumps, and an emphasis on shared amenities and encouraging community. While none of the policy regimes achieved all that had been envisaged by their legislators, housing policy played a very important part in Swedish social democracy, benefiting from and helping to maintain its relatively low levels of social stratification.

Conclusion

History demonstrates the inability of the market to provide decent housing for a large section of the population, even when tempered by a more philanthropic capitalism; and shows how pragmatic concern for a healthy society, combined with pressure from below, can persuade the most reluctant free marketeer of the need for government intervention. We can see how the growth in homeownership has been the result of politically motivated policy decisions, including large amounts of effective government subsidy; and how this, together with the squeezing of resources for public housing, can help reduce that public housing to a second-choice tenure. And, most importantly, we can remember how, through improvements in living conditions that have come to be taken for granted, subsidised public housing provided the base for the development of vigorous and cohesive communities.

Further Reading

Cole, Ian and Robert Furbey (1994) *The Eclipse of Council Housing* (London and New York: Routledge).

Forrest, Ray, Alan Murie and Peter Williams (1990) *Home Ownership: Differentiation and Fragmentation* (London: Unwin Hyman).

Goodwin, John and Carol Grant (1997) (eds) *Built to Last? Reflections on British Housing Policy* (London: ROOF).

Malpass, Peter (2005) *Housing and the Welfare State: The Development of Housing Policy in Britain* (Basingstoke: Palgrave Macmillan).

Notes

1. In the US, even housing benefit can be dependent on compliance with Workfare schemes; however, when, in February 2008, the English housing minister floated the idea of making unemployed council tenants seek work as a condition of their tenancy, she was attacked from all sides (*Guardian*, 5 February 2008).
2. Stedman Jones, Gareth (1976 [1971]) *Outcast London: A Study in the Relationship Between Classes in Victorian Society* (Harmondsworth: Penguin), p. 178.
3. Quoted by Jerry White in 'Business out of Charity', in John Goodwin and Carol Grant (1997) (eds) *Built to Last? Reflections on British Housing Policy* (London: ROOF), p. 11.
4. The Peabody Trust was a bit different in that its initial funding was a charitable donation, allowing it to charge lower rents; however, its housing was still designed to make a profit to reinvest in further building.

5. Lowe, Stuart (2004) *Housing Policy Analysis: British Housing in Cultural and Comparative Context* (Basingstoke: Palgrave Macmillan), p. 165.
6. Wohl, A.S. (1971) 'Octavia Hill and the Homes of the London Poor', *Journal of British Studies* 10(2): 119.
7. Hill, quoted in Wohl, 'Octavia Hill', p. 113.
8. Wohl, 'Octavia Hill', p. 131.
9. Stedman Jones, *Outcast London*, pp. 224–5.
10. Morton, Jane (1991) 'The 1890 Act and its Aftermath – The Era of the "Model Dwellings"', in Stuart Lowe and David Hughes (eds) *A New Century of Social Housing* (Leicester: Leicester University Press), p. 29. They were still beyond the reach of the very poor.
11. Ibid., p. 16. He specifically mentioned building cheaper than Peabody.
12. Royal Commission (1918) *Report of the Royal Commission on the Housing of the Industrial Population of Scotland Rural and Urban*, paras 2230 and 2223.
13. Ibid., paras 1945–48 and 2237.
14. Quoted in Ravetz, Alison (2001) *Council Housing and Culture: The History of a Social Experiment* (London: Routledge), p. 77.
15. Swenarton, Mark (1981) 'An "Insurance against Revolution": Ideological Objectives of the Provision and Design of Public Housing in Britain after the First World War', *Historical Research* 54(129): 92.
16. Royal Commission (1918) *Report*, para 2237.
17. See discussion of this debate by Peter Kemp in 'The Origins of Council Housing', in Goodwin and Grant, *Built to Last?*, pp. 47–53.
18. Engels, Friedrich (1987) 'Preface to the English Edition' [1892] of *The Condition of the Working Class in England* (Harmondsworth: Penguin), p. 42.
19. Stedman Jones, *Outcast London*, p. 227.
20. *The Housing Journal*, August 1915, p. 3.
21. *Picture Post*, 4 January 1941. I am grateful to Peter Ambrose for drawing my attention to this.
22. Jefferys, Kevin (1991) *The Churchill Coalition and Wartime Politics, 1940–1945* (Manchester: Manchester University Press).
23. It has been argued that such a fundamental form of private property was particularly resistant to decommodification (Malpass, Peter (2005) *Housing and the Welfare State: The Development of Housing Policy in Britain* (Basingstoke: Palgrave Macmillan), p. 23), but similar arguments could, perhaps, have been made about the coal, electricity and railway industries before they were nationalised.

24. Quoted in Foot, Michael (1973) *Aneurin Bevan: A Biography* (Vol. II) (London: Davis-Poynter), p. 80.

25. Ibid., p. 86.

26. Quoted in Ambrose, Peter (1984) *Urban Process and Power* (London: Routledge), p. 88.

27. Quoted in Short, John R. (1982) *Housing in Britain: The Post-war Experience* (London: Methuen), p. 118.

28. Cole, Ian and Robert Furbey (1994) *The Eclipse of Council Housing* (London and New York: Routledge), p. 69.

29. Malpass, *Housing and the Welfare State.*

30. Community Development Project (1976) *Whatever Happened to Council Housing?* (London: Co-operative Press Ltd), p. 12.

31. See Labour Party Housing White Paper (1965), and Housing Green Paper (1977).

32. Kemeny, Jim (1981) *The Myth of Home Ownership: Private versus Public Choices in Housing Tenure* (London: Routledge and Kegan Paul), pp. 102–6.

33. Forrest, Ray, Alan Murie and Peter Williams (1990) *Home Ownership: Differentiation and Fragmentation* (London: Unwin Hyman), p. 45.

34. Ravetz, *Council Housing and Culture*, p. 175.

35. People also complain about the workings of the health service, but would not want to lose it.

36. This was designed by the Swedish architect, Ralph Erskine, and constructed in the early 1970s.

37. Scott, Suzie (2000) 'The People's Republic of Yoker: A Case Study of Tenant Management in Scotland', *Co-op Studies Journal* <http://www.co-opstudies.org/Journal/April%2000/suzie_scott_article.htm>.

38. Ambrose, *Urban Process and Power*, p. 42.

39. Malpass, *Housing and the Welfare State*, p. 20.

40. There are examples of the compulsory purchase and reuse of existing housing by local authorities, but these are relatively insignificant.

41. Conservatives would argue that this ignores the promotion of homeownership as a tool to boost the economy. The theory is that new aspirations and pressures encourage the work ethic – or, in Marxist terms, allow greater exploitation. The political impacts of homeownership are discussed further in Chapter 2.

42. Report of a Special Committee of the Surveyors' Institution, December 1916, quoted in Royal Commission, *Report*, para 1992.

43. Lowe, *Housing Policy Analysis*, p. 167.

44. The Workmen's National Housing Council compared homes built by these associations to tied company housing (*The Housing Journal*, August 1917, pp. 2, 3, 7).

45. Headey, Bruce (1978) *Housing Policy in the Developed Economy: The United Kingdom, Sweden and the United States* (London: Croom Helm), p. 23.
46. See ibid., and Kemeny, *The Myth of Home Ownership*.
47. Owners paid a tax on their notional rental income, but this was much smaller than their tax relief, particularly for high earners paying large taxes. Similarly, capital gains tax on house sales could be made to disappear through generous allowances for repairs, maintenance and improvement.

2

NEOLIBERALISM'S HOME FRONT

Sarah Glynn

Although it is true that neoliberalism conveys an ideology and a propaganda of its own, it is fundamentally a new social order in which the power and income of the upper fractions of the ruling classes – the wealthiest persons – was re-established in the wake of a setback.

Gérard Duménil and Dominique Lévy, 2005[1]

The first step towards addressing housing's inadequacies and inequalities is to attempt to understand the economic system that is creating them. The key to understanding this system is found in the interpretation of neoliberalism as a system geared towards the restoration of the power of economic elites. 'The main substantive achievement of neoliberalization', as David Harvey explains, 'has been to redistribute, rather than to generate, wealth and income.'[2] Neoliberal theory is diametrically opposed to anything that interferes with the uneven wealth distribution of capitalism. In dismantling the regulatory and redistributory structures of the Keynesian mixed economy, neoliberalism makes the rich richer through the appropriation of a larger proportion of overall wealth. Naturally, such a theory has always had wealthy and powerful backers, but it would be wrong to claim that all, or even a majority, of those who have come to be involved in implementing neoliberal policies would regard themselves as in favour of the redistribution of wealth from the poor to the rich. How neoliberalism has come to be accepted as common sense and the only possible alternative is looked at later in this chapter. However, neoliberal economic policies do not, as their supporters claim, provide an efficient solution to the problems of economic slowdown, as was clear well before the current crisis. Neoliberalism is commonly portrayed as a necessary medicine for the general good, but it has not only generated a massive increase in the gap between rich and poor and brought significant numbers into social deprivation, it has also proved a bad, and exceedingly risky, basis for sustained economic growth. Unregulated markets encourage the development of speculative or finance capital, which is notoriously predatory – geared towards quick returns rather than long-term investment – and extremely volatile. The last three decades have been characterised by ruthless asset-stripping, bursting 'bubble' economies and – as market barriers are torn down – increasingly contagious financial crises. Looked at overall, world growth of GDP per capita since the early 1970s was unimpressive, even before the recent collapse, with periods of economic advance in some countries generally being at the expense of others.[3] Where growth has been more substantial, this has been due to more traditional investment in manufacturing (China), or rising oil prices (Russia), but it has been accompanied by social turmoil reminiscent of the Industrial Revolution. And China, like the earlier Asian Tigers, has benefited from relatively protected markets, as well as major government-funded infrastructural projects, so it is hardly an example of pure neoliberalism.

As an economic theory, neoliberalism was developed by the Mont Pelerin Society, founded in 1947 by the group around Friedrich von Hayek to defend nineteenth-century ideas of neoclassical free-market economics. Their ideas were propagated through think-tanks supported by corporate leaders (often from the US), and increasingly through the academy – especially by Milton Friedman and his followers in Chicago. The first opportunity to put their ideas into practice came in 1973 when Pinochet's *coup* allowed Chile to become a brutal laboratory in which to test neoliberalism's tenets. In the 1980s, after further Latin American experiments, neoliberalism was enthusiastically embraced by the leading capitalist economies – notably under Thatcher and Reagan – who proclaimed it a way out of the economic crisis of social democracy, in opposition to growing left movements. The new system was welcomed by the international business class, especially by the growing breed of finance capitalists, and aggressive business tactics were backed up by international organisations such as the International Monetary Fund (IMF) to force more and more countries to play by the new rules. While neoliberalism on the ground reflects geographical and historical realities, different places share not only an ideological and economic dominance by finance capital, but also systems of organisation and practical policies, as they learn from each other.

Redistribution to the increasingly powerful business elite is put into practice by prioritising private property, and by promoting wealth accumulation through speculation and through what David Harvey describes as the dispossession (or privatisation) of common rights.[4] The role of government becomes the facilitation and protection of these processes. This understanding of the meaning and practice of neoliberalism can help to throw light on what is happening in housing. And, while this book focuses on housing issues, it is important to remember that changes in housing have been taking place in the context of an overall attack on the working class, which is regarded as a source of actual and potential resistance to the new order. Beyond set-piece battles – such as Margaret Thatcher's against the miners or Ronald Reagan's against the air-traffic controllers – workers have faced a prolonged erosion of hard-won rights and conditions. Large-scale unemployment, casualised labour and (in response to declining opportunities) growing levels of drug addiction have all had a devastating effect on working-class power and working-class neighbourhoods.

Commodification and Speculation

At the heart of today's housing crisis is the prioritisation of the house as investment rather than as home, that is, of its exchange value over its use value. Housing forms a large proportion of a country's wealth (in 2007 an estimated 60 per cent of Britain's wealth was in property), and property speculation plays an important part in today's regressive wealth redistribution. Deregulation of banks and building societies, designed to set loose the forces of finance capital, has allowed money to be poured into property. In a highly competitive money market, mortgages have been made available to a much wider range of people than before, and people have been able to borrow much higher sums. The dramatic price rises that followed this increase of funds were many times the rise in average income, and the promise of high returns attracted major investors who put even more money into the system, pushing prices up further. While mainstream commentators have laid the blame for high house prices on limited housing supply (and this view has formed the basis of British government policy), it is clearly not as simple as that. If all houses were the same, then we need only be concerned with the total number, but this is not the case. House types and values vary hugely, and so long as prices rise there is scope for those with money to use houses as a medium for making more money.

House price rises are often portrayed as beneficial to all homeowners, but most are unable to realise any gains except as a collateral for often unsustainable borrowing. Those who truly benefited were those who already owned more property than they needed to live in (or the money to invest in it); the more they owned, the more they benefited. Their gains were made at the expense of those starting off with fewer resources. The losers include households excluded from the possibilities of the bonanza by their inability to buy a home in the first place, who have been left to rely on a diminishing stock of social housing, or who pay high rents to the new class of buy-to-let landlords. They also include families whose lives are in harness to the need to repay ever more disproportionate mortgages as well as the increasing numbers who have lost everything in the battle to pay back their mortgage debt. Peter Malpass has shown how the shared prosperity of the welfare state actually provided a golden age for the growth of private homeownership,[5] but now that homeownership is being forced on those who have not yet bought, and can often least afford to do so, more and more people are facing an insecure economic future where homeownership becomes an additional burden.

Altogether, this is a very efficient system for increasing disparities of wealth and opportunity, with long-term and indirect effects as well as more immediate ones. Being stuck in poor and expensive housing can mean poor health, lack of money for other things (even for a healthy diet or decent heating), lack of space for homework, pressures for both parents to work and delay having children, pressures on older parents who have used their own savings to help their children, inability to move to a better job, and all the knock-on effects of living in a poorer area with poorly resourced schools and services. It can mean huge amounts of worry and stress – as documented in the case study from Australia discussed in Chapter 9 – and these are compounded if something goes wrong and tips an already precariously balanced budget over the edge.[6] Chapter 1 has already noted some of the wider consequences of the poor housing conditions of earlier periods, and Christopher Addison, the minister responsible for Britain's first state-subsidised council housing after the First World War, actually tried to put a figure on the exported health costs of poor housing to support his argument for continued investment after those subsidies were cut.[7] The social significance of the new realignment of wealth was spelt out in Thomas and Dorling's report for the UK housing charity, Shelter, where they pointed out: 'A child will not easily be able to earn their way out of their social position in the future. A social position that will be increasingly determined by their parents' housing wealth.'[8]

Over and above the gains of individual winners have been the gains made by the real estate business. This includes not only the developers of new homes and the agents who sell them, but also the huge financial services industry that supports and feeds off them, and off millions of heavily indebted individual borrowers. Private businesses, and especially businesses geared towards the financial sector, are the primary vehicles for the rapid development of elite wealth and power, and their needs form the core of neoliberal policy. This results in a very predatory form of wealth creation. From the point of view of the investor, it does not matter whether money is made through building homes for people to live in or by speculation on land and buildings. That is why developers (who are more and more involved with finance capital rather than productive capital) may prefer to sit on large land banks rather than address immediate housing needs, and why new flats may be left empty as their speculative purchasers have not found it financially worth their while to rent them out before reselling them. With the emphasis on quick profit, the majority of speculative building tends to be banal and cramped. In Britain, the volume house-builders have used their industrial muscle to force the government to let them build to lower environmental standards than are compulsory for subsidised social housing.

Neoliberalism favours the financial consolidation and 'rationalisation' represented by mergers and takeovers and vertical disintegration (or outsourcing). As in other areas of business, the housing industry (in all its different parts) is increasingly dominated by large firms and the practice of subcontracting. Just as ordinary overstretched borrowers can often find themselves the people most exposed to fluctuations in the housing market, those at the bottom of the production chain – exemplified by increasingly casualised building workers – are expected to carry the greatest risk. This can mean the growing physical risk of industrial accident as well as the risk of losing their job.

The priority given to exchange value is perhaps most explicit in the programmes of mass 'regeneration' – or government-sponsored gentrification – that form the subject of the next chapter. Rises in property value are used as measures of regeneration success, and even the veneer of social rhetoric has been increasingly sidelined. So, for example, it has hardly been felt necessary to disguise the real aims of the processes of 'Housing Market Renewal' taking place in the north of England. Thousands of homes face compulsory purchase and demolition, even though they are used or potentially useable, in order that the land they occupy may be made available for more high-yielding developments; and, with supply reduced, remaining homes become more valuable.

The new economic system favours private renting, and in Britain, this has increased for the first time since before the First World War. Many countries have seen a weakening of rent regulation that has encouraged a new class of small landlords, as well as bigger property companies. (There has been no rent control for new private lets in Britain since 1989.) Private renting provides a further method of regressive wealth distribution, with (generally poorer) tenants who are unable to purchase their own home contributing to the profits of those with property to spare. As in the past, the profit motive demands minimum expenditure on maintenance and maximum flexibility for the investor – most British 'buy-to-let' mortgages actually insist on tenants being given only short-term tenancies. Families suffer the consequences of the resultant insecurity, forced moves and accompanying stress. If buy-to-let owners are forced to sell up, or if they default on their mortgages, it is their tenants who may find themselves on the street. New developments especially designed to attract private investors include student flats that may look similar to traditional halls of residence but require student rents to cover an element of private profit.[9]

Investment in property has been further encouraged by the promotion of Real Estate Investment Trusts. First conceived in the US in 1960, REITs have only become prominent in recent years. They have become vehicles for large-scale international investment, and more and more countries have wanted to be in on the action (there are even Islamic REITs based in Dubai). These trusts are geared towards short-term financial profit, making them ideal embodiments of neoliberal business practice. They are exempt from corporation tax so long as a high percentage of their profit is paid out to their shareholders (at least 90 per cent in the US and Britain). This means that not only do they provide minimal tax revenue, but they also discourage long-term investment in favour of asset stripping – which can involve large-scale evictions of existing tenants. As they seek out property that can be used to bring in rapid high returns, they have become an important tool in the break-up and sell-off of public housing. Tenants' groups in the United States have recorded how REITs who bought public housing have used every trick in the landlords' book to squeeze the tenants and eventually force them to leave and make way for more profitable development.[10]

Accumulation by Dispossession

Privatisation – especially when it involves evicting tenants onto the street – is the most blatant form of wealth transfer. Harvey has described this as 'accumulation by dispossession', in conscious imitation of Marx's term 'primitive accumulation', used to describe 'the expropriation of the agricultural producer, the peasant, from the soil, [which] is the basis of the whole process' of capitalism.[11] Privatisation in the countries covered in this book cannot compete with the scale of what is happening in China or the former Soviet Union, but it remains hugely significant. Not all privatisation is immediately obvious and the dispossession of commonly owned property is often a piecemeal process that avoids public attention.

Just as there were many different forms of social housing, some of them existing side by side, so there are many different roads to privatisation: but they all lead in similar directions. Social housing of all kinds may be sold *en bloc* to private property companies, or individual dwellings may be sold to their tenants or on the open market. Not all transactions proceed all the way down the privatisation road. A large proportion of British council housing has been sold to the housing association sector (as discussed below), while some Swedish social housing blocks have become co-ownership co-ops. However, almost everywhere, at the same time as social polarisation and soaring house prices have led to a growing need for cheap rented housing, social housing stocks have been restrained or often actively cut back. Moreover, social housing stocks that remain are often starved of funds, depriving them of all but minimal repair and maintenance. There is much talk about providing and improving social housing, but this has rarely been backed by the necessary finance or action.[12] Even the new recognition of the importance of social housing that has been engendered by the collapse of market alternatives has resulted only in sticking-plaster policies such as bringing forward future budgets and buying unsold speculative developments.

Public goods may also be opened up to market forces and more strongly tied into private finance without change of ownership.

Chapter 1 has already shown how Conservative governments tried to bring market forces to bear on council housing, and these tactics have only increased. The new social-rent formula introduced in England in 2003 even factors in property value. At the same time, housing associations are being forced to conform to market rules and blur the boundaries between the non-profit and open-market sectors. Dutch housing associations provide a thoroughgoing example, having run since 1995 without any government subsidy: many of the old regulations have been relaxed and rents have been 'liberalised' within an overall maximum.[13] It has become common practice for new social housing to be made to ride on the back of private development (as described below), and housing associations have become dependent on borrowing in the financial markets. All this makes social housing itself immediately susceptible to the impacts of the credit crunch and the collapse of housing-market speculation, more than negating any gains from the sticking-plaster measures outlined above.

There has been an international tendency to cut supply-side (or bricks-and-mortar) subsidies, so pushing up social rents and forcing low-income households to rely on demand-side subsidies, such as housing benefit, which can also be used to subsidise (and push up) private rents. This reduces the difference between social and market rented housing. It can also prove expensive for the public purse. Subsidies for private rents must cover the added costs of the landlords' profits, and even subsidies to social sector tenants have secondary financial – as well as social – costs. The British Conservative government was forced to acknowledge in 1995 that 'To increase [social sector] rent much further could increase the cost to the taxpayer, because of the increased benefit bill and damage to work incentives.'[14]

While higher-earning social tenants bear the full brunt of rent rises, and are in effect helping to subsidise the system, others are forced to undergo a means test. Benefits tend to fall off sharply with increases in income, putting many families into a poverty trap where it is simply not worth working – almost every extra penny earned is taken away in loss of benefits of different kinds. This system introduces even more stress factors – especially when benefit agencies pay late, causing tenants to go into arrears – and, like other benefits, is not taken up by all who are eligible.[15] Since Thatcher's 'reforms', English council housing has been used to provide a net income *to* government, which has been used to help pay for housing benefit. More recently, many Swedish municipalities have been happily making a profit on their housing.

Alongside the increasing residualisation of the majority of what remains of social housing as housing of last resort, many places have also seen a new tendency to direct social housing funding to better-off households who are not quite able to reach the bottom of the housing ladder. In France, increasing proportions of subsidy are being given to 'upper social housing', and other schemes, such as those in Britain and the Netherlands, involve various forms of part-ownership. All this raises concerns that these 'intermediate' subsidies are being given at the expense of subsidies to those with the greatest need, amounting to a reallocation of common goods up the income scale. A worrying trend in British planning has been the tendency to substitute requirements for provision of 'social housing' with requirements for 'affordable housing' – a term that can include various subsidised or unsubsidised forms of (relatively) low-cost housing for sale.

Other, more insidious processes of dispossession include increasingly regressive tax systems (so that the remaining public services are disproportionately paid for by those on the lowest incomes),[16] and the increasing use of public subsidy to promote private interests. A high-profile example of prevailing approaches to taxation was provided in Britain by the unseemly battle between Conservatives and Labour to claim credit for the proposal to raise the threshold for inheritance tax. The argument for this change was that this allowed people to pass on their increasingly valuable homes to their children (and so perpetuate wealth inequalities). Grants, subsidies and tax relief can all be used to channel public money to private property interests. In France, gross government expenditure on private rented housing has overtaken that on social rented housing, and both receive considerably less help than is given to owner-occupation.[17] Dutch local authorities have given public land to subsidise housing for owner-occupation. England has seen the development of heavily subsidised schemes for first-time buyers and so-called 'key-workers', which helped those individuals but also helped fuel the already overheated market and boost prices for everyone else. Of the 'affordable housing' subsidised by the Housing Corporation in England in 2007–08, only 58 per cent were rental properties, with the rest forming part of various low-cost ownership or shared equity schemes.[18] And there has been concern that many of those who have benefited are not even the key workers flagged up in government statements, let alone those most in need of help.[19]

Even beyond the obvious public losses of the various forms of privatisation, support for neoliberal housing policies can involve considerable extra public expenditure, and this appears to be simply absorbed without question as a price worth paying for promoting private business interests. In Chapter 5, we see how in Scotland public money may be made available for council-house demolitions and to subsidise very limited amounts of new, primarily housing association, housing, but not for the much more cost-efficient improvements that would allow the maintenance of existing council housing stocks. Where policies have met resistance (as with the transfer of council housing to housing associations, which requires tenant support), then the public can end up paying for expensive propaganda campaigns.

Public-private partnerships have become a familiar form of privatisation in many sectors. They have also been the subject of considerable critical analysis for their inefficiencies and for their ability to make large private profits at public expense, while shifting financial risk to the public sector.[20] Public-private partnership in housing can take different forms. Chapter 4 analyses the devastating affect of their use for regeneration in the English city of Leeds, and shows how, through taking on the financial risks associated with such development, the city council has been forced to tie itself into a regime of tight neoliberal economics that extends far beyond the original partnership.

Public-private partnerships have become the main source of new social housing in England. Provision of a certain proportion of social housing has become a condition of planning permission for new housing development, giving rise to a new profession of consultants who can advise property companies on how to negotiate the most advantageous deals. Similar systems operate in Ireland, Scotland and German municipalities. (The crisis of speculative building following from economic slowdown has exposed additional systemic dangers of relying on developers for the provision of social housing.) There have also been all sorts of *ad hoc* public-private partnerships, as housing authorities have made deals with private landlords to accommodate households who would otherwise be homeless; and reliance on private landlords looks set to increase. Some British local authorities have even found themselves renting back former council homes. A *Guardian* report from 2006 gives an indication of the wastefulness of housing policy 'modernisation' and the complexity of the schemes evolved to provide a basic safety net of social housing within current rules. The report described the role of a new housing association, part funded by a London borough council. The association was being contracted by that council to buy homes, including ex-council houses, from private landlords who were currently renting them out to local authorities to house homeless families. The council then leased the homes from the housing association, to which it had also transferred some of its own properties.[21]

Malpass argues that what is happening to housing has provided a model for welfare changes more generally;[22] and privatisations and welfare cuts in other areas can have knock-on effects on housing as well. One area where the effect is most direct is cuts to the value of pensions. Concerns about future financial security have been exploited to promote investment in property, especially boosting the buy-to-let market. This has contributed to the increase in private renting and to rising house prices at the bottom of the housing ladder.

The most dramatic privatisation in British housing began in 1980, when the Thatcher government gave council tenants the right to buy their homes, for which they were given a heavy discount. This was popular among the many who personally benefited from the policy, but it successfully decimated a public housing stock that represented decades of public investment and housed one-third of the population. Today, its impact is being felt more and more by council tenants and would-be tenants, who have been left with a limited supply of houses – generally the least attractive ones. Those who have bought their homes under the Right to Buy scheme are hardly the economic elites referred to by Duménil and Lévy (and some are struggling to cope with heavy maintenance and service charges), but a general increase in homeownership nevertheless serves elite interests well. Most immediately, it was used as a way to extract money back from local authorities (who were not allowed to reinvest the proceeds in housing), and it expanded the housing market as a potential source of speculative profit. It also had strategic importance for power and control.

As early as the 1880s, Tory landowners were arguing that the active promotion of many small property owners would build up a rampart of support for property interests more generally. As Lord Halsbury explained:

> If there is to be an attack on property it will be resisted with much greater force if it is possible to say that it includes all property, not merely property which has any peculiar privilege, because then it can be said that an attack on property is an attack on property of all kinds.[23]

The wide media support for the plans to raise the threshold of inheritance tax, mentioned above, demonstrates that this argument is as true now as when it was first made.

The implications of homeownership for social control were recognised early on by both sides of the political spectrum. Also in the 1880s, Engels warned:

> Give [workers] their own houses ... and you break their power of resistance to the wage cutting of the factory owners. The individual owner might be able to sell his house on occasion, but during a big strike or a general industrial crisis all the houses belonging to the affected workers would have to come on the market for sale and would therefore find no purchasers or be sold off far below their cost price.[24]

The problems, from the workers' perspective, of being tied to one locality through homeownership, and unable to move to new employment were still being discussed in 1919.[25] From a more conservative viewpoint, Samuel Smiles had observed back in 1864 that 'the accumulation of property … weans [thrifty men] from revolutionary notions, and makes them conservative',[26] a view that was later famously espoused by Neville Chamberlain, who actively promoted homeownership in the 1920s and claimed that 'Every spadeful of manure dug in, every fruit tree planted … converted a potential revolutionary into a citizen.'[27] The promotion of homeownership played an important role in preventing resistance to the severe 'rationalisation' of British industry that was begun under Thatcher; and today, workers committed to the repayment of large mortgages will be especially unwilling to risk losing their jobs and incomes through industrial action.

The transfer of British council housing to housing associations demonstrates a more staggered form of privatisation, though it may take place on a massive scale (for example, the transfer of 81,000 homes in Glasgow in 2003), and has affected a total of 1.1 million homes over 20 years. Modern British housing associations are private not-for-profit organisations that receive considerable sums of public money. They are also heavily dependent on private funding and are expected to produce a surplus. They are made to compete for housing grants in a quasi-market, and this, along with wider market pressures, increasingly favours large housing associations and encourages takeovers, so that the sector has followed the neoliberal pattern and become dominated by larger and larger organisations. British housing associations are subsidised to build for low-cost ownership as well as social rental and, besides working in partnership with independent private developers, they are encouraged to set up their own market divisions, which carry out unsubsidised development for profit.

Council homes transferred to housing associations are still social housing, but housing stock transfer has removed them from public ownership and control. This form of privatisation does not, however, actually decrease the total amount of welfare subsidy. Funding through housing associations is generally more expensive than through local authorities,[28] and when some of this cost is passed on in higher rents, these are reflected in higher housing-benefit costs. However, a bigger proportion of this subsidy represents profits for business interests, be they those of the private finance companies or housing association directors on private-sector salaries.[29] (The promotion of arm's-length management organisations as more palatable alternatives to stock transfer, as in our example from Leeds in Chapter 4, introduces another stage into the privatisation process, but the direction of travel remains the same.)

Housing stock transfers do not reflect the market value of the huge public assets involved. Houses may be sold for pennies or even given with a substantial dowry from public funds. The argument is that this is needed to cover running costs, but, as with other privatisations, financial arrangements are designed to shift maximum risk onto the public sector, leaving private capital free to make a profit. This public asset stripping becomes most obvious when parts of the transferred property are subsequently sold off for large sums to private developers.

The anomalous position of the modern British housing association has been highlighted by Malpass, who points out:

> ... on the one hand, actively growing [housing] associations have been under pressure to become more businesslike and competitive, while on the other hand they have become ever more obviously and deeply entrenched within the structure of the state apparatus for meeting social needs.[30]

While Malpass stresses the conflicting pressures this puts onto the housing associations, it has also provided them, and the financial organisations that invest in them, with huge business opportunities. And though the associations are very much tied to government policy, this has been policy formulated around speculative business interests. At the same time that housing associations are being made to conform to market practices, English private developers have been permitted to compete with them for social housing grant. All these changes are symptomatic of a general situation where business and government are increasingly intertwined and, as will be discussed later, the public/private boundary has become blurred.

Dispossession is often facilitated by regeneration schemes that involve the demolition of social housing – and also (as on much of the land designated for Housing Market Renewal) cheap private housing – and its replacement with developments that include a high proportion of more expensive private homes and considerably less social housing than would be needed to house those displaced. Changes of this kind are taking place throughout the world – often on an immense scale – and are the subject of Chapter 3. City-centre housing schemes, or those in other areas with high land value, are particularly susceptible to such developments, which are openly conceived as ways to attract richer new residents rather than improve conditions for existing residents. Yet again, the main beneficiaries are the developers and financiers, while the main losers are those with the least money to spend on housing.

The Role of Government

Government action is needed to facilitate and protect the neoliberal economy, and so-called 'free markets' demand a great deal of interference. Like capitalism more generally, neoliberalism is not a static system but constantly changes in response to external forces and internal contradictions. Peck and Tickell have observed how earlier forms of 'roll-back' neoliberalism instigated by the United States and Britain were superseded by a 'roll-out' neoliberalism concerned with 'the aggressive reregulation, disciplining, and containment of those marginalized or dispossessed by the neoliberalism of the 1980s'.[31] When Thatcher talked about rolling back the frontiers of the state, what she meant was the dismantling of the Keynesian welfare state (including the privatisation of council housing and the lifting of rent control), but older regulations have been and are being replaced by new structures. Many of these were developed to contain the social consequences of marketisation and are increasingly authoritarian (see below). All are concerned with opening up more and more areas to competitive market forces, and this has resulted in fundamental changes in governing structures. The underlying logic of these changes is to give greater power to the (unelected) representatives of big business, who are portrayed as somehow above politics. This has led some people to talk about a new corporatism, in the sense of a government dominated by business corporations.[32] Significantly, neoliberal systems are characterised by an unquestioned acceptance of monetarist 'science', and economic policy tends to be reduced to an issue of technocratic management in which politicians have no place.

Neoliberalism has developed various organisational char-acteristics: international agreements tying governments to business-friendly rules; new roles for business in both the creation of policy and the delivery of services; development of partnership models of local governance; organisational restructuring as a method to force marketisation and increase overall central control; the use of voluntary or 'not-for-profit' organisations to promote neoliberal objectives, and the introduction of quasi-markets and financial audit into remaining public services. These all have a direct relevance to housing.

European Union legislation is guided by the neoliberal principles of free trade, and may make it harder for states to subsidise social housing that performs more than a residual role. This is an issue that is still being fought over, with private developers lobbying for a restrictive interpretation.[33] Chapter 7 illustrates, through the example of Sweden, how EU law can be invoked by politicians to support their views.

Private businesses play an active role in both strategic planning and policy implementation. The big developers can be sure of a ready ear for their concerns, through organisations such as the English Home Builders Federation, and are always consulted as key 'stakeholders' (see Figure 2.1); meanwhile, private organisations are taking on the management of housing-related functions. Some of these organisations, such as the housing associations, are not profit-making, but there is growing use of contracted-out services.

We are increasingly seeing the use of the term 'governance' to include the 'networks' and 'partnerships' (including interest groups, businesses, the voluntary sector) that are playing a growing

Figure 2.1 'Consulting with stakeholders'.

role alongside more regular local governmental structures. The impact of these changes will be discussed more fully in the next chapter, but one aspect of the new partnership arrangements has been the decreasing power of local democracy, with local government reduced to little more than the strategic management of the private companies employed to carry out a centrally set agenda. In Britain, the reduction of council housing has itself made a considerable dent in British local authority power. It is not incidental to this that the municipal town halls are commonly regarded as impediments to neoliberal reform and are remembered as a traditional base of more left-wing influence.

Some places have seen an ostensible localising of power, but, as in our Canadian example discussed in Chapter 11, this is often done in such a way as to force marketisation and offload responsibility for its consequences. Tight fiscal control means that local politicians have little room to manoeuvre within a centrally set agenda, and decentralisation is used to push different regions into economic competition.

Voluntary and not-for-profit organisations play increasing roles in the new partnership structures and also in service delivery. This not only helps incorporate possible sources of resistance into the neoliberal project (of which more below), but also provides a way of displacing the welfare state and hollowing out local government. A prime example of what Harvey calls 'privatization by NGO' is provided by the British housing associations. A movement largely conceived in the spirit of community self-help has been turned into a vast industry and 'the main vehicle for the break up of the local authority sector'.[34] These housing associations are also being encouraged to move into other areas of service delivery that were once the sole preserve of the elected local authorities.

Not only are many functions of government being devolved to non-elected organisations, but government itself – at all levels – increasingly is run along business principles and regulated by the priorities of financial audit. These are portrayed as scientifically neutral and beyond politics, but they are actually concerned with avoiding financial risk and take little account of less measurable social concerns. This financially driven regulation has now become internalised by those involved.[35] Performance indicators and targets ensure a strictly controlled hierarchical structure, with limited, tightly set goals and little room for initiative.[36] Housing departments produce glossy newsletters replete with graphical representations of targets and achievements – such as how quickly they can turn around a council-house sale[37] – but they are ill-equipped to address the complicated problems of social reality. This is a culture that thrives on statistics, but statistics are notoriously easy to misuse. Market 'research' is employed to create data that supports favoured policies;[38] meanwhile, real information on the nature of the housing stock and house allocations may not be properly collected – as I found when I requested details of the housing waiting list in Dundee.[39]

Manufacturing 'Consent' and the New Authoritarianism

In creating a climate for financial accumulation in a democracy, a significant proportion of people (including politicians) must convince themselves that what is happening is for the general good. Government also must contain the social consequences of an increasingly unequal society.

As Harvey has shown in *A Brief History of Neoliberalism*,[40] a carefully orchestrated campaign over decades, carried out through policy groups and the academy and later through powerful political leaders and organisations, has led to a general acceptance of neoliberal ideas as good common sense or as just the way the world works. Presumably, many of those now pushing forward neoliberal policies believe that they are acting in the wider public interest, or at the very least that there is no possible alternative. The fundamental idea that has allowed neoliberalism to be portrayed as a system based on core values of civilisation, is that of individual freedom. Despite the contradictory nature of freedom (which Polanyi points out includes bad freedoms such as 'the freedom to exploit one's fellows'[41]), it remains a hugely emotive concept. It is this idea of individual freedom that has allowed individual homeownership to be increasingly portrayed as natural.

People are portrayed as free to succeed and also free to fail – and, in an argument evoking nineteenth-century concepts of the undeserving poor, lack of success is attributed to personal failure, which should not be rewarded. Political rhetoric appeals to populist moral values: Keynesian housing policies are portrayed as favouring drug addicts and teenage mothers at the expense of hard-working families. Such arguments are used to prevent those who have done better under the system (and perhaps bought their own home) from identifying with those less well-off, and to reduce the concept of welfare to a minimal safety-net – as is increasingly the case with social housing. At the same time, social housing tenants have themselves been rebranded as consumers in an attempt to make them take on more of the responsibility for their situation.[42] Neoliberalism is profoundly individualising, and even when it engages with ideas of community development it does so in such a way as to suggest that the burden of change lies with the individual and not the system. There is much talk of the concept of 'social capital', but this has become divested of its original meaning, which emphasised relationships of power. Instead, it is deemed sufficient to prescribe participation in (non-political) community groups as the key to neighbourhood improvement, regardless of the impacts of wider economic structures.[43]

Belief in the value of the welfare state is hard to shift, but there have been plenty of attempts to blame the 'nanny state' and 'welfare dependency' for current problems. Such arguments are exemplified in a recent study of London's East End that lays much of the blame for the current housing crisis not on under-investment in public housing, which has left different groups competing for limited stock, but on reliance on the public housing system in the first place.[44] More generally, it has become fashionable to scorn what the East End study calls 'a culture of entitlement';[45] and when it comes to social housing, decades of achievement (despite chronic under-funding) are increasingly ignored in favour of the view that it has been a failed experiment. Poor management and excessive bureaucracy are regarded as integral to public housing, rather than as things that can be (and sometimes have been) successfully addressed.[46] Of course, bad news has always made headlines, but negative views have been reinforced by the residualisation of social housing as the poorest homes for the poorest people. There is a tendency to confuse cause and effect and to attribute the poverty and its attendant problems to the nature of the tenure: if a disproportionate number of the poor and unemployed live in social housing, then social housing must be to blame. The image of the 'failed estate' has developed a firm identity in popular mythology that is reflected in and reinforced by government thinking. Thus, when the new Scottish Housing Minister was asked in 2007 about the possibility of building more council housing, his immediate response was that we do not want more 'sink estates'.[47]

Besides, or *despite* this rhetoric of freedom, the other outstanding appeal of neoliberal economics is (as we have seen) that it is not a political system at all, but a science based on immutable laws. This relieves politicians of their responsibilities, with the implication that there is no alternative – they cannot hope to buck the market. Such a view is reinforced by the conflation of alternative economic models with the failed Soviet system.

Chik Collins and Peter Jones have shown how carefully chosen language can be used to present a pragmatic capitulation to business-based policies as something progressive, or even socialist.[48] Their example concerns the transfer of some of Glasgow's council housing to housing associations in the mid-1980s. Conservative central government was starving public housing of funds, but even so, Glasgow's Labour Party, which had led the way in housing provision, seemed unlikely to agree to get rid of any of its homes. That was until a council officer rebranded the sales as a 'socialist case for community ownership', drawing parallels with the co-operative movement. This proved to be only the first stage in the adoption of these ideas by the British Labour hierarchy, which now promotes them wholesale and with enthusiasm. Neoliberal ideas are being accepted step by step, and this piecemeal acceptance – sometimes as the least worst option – has made resistance increasingly difficult.

All these arguments and images play a crucial part in allowing those who impose neoliberal policies to justify their actions (not least to themselves), but they will hardly persuade all of those who are at the receiving end of those policies. For them, governments have employed a mixture of persuasion and incorporation, co-option, and divide and rule and, not least, the strategic use of neglect, and fear.

Central to neoliberal techniques of persuasion and of incorporation into the system is the encouragement of consumerism. Occasional concerns about the growing burden of personal debt are vastly outweighed by a vision that regards consumer spending as the main driving force of the economy, and the promotion of consumerism as a way to instil more individualistic values and provide ready satisfactions – a sort of government-approved retail therapy. Old solidarities are being replaced by the freedom to express our individuality through our purse. We are to be judged not by our lives, but by our lifestyles, and central to these lifestyles is our private home. In recent years (pre-credit crunch), television schedules have been crowded with programmes on home improvements – though it was soon realised that rather than consuming goods, it was even better to sell them at a healthy mark-up and the improvements began to be aimed at realising profit.

The various media are integral to consumer society, boosting, and benefiting from, the explosion of lifestyle publications of all kinds. The media also decide how and what stories are told and, importantly, what are omitted. While government dependence on media spin is notorious, business and government sources are also proving ever more efficient at influencing news coverage. Tight market competition within the media industries has encouraged an often uncritical reliance on press releases. An analysis of British journalism, carried out by researchers at Cardiff University, uncovered a world of increasingly desk-bound journalists under pressure to produce growing amounts of copy. These journalists are forced to rely more and more heavily on recycled press releases or agency reports, that themselves may be based on press-release material. The Cardiff survey suggested that '60% of press articles and 34% of broadcast stories come wholly or mainly from one of these "pre-packaged" sources'.[49] Little wonder then that reports on major redevelopments or 'problem estates' tend to present the same official views. (Or there is always a more direct approach, as demonstrated by the government-sponsored *Guardian* 'supplement' on the regeneration in the north of England.[50]) Those directly involved in housing campaigns know there is another story besides the official version, but also know that few will hear it.

Incorporation can also be more targeted. Independent organisations, professionals (including journalists), and even grassroots groups that could provide potential sources of opposition are all brought on board the neoliberal project. This is often facilitated by the new forms of partnership governance. We have already seen the role that has been given to housing associations, and a particularly telling example of incorporation has been provided by Britain's major housing charity, Shelter. Like other charities, Shelter provides some public services on a contract basis, and it has found itself in fierce competition with private-sector companies. (Charities may even lose money on such contracts, in effect subsidising the government.[51]) Shelter's management argued that in order for them to be able to compete efficiently as providers of legal aid, their junior staff should accept changes in employment conditions, an increasingly audit-based culture, and what amounted to a major cut in pay. These relatively low-paid workers, worried about their own tight housing budgets, felt they had no choice but to come out on strike. For others, incorporation can come with considerable financial gain. Civil servants can be rewarded with large pay rises if their departments are privatised or they transfer to firms providing privatised services. Others may accept incorporation as the price of financial support. Increasingly, commercialised funding methods have impacted on academic independence and steered academics within narrow, policy-dictated parameters. And in both England and Scotland, tenants' organisations are being enticed with funding and practical assistance to become part of a registered network, where government bureaucrats set the agenda. Such controlled organisation is not only highly restricted in what it can achieve itself; its existence also inhibits the growth of genuinely independent representation. It sucks in the energy of its volunteers and assumes the role of tenants' representative. Tenant activists are also being encouraged onto housing association boards, where they find themselves legally bound to work not for the interests of tenants, but for the association.[52] Many of these processes are examined further in the next chapter.

Neoliberalism appeals to individual self-interest over wider community interests. In its very nature, it sets the individual up in opposition to the old sources of solidarity in the community; its implementation breaks down the older sites of community building and shared experience. It is no accident that it is hard for homeowners and tenants to make common cause, and that the revival of concepts of 'deserving' and 'undeserving' poor creates resentment rather than unity. More visibly, gentrification, especially through large-scale regeneration schemes, is leading to the physical dispersal of existing communities and activists. Those who do make a stand against neoliberal development must be prepared to face the full impact of a professional PR machine paid to discredit their integrity and character and blame them for holding back progress.

Those attempting to exert their freedom by rejecting the choices made for them by powerful combinations of governing authorities and developers soon discover the real limits to freedom of choice. When it came to the transfer of British council housing to housing associations (which needed the vote of existing tenants), bullying was an overt and central part of the process. Vote for transfer, and your much-neglected homes will be brought up to modern standards; vote against, and there will be no money for improvements. (At the same time, some of the supposedly neutral housing officers organising the votes stood to gain large salary increases if a 'yes' vote meant they became housing association employees.)

More often, pressures are harder to prove. People in areas targeted for potential redevelopment can find themselves facing a long war of attrition and malign neglect. It is well known that poorer areas (with less political muscle) tend to have poorer public services, and that public housing allocations have tended to match quality of housing with 'quality' of tenant. It may be difficult, even for those actively involved, to detect where the line has been crossed between this and a more deliberate running-down of a neighbourhood to a point where it can be argued that the only solution is comprehensive redevelopment. A Dublin community activist, working in an area scheduled for redevelopment where at least 120 children had died of heroin, suggested that this was not a coincidence 'that the establishment ... did nothing about open [drug] dealing in an area that they wanted – that their class wanted?'[53] In the Housing Market Renewal area of Kensington in Liverpool, which was largely made up of a mixture of housing association homes and low-cost homeownership, social tenants were moved out and the resulting empty properties used as evidence of the area's failure.[54] This provided the justification for the imposition of compulsory purchase orders on the remaining, primarily working-class, residents, so that the area could be cleared for 'regeneration'. Those who obstinately try and remain in areas designated for 'better' things face all the discomforts of an increasingly run-down neighbourhood and pressures to get out soon or face even more restricted options.

Naomi Klein has shown how the political and corporate leaders of neoliberalism (often one and the same) have consistently regarded crisis and confusion as the perfect opportunity for the imposition of extreme forms of neoliberal economics – what she calls 'disaster capitalism'. Are similar processes at work in these less dramatic fields? Harvey had already used the phrase 'the management and manipulation of crises' to describe the imposition of structural adjustment programmes, and had compared the bankruptcy and subsequent restructuring of New York in the 1970s to Pinochet's *coup* in Chile.[55] More recently, Chris Allen and Lee Crookes have argued that Housing Market Renewal is 'disaster capitalism *par excellence*, with state-sponsored gentrification being legitimated by the manufacture of a "disaster" myth',[56] and a similar case could be made for other regeneration schemes. Indeed, we are looking at the manufacture of more than a myth. Sustained neglect (avoidable if not necessarily planned) has, as in Klein's examples, manufactured actual disasters that make it easier to impose a radical solution.

Despite all the rhetoric, most people do not freely choose to support the new neoliberal world order. Generally they are given no alternative. And it is not just the initial imposition of neoliberalism that sits uneasily with its ostensible ideology of freedom. The contradictions thrown up by neoliberal economics in practice have prompted the emergence of a growing neoconservative authoritarianism. Political authorities have evolved an expanding web of structures and controls designed to prevent any resurgence of working-class power and to quash resistance to the new order – whether that resistance be in the form of organised campaigns, or the more nihilistic actions of some members of an increasingly frustrated underclass. New forms of governance curtail opportunities for real political debate or for dissident voices, and can be used to destroy existing independent organisations. Employment laws have effectively weakened the power of organised labour, enabling an erosion of workers' rights and conditions that has further undermined possibilities of effective labour organisation. And, at the same time as welfare is being cut, the programmes that remain are, as Wacquant put it, 'increasingly turned into instruments of surveillance and control'.[57] The US system of Workfare, or Britain's 'welfare to work', provide prime examples of this, and in the US, housing benefit can be dependent on compliance with Workfare schemes. Recently, the English housing minister also floated the idea of making unemployed council tenants seek work as a condition of their tenancy, but had to back off after being attacked from all sides.[58] There is pressure to clamp down on breaches of social security regulations and to take tenants to court at the first sign of rent arrears, escalating problems into tragedies.[59]

Widening inequalities, and the breakdown of older communities and forms of organised resistance, have encouraged a growing black economy, and destructive anti-social behaviour. Rather than address the structural conditions that are the cause of this behaviour, the state and authorities at all levels have developed new methods of surveillance and control to hold it in check and, specifically, to prevent damage to elite interests. This has been well documented in the now-extensive literature on what Neil Smith has called the 'revanchist city': the city recaptured by a vengeful right wing, prepared to exclude those of other views and backgrounds. 'Social mix' may be a useful rhetorical concept for authorities wanting to justify the gentrification of poorer areas occupying prime land, but on the ground, we are witnessing a new geographical marginalisation of the poor, who are pushed out of sight and out of mind. Gentrifiers, like colonial settlers, are protected by gates and security systems, and surveillance of public spaces drives anti-social behaviour into areas where it will not impact on those who are better off. In Britain, 'deviant' behaviour, such as kids gathering on street corners, can lead to an anti-social behaviour order (ASBO) – the breach of which results in a criminal record.

Another outlet for frustration – and especially frustration around the lack of good, genuinely affordable housing – is in xenophobia and racism. This is a classic example of the right-wing populism that has been taking root in the ground vacated through the erosion of the left. Some politicians (including those who once called themselves socialists) have found it easier to attempt to appease these views than accept the need to address the structural housing crisis that encourages them.[60] Their approach merges easily with the new attitudes towards immigration control encouraged by the 'War on Terror'.

Much has been written about the increasing constraints on public protest, and protest about housing is no exception. Authorities have become adept at the creative use of rules to suit new ends. My own local housing action group in Dundee was recently told we could not set up a stall in the city square because we did not have public liability insurance. We went ahead anyway, rightly assuming that the council would prefer not to garner further bad publicity by stopping us. However, as I subsequently discovered, this is a method of shutting down protest that is becoming common across Britain. Although in our case it proved a toothless threat, this is symptomatic of a new attitude to democratic freedoms in our increasingly 'Big Brother' society.[61]

After the 'Crunch'

As I write this, we are going through a period of economic crisis. The story is now well known. Intense competition in the mortgage market encouraged US lenders to make loans to households with low and insecure incomes (the so-called 'subprime' loans). With house prices rising, these were deemed relatively secure, and anyway the risks were spread through bundling up collections of debt, good and potentially bad, and selling them on through a highly profitable web of speculative investment all round the world. This began to unravel when interest rates were raised (in order to control inflation). It became harder to sell houses and households began to default on their loans. Soon, the result was a vicious spiral of falling house prices and mortgage foreclosures. Those who had bought the debts found that they were backed by homes worth much less that the original sum borrowed, and because the repackaging of the debts had been so complicated, no one was quite sure where the bad debts would turn up. Financial investment packages had been changing hands for growing sums, but the speculative bubble had burst. These packages had provided the security for much of the lending that lubricated the neoliberal economy. Now, existing lenders wanted their money back and new loans were hard to secure. This restriction on loans (or 'credit crunch') was not restricted to the rarefied world of financial speculation and has impacted on all sections of the economy, triggering a recessionary spiral. The international nature of modern capitalism has meant that the effects have spread quickly across the world, raising comparisons with the stock market crash of 1929.

This is a cautionary tale of unregulated finance capitalism, but will it put a damper on neoliberalism? All the evidence from past crises suggests that neoliberal capitalism will try to transform itself to master the new situation. Governments cannot afford to let their major financial institutions crash; despite all the free-market rhetoric, a huge amount of public money is being used to bail out the major players – just as it was in previous crises. These organisations have proved very ready to transform their attitudes to government intervention when they stand to benefit – and governments have been careful not to tie public money to public control, as in socialist nationalisations. In fact, as we have seen, neoliberal fundamentalists can be very pragmatic in the pursuit of profit, and crisis and disaster are regarded as opportunities for instigating new 'reforms' on the back of the emergency. There have been setbacks in the past, and even, as in New Zealand, a forced change of pace. We can expect to see changes – including a stay on some regeneration schemes where finances no longer add up, and a greater recognition of the need for the social housing safety net – but solutions to the current crisis are still being sought within the neoliberal paradigm. Even plans for building new council housing are being conceived as public-private partnerships.[62] One early way the system adjusted was to shift to speculation in commodities – contributing to serious increases in the costs of food and oil that gave rise to headlines of 'heat or eat'. Falling demand due to the recession soon brought oil prices down again, but finance capital remains ready to exploit a volatile situation.

Crises are inherent to neoliberalism, but we cannot just wait for the system to self-destruct. There are many powerful players with a great deal to lose, and they will not give up without a fight. If we do not like what is happening we need to understand it, resist it, and through resisting it create a better alternative.

Further Reading

Duménil, Gérard and Dominique Lévy (2005) 'The Neoliberal (Counter-) Revolution', in Alfredo Saad-Filho and Deborah Johnston (eds) *Neoliberalism: A Critical Reader* (London: Pluto Press).

Harvey, David (2005) *A Brief History of Neoliberalism* (Oxford: Oxford University Press).

Klein, Naomi (2007) *The Shock Doctrine: The Rise of Disaster Capitalism* (London: Penguin).

Peck, Jamie and Adam Tickell (2002) 'Neoliberalizing Space', *Antipode* 34(3): 380–404.

Notes

1. Duménil, Gérard and Dominique Lévy (2005) 'The Neoliberal (Counter-) Revolution', in Alfredo Saad-Filho and Deborah Johnston (eds) *Neoliberalism: A Critical Reader* (London: Pluto Press), p. 9.
2. Harvey, David (2005) *A Brief History of Neoliberalism* (Oxford: Oxford University Press), p. 159.
3. See <http://earthtrends.wri.org/searchable_db/index.php?theme=5&variable_ID=641&action=select-_countries> [accessed 1 August 2008]; Harvey, *A Brief History of Neoliberalism*, pp. 155–6, and Duménil and Lévy, 'The Neoliberal (Counter-) Revolution'.
4. Harvey, *A Brief History of Neoliberalism*.

5. Malpass, Peter (2005) *Housing and the Welfare State: The Development of Housing Policy in Britain* (Basingstoke: Palgrave Macmillan), p. 213.

6. For an examination of the wider impacts of poor housing, see Ambrose, Peter and Dee MacDonald (2001) *For Richer, For Poorer? Counting the Costs of Regeneration in Stepney* (Brighton: Health and Social Policy Research Centre, University of Brighton), Zacchaeus 2000 Trust (2005) *Memorandum to the Prime Minister on Unaffordable Housing* <www.z2k.org> [downloaded 17 August 2008], and ongoing research by John Bone (Aberdeen) and Karen O'Reilly (Loughborough).

7. Peter Ambrose and Sian Griffiths in Zacchaeus 2000 Trust, *Memorandum*, p. 63.

8. Thomas, Bethan and Danny Dorling (2004) 'Knowing Your Place: Housing Wealth and Equality in Great Britain 1980–2003' (London: Shelter), p. 6.

9. See, for example, 'Invest in Student Accommodation for Attractive Tax Breaks', *Independent*, 19 July 2006.

10. Unger, Knut (2006) 'Right but REITs: Opposing the Global Introduction and Consequences of Real Estate Investment Trusts (REITs)', Case study for Habitat International Coalition (from <http://www.hic-net.org> [downloaded 2 August 2008]); <http://www.lincolnplace.net> [accessed 4 August 2008], includes a video of forced evictions.

11. Marx, Karl (1999 [1887 in English]) *Capital*, Vol. 1, Part VIII, Chapter 26 <http://www.marxists.org/archive/marx/works/1867-c1/ch26.htm> [accessed 4 August 2008].

12. Whitehead, Christine and Kathleen Scanlon (eds) (2007) *Social Housing in Europe* (London: London School of Economics), pp. 6 and 10–11.

13. Ibid., p. 134.

14. *Our Future Homes*, White Paper produced by the Conservative government in 1995, quoted in 'Rent Levels, Affordability and Housing Benefit', House of Commons Research Paper 98/69 (1998), p. 25.

15. See Ambrose, Peter and Paul Nicolson (2005) 'Appendix 7 – Some Problems of Demand Side Support' in Zacchaeus 2000 Trust, *Memorandum*.

16. Higher rates of tax have been cut and blanket taxes, such as sales tax, which impact disproportionately on the poor, have been increased.

17. 2004 figures from Whitehead and Scanlon, *Social Housing in Europe*, p. 83.

18. Housing Corporation, *Annual Report and Accounts 2007–8*, p. 8.
19. See investigation by BBC Five Live, 15 October 2006 <http://news.bbc.co.uk/1/hi/business/6048982.stm> [accessed 8 August 2008].
20. See, for example, Monbiot, George (2000) *Captive State: The Corporate Takeover of Britain* (Basingstoke: Palgrave Macmillan), and Pollock, Allyson M. (2004) *NHS plc: The Privatisation of Our Health Care* (London: Verso).
21. *Guardian*, 'Society', 26 July 2006. The British government argues that it is better for housing associations to borrow money than for local authorities to do so because then it does not count as public-sector borrowing, upon which they have set strict limits. Of course, as government, they could always change their own accounting rules.
22. Malpass, *Housing and the Welfare State*, p. 24.
23. Quoted in Forrest, Ray, Alan Murie and Peter Williams (1990) *Homeownership: Differentiation and Fragmentation* (London: Unwin Hyman), p. 69.
24. Engels, Friedrich (1936) *The Housing Question* (London: Lawrence and Wishart), p. 46.
25. Forrest et al., *Homeownership*, p. 60.
26. Quoted in Cowan, David and Morag McDermont (2006) *Regulating Social Housing: Governing Decline* (Abingdon: Routledge-Cavendish), p. 165.
27. Quoted in Forrest et al., *Homeownership*, p. 60. This comment was made three years before his 1923 Housing Act.
28. House of Commons Council Housing Group (2005) 'Support for the "Fourth Option" for Council Housing: Report on the Enquiry into the Future Funding of Council Housing 2004–2005' <http://www.support4councilhousing.org.uk/report/resources/HoCCHG_report.pdf> [accessed 18 August 2008] p. 8; Glynn, Sarah (2007) 'But We Already Have Community Ownership – Making Council Housing Work', in Andy Cumbers and Geoff Whittam (eds) *Reclaiming the Economy: Alternatives to Market Fundamentalism* (Glasgow: Scottish Left Review Press), p. 144.
29. See, for example, 'Chief Executive Pay Hits a New High', *Inside Housing*, 8 August 2008. Two months later (24 October), *Inside Housing* reported that the same housing association had capped the pay of its sheltered housing managers and derecognised their union.
30. Malpass, Peter (2000) *Housing Associations and Housing Policy: A Historical Perspective* (Basingstoke: Palgrave Macmillan), p. 240.

31. Peck, Jamie and Adam Tickell (2002) 'Neoliberalizing Space', *Antipode* 34(3): 389.
32. See, for example, Klein, Naomi (2007) *The Shock Doctrine: The Rise of Disaster Capitalism* (London: Penguin), p. 15.
33. FEANTSA (2006) 'EU State Aid Rules and Social Housing: FEANTSA Calls for Action to Make Social Housing Accessible for the Most Vulnerable' <http://www.feantsa.org/files/Housing%20Policy%20st atements/EU%20State%20aid%20rules%20and%20social%20hou sing_Feantsa.pdf>[accessed 12 October 2008]). FEANTSA stands for Fédération Européenne d'Associations Nationales Travaillant avec les Sans-Abri, or European Federation of National Organisations Working with the Homeless.
34. Malpass, *Housing Associations and Housing Policy*, p. 183.
35. Cowan and McDermont, *Regulating Social Housing*.
36. Jacobs, Keith and Tony Manzi (2000) 'Performance Indicators and Social Constructivism: Conflict and Control in Housing Management' *Critical Social Policy* 20: 85.
37. See Dundee City Council's *Housing News*.
38. See, for example, Potter, Bob (2008) 'Damned Lies and Statistics', *Weekly Worker*, 12 June.
39. The information I received was both incomplete and contradictory – for example, the number of overcrowded households was given as 565 from one source, and 2,033 from another.
40. Harvey, *A Brief History of Neoliberalism*.
41. Quoted in ibid., p. 36.
42. Cowan and McDermont, *Regulating Social Housing*.
43. DeFilippis, James (2001) 'The Myth of Social Capital in Community Development', *Housing Policy Debate* 12: 4 <http://www.fannie-maefoundation.org/programs/hpd/pdf/HPD_1204_defilippis.pdf>.
44. Dench, Geoff, Kate Gavron and Michael Young (2006) *The New East End: Kinship, Race and Conflict* (London: Profile Books).
45. Ibid., p. 231.
46. Glynn, 'But We Already Have Community Ownership'.
47. Stewart Maxwell MSP, interviewed by Lesley Riddoch on BBC Radio Scotland, 20 July 2007.
48. Collins, Chik and Peter Jones (2006) 'Analysis of Discourse As "a Form of History Writing:" A Critique of Critical Discourse Analysis and an Illustration of a Cultural-Historical Alternative', *Atlantic Journal of Communication* 14(1&2): 51–69.
49. Lewis, Justin et al. (2008) 'The Quality and Independence of British Journalism: Tracking the Changes over 20 years', report published by the Mediawise Trust <http://www.mediawise.org.uk/files/uploaded/

Quality%20&%20Independence%20of%20British%20Journalism.
pdf> [downloaded 16 August 2008].

50. *Guardian* supplement, 'Promised Lands', 14 March 2007.
51. Patrick Butler, *Guardian*, 5 March 2008.
52. This has been the subject of many bitter postings on the *Inside Housing* internet forum (downloaded October 2007).
53. Quoted in Punch, Michael (2005) 'Problem Drug Use and the Political Economy of Urban Restructuring: Heroin, Class and Governance in Dublin', *Antipode* 37(4): 771–2.
54. The official phrase was that the area was 'under used and unsightly'.
55. Harvey, *A Brief History of Neoliberalism*, pp. 162 and 45.
56. *Morning Star*, 30 July 2008.
57. Wacquant, Loïc (1999) 'Urban Marginality in the Coming Millennium', *Urban Studies* 36(10): 1643.
58. *Guardian*, 5 February 2008. Unlike in the US, British councils have a duty to make sure families are housed.
59. For examples, see Ambrose and Nicolson, 'Appendix 7 – Some Problems of Demand Side Support', pp. 49–50.
60. See Margaret Hodge in the *Observer*, 20 May 2007.
61. See, for example, Jenni Russell, 'The All-seeing State is About to End Privacy as We Know It', *Guardian*, 8 October 2008.
62. *Guardian*, *Society* section, 13 August 2008.

3

REGENERATION AS A TROJAN HORSE

Sarah Glynn

You take down the dwellings of the poor, build houses in their place for which only the middle classes can afford to pay the rent, and thus by diminishing the amount of cheap house accommodation, increase the rents and aggravate the evil you attempted to cure.

William Farr, 1841[1]

'Regeneration' sounds as though it could only be a good thing, but it is being used as a Trojan horse for state-sponsored 'accumulation by dispossession' on a massive scale. For Neil Smith, 'the victory of this language [of regeneration] in anesthetizing our critical understanding of gentrification in Europe represents a considerable ideological victory for neoliberal visions of the city'.[2] This chapter examines the arguments and methods used by regeneration's protagonists to investigate how wholesale changes that benefit elite interests have become widely regarded as the incontestable future.

Something Needs to Be Done

Most people would agree that intervention of some kind is necessary because huge disparities in wealth have left many areas struggling under multiple deprivation. However, as Gough and colleagues have argued, even regeneration schemes that would appear to be most focused on uplifting disadvantaged communities are doomed to failure and are also largely conceived as damage limitation exercises dictated by elite interests. As these authors explain, poverty and exclusion are 'logical outcomes of capitalist societies'.[3] The social-democratic welfare state attempted to

72

temper this through a measure of redistribution; however (as we saw in Chapter 2), the last 30 years have seen 'an offensive by capital to restore both its authority and its rate of profit',[4] and redistributory mechanisms have been cut. While most legislators express concern about poverty, active responses to it have, as in previous centuries, generally had more pragmatic origins. They have been prompted by fear of disorder, desire to improve the usefulness of the reserve army of labour,[5] and in reaction to organised pressure from below[6] – though such organised pressure has been badly weakened. Gough and colleagues argue that British government policy on social exclusion 'accepts the main thrust of neoliberalism'[7] but, in response to these pressures, seeks to mitigate its worst excesses through piecemeal interventions.

Progressive-sounding concepts, such as New Labour's 'Neighbourhood Renewal', do move beyond the 'bricks-and-mortar' approaches of previous regeneration schemes to look at social issues, but they are doomed to remain relatively ineffective so long as the major structural forces of neoliberalism remain unchecked. So, for example, government-sponsored schemes provide basic training that ensures a ready supply of potential workers, but not well-paid jobs. Interventions are officially portrayed as examples of 'joined-up thinking', but political and geographical restrictions mean that they can only ever address the symptoms of what is going wrong, and not the underlying malaise. The consequent failures have themselves been used to justify a new approach. If existing communities obstinately refuse to renew themselves, then they should be dispersed and replaced by a better class of people. Structural inequalities continue to be ignored in favour of a 'false choice' between degeneration and gentrification;[8] like other responses to neoliberal failure, the new solution involves a heavier dose of yet more neoliberalism.

The Entrepreneurial Local State

Through an analysis of the reincarnation of Newcastle, England, Stuart Cameron has shown how the ideas of people-focused community development that were trumpeted in the late 1990s have come into direct conflict with new theories of housing-led regeneration. This new orthodoxy has little time for working with the people now living in the areas concerned. In fact, as Cameron explains:

> [It] is not, in general, an approach that is directly concerned with the housing conditions or economic well-being of existing residents. It is an approach to regeneration which seeks to solve the problems of a locality through the introduction of a new, more affluent, population, rather than directly addressing and seeking to solve the economic and social problems of existing communities and neighbourhoods.[9]

At local and regional levels, different areas are increasingly competing with each other to attract new, wealthier, home-owning, tax-paying residents and also the economic spin-offs of large-scale construction. The drive to increase council tax yields awakens echoes of nineteenth-century slum clearances that were similarly driven by the desire to raise rates and also to offload the cost of looking after the poor onto neighbouring areas.[10]

Local political leaders have become caught up in the competitive drive. Peter Brooks, the Labour deputy leader of Greenwich Council, which is presiding over a major regeneration scheme to replace a large council estate, told *ROOF* magazine:

> Kidbrooke could be a key place to live and work in London so I suspect that a different type of person will want to move in. I do understand that communities have been torn apart and I think that's the part of it you regret. But what I am trying to do is form a new community. I see it as a fantastic opportunity for people who live in and around Kidbrooke and on an estate that is going nowhere. It is unfortunate that we have had to move people to do this. I wouldn't like it I suppose if I lived here.[11]

This is all part of what Jason Hackworth and Neil Smith have defined as 'third-wave gentrification': large-scale gentrification that is expanding into new areas and is being carried out by big developers actively supported by local government. Such projects have become possible, they argue, because of the dismantling of both the institutional structures designed to restrict uneven development, and the physical structures of social housing that literally stood in its way.[12] Poorer neighbourhoods on prime sites are expected to make way for more profitable development, and although this will be officially portrayed as in the wider interests of the city or region, there is little in the way of redistributive mechanisms, while local government investment tends to be geared towards attracting more private investment. Regeneration is big business, with money to be made not just in the actual development but also through the promotion of high-yielding economic sectors such as the retail trade or tourism and – most importantly – through the associated financial services and speculative activities. In Scotland, Chik Collins has shown how the Scottish government's Regeneration Policy Statement took its lead from a report by the Royal Bank of Scotland that promoted 'regeneration' as an opportunity for the growth of private business through the privatisation of public services.[13]

Unpicking the Arguments

The Problem of Low Demand

Looking at the example of Britain (and similar practices obtain elsewhere), we find that this social engineering through housing policy is being promoted on the back of four main arguments that serve to disguise the bigger picture under a rhetoric of social good. The arguments are: the problem of 'low-demand' housing, the desirability of 'mixed-income' neighbourhoods including 'tenure mix', the improvement of housing standards, and the need for 'modernisation'.

Low-demand housing has come to be seen as not just a symptom of area decline, but a cause of it, that needs to be dealt with explicitly. Reasons for an area becoming unpopular are incredibly complex and it is difficult to isolate the effects of different interrelated causes. Bramley and Pawson – key proponents of this argument – suggest three principal reasons: demographic trends such as out-migration, changes in housing preference (especially away from social housing), and area stigmatisation.[14] None of these is straightforward. Even if we accept, as they do, the neoliberal *laissez-faire* argument that regional planning policies are no longer feasible,[15] and even if some out-migration and population loss is seen as unavoidable, what groups are leaving and how does this relate to need for different housing types? What happens when, as now, the housing market declines and a higher proportion of people want and need affordable rented housing?

'Preference' for other tenures, as opposed to social housing, is affected by the quality, cost and ease of availability of social housing. Social rent levels have risen dramatically, basic repair and maintenance has often been starved of funds, and waiting lists for good social housing can, nevertheless, be prohibitive. Meanwhile, as shown in Chapter 2, there has been a big economic imperative for those who can to get a foot on the housing ladder, even though promotion of homeownership as the natural and desirable state may be far from beneficial for many of those pressured to take on a mortgage, as well as for those unable to do so. In fact, the drive for ownership has been taken so far that even the relatively conservative Chartered Institute of Housing found in a survey of its members carried out in 2007 (before the credit crunch) that 83 per cent of respondents agreed that 'there is too much emphasis on home owning at the expense of renting'.[16] Promoting preference for ownership is government policy, and any such preference should be seen to a considerable extent as the result of housing policy, not an independent factor feeding into it. Homeownership was rising almost everywhere, even in countries such as Germany that have long had a much higher proportion of rented homes.[17]

Area stigmatisation is a different kind of problem, as it implies not that homes are not needed, but that particular homes are seen as undesirable. Even where this is true – and the label of low demand is often used on very little evidence – the reason may have little to do with the buildings themselves, and should be properly investigated in each case. Bramley and Pawson stress the importance of concerns about crime and anti-social behaviour, and these need to be understood and addressed in themselves. Otherwise, we will see whole areas being destroyed because of a few troublemakers, while the problems are simply moved on elsewhere. It is also easy for an area, once it gets any sort of bad name, to slide downhill. This is not just because more socially mobile people will leave and others will be unwilling to take their place, but also because, as discussed in Chapter 2, the estate may become used as a 'dumping ground' for 'problem' tenants.

Bramley and Pawson appear to disregard their own observation that 'demand projections for more than about five years ahead are difficult and would not carry great credibility'.[18] They argue that a logical conclusion of research into low-demand housing is the diversion of investment away from some of the worst areas, which are seen as fit only for demolition, so enabling councils to reduce their housing stock.[19] Arguments about housing preference allow this loss of council housing stock to be portrayed as a positive outcome. In a report for the government in 2000, DTZ Pieda estimated that in England growing levels of demolition brought down around 40,000 (or 1 per cent of) local authority homes between 1991 and 1997.[20] They recorded a significant net loss of dwellings, an even greater reduction in the amount of social housing, and a net shift from local authority housing to housing with registered social landlords (generally housing associations).[21] Reasons for demolition given by the councils concerned included reducing the stock of social housing and promoting tenure mix. It has also been shown that where areas designated for regeneration extend over a mixture of tenures, then it is enormously cheaper to demolish public housing than negotiate compensatory packages for private owners.[22] However, council house demolitions have coincided with growing housing waiting lists.

The Panacea of Mixed-income Neighbourhoods

Tenure mix – and mixed-income housing more generally – is often promoted simply as an unquestioned good. This is an idea with a long pedigree. A parliamentary Select Committee of 1838 argued that seclusion from 'the observation and influence of better educated neighbours' in the dense London slums resulted in a 'state of moral degradation';[23] and later in the century, belief in the beneficial influence of middle-class neighbours inspired idealistic university students and graduates to live in settlements in the slum areas so as to work on improving the poor. It would seem to be no accident that the push for income mix today has coincided with a retreat towards past levels of inequality as governments abandon the idea that equality is possible, or even desirable. Income mix has become a substitute for income equality – which is a very different thing from Nye Bevan's vision of council housing for all as part of a wider plan of wealth redistribution. The current incarnation of the idea of income mix is based around the argument for area effects – that is, that it is worse to be poor in a poor area than poor in an area of mixed prosperity. This is an idea that developed in the United States and has become generally accepted, acquiring the status of a common-sense truth. However, it was based more on intuition than evidence, and recent research – both qualitative and now quantitative – has put its validity into question.

Atkinson and Kintrea carried out a comparative study in two different areas in Glasgow and two in Edinburgh in 2000. It is difficult to isolate similarly poor households in different areas; however, they found that the poorer areas did not conform to the model stereotype of an isolated and inward-looking place where criminal behaviour is normalised, though they did uncover a very strong belief that an address in an area with a poor reputation made getting a job more difficult.[24] A follow-up paper, based on interviews with local community workers of various kinds, gave a more complicated and sometimes contradictory picture of both negative and positive area effects. Stigmatisation and discrimination, lack of useful external contacts and an aggressive territoriality were combined with, and could be set against, the benefits of sharing a similar socio-economic position with others in the neighbourhood, support of local friends and family, and sense of community.[25] More unmitigated disadvantages arose from overloaded and under-funded welfare services, which are often much worse in poorer areas; but these are problems that should be addressed directly and are more to do with how resources are allocated than area effects *per se*. There is little here to suggest that new, wealthier neighbours would improve the lives of those in poorer areas.

Butler and Robson have interviewed middle-class gentrifiers and found social networks in Lewisham that were 'largely exclusive of non-middle-class people' and a social structure in Brixton 'which celebrates diversity in principle but leads to separate lives in practice'.[26] Similarly, Davidson and Lees' qualitative examination of new-build gentrification in Brentford, on the bank of the Thames, found no evidence of the social mixing that was supposed to result from the Greater London Authority's plans.[27]

Uitermark and colleagues, looking at the introduction of owner-occupied housing into a social housing estate in Rotterdam, concluded that attempts to build social cohesion between old and new residents were doomed to failure since the 'acceptance of demolition as a solution for social problems pitted residents of new and old housing blocks against each other'. They found that 'Many tenants in less attractive social housing were considered as a nuisance to other neighbourhood residents', and that 'the result of restructuring ... is not a cohesive living environment, but rather a neighbourhood where people live their own lives and avoid confrontations with members of other groups'.[28] Pierre Gilbert predicts similar outcomes from the urban renewal of a large housing estate in the troubled Lyon suburb of Minguettes. Tenants with greater social mobility have been able to use the opportunity of the demolitions to move away, while others with more precarious incomes and employment have been allotted homes within the estate that are similar to those they have left; so the initial effect has been to concentrate poverty and increase stigmatisation. This will make it harder to attract new residents and also encourages attitudes that preserve social distance.[29]

Doherty and colleagues have recently completed a significant large-scale quantitative study that looked at indices of social well-being using UK-wide data from the 1991 and 2001 censuses and Scottish data from the Scottish Longitudinal Study. Although (after taking account of the characteristics of the population) they found better than average results for wards where the level of social renting was between 10 and 30 per cent and significantly worse results when the level of social renting was over 50 per cent, it was impossible to tell which groups were affected. When they looked at social mix on a more local scale – that is, the 'pepper-potting' of different types of housing – they found more evidence for negative results of mixing than positive. And when they attempted to predict employment levels based on tenure mix using Scottish neighbourhood statistics, they found no consistent pattern, suggesting that other factors were more significant. As a result, Doherty and colleagues were 'forced to conclude that the policy of deliberately mixing tenures in housing developments in order to improve social well-being remains largely unsupported by the research evidence so far available'.[30]

Tenure mix can also generate problems of its own. Social tenants complain of private owners who hinder general improvements through failure to contribute their share of the costs, while homes planned for owner-occupiers, who would put down roots in an area, can attract buy-to-let absentee landlords and a shifting population on short-term tenancies.

Neoliberalism has proved to be generally less concerned about helping the poor than controlling them; and tenure mix is also promoted as a way of breaking up communities that do not comply with middle-class mores. The new middle-class neighbours thus become instruments of social control.[31]

The mantra of 'tenure mix' has become an important tool for those promoting the replacement of well-located social housing with developments that concentrate on private housing for sale; however, there is very little pressure to bring social rented housing into areas of private ownership. An exception to this is provided by the social housing that developers, especially in Britain, have been obliged to provide as a condition of building larger private developments. This housing, however, tends to be tucked away in less attractive corners, if it cannot be built on an entirely different site. People who buy their homes do not want social rented tenants next door, not necessarily for social reasons, but because of the effect on property values. This is a long-standing prejudice, as evidenced by the notorious Cutteslowe walls built by a developer across an Oxford road to separate his private houses from the council houses beyond. Erected in 1934, the walls were not finally removed until 1959.[32] Such prejudices are only increased by the residualisation of social housing and the growing importance of property value.

One reason why arguments about tenure mix have come to the fore is the concentrations of poverty resulting from the residu-alisation of social housing, which shows up statistically as an increasing proportion of those in social housing being on low incomes and state benefits. This narrowing of the social group does have a real effect on the situation of those who remain. It removes a layer of people most likely to be able to contribute to community life, and it increases segregation between those who can afford to buy into the new marketised system and those who cannot. Tenure mix will not break down this division, which *would* be addressed by a re-expansion of social rented housing to take in a wider range of people,[33] and by an end to the fetishisation of homeownership (see Chapter 13).

Improvements and Aspirations – For Some

No one would dispute the need for improved standards for social housing, especially in post-Thatcherite Britain after decades of under-investment, but here we find that the nature and limits of funding mean that new standards are being used to force through mass privatisations and demolitions. Councils are anxious to divest themselves of homes they cannot afford to improve; rather than being a means of upgrading council housing, the new standards are driving another nail in its coffin. Statutory improvement targets have forced some councils to accept the government bribe of the write-off of their accumulated housing debts, a write-off given on condition that councils transfer their housing stock to private non-profit housing associations. And, with or without stock-transfer, business plans by housing associations and councils are increasingly forced to depend on large-scale demolitions. Long-overdue improvements to some homes will only be achieved through the total destruction of others. This point was raised in Parliament by Labour MP Lynne Jones, who stated:

> The only way that the Government have any chance of meeting the decent homes standard without more resources is by demolishing a great deal of

houses that are not decent. We now have a crisis, not only because of the condition of homes, but because of homelessness: hundreds of families are now in temporary accommodation.[34]

As will be shown in Chapter 5, this approach does not actually result in an overall saving in public expenditure. Rather, it is another significant example of the application of regressive subsidy, with the largest benefits going to private developers.

Arguments about 'low demand' are still being used, but after interviewing regeneration practitioners in the north-east of England, Cameron noted that the discourse around the policies was changing. He observed a new emphasis on the need for 'modernisation' of housing stock and tenure to meet 'new aspirations'.[35] This is the language being used to promote Housing Market Renewal. It suggests that the neoliberal hegemony is such

Figure 3.1   Housing campaign illustration.

that its proponents feel able to adopt a much more obviously market-based agenda, and it allows the renewal approach to be rolled out across much wider areas. In Dundee, we were told that no one wants to live in high flats because they want small family houses; in the north of England, terraces of small family houses (in mixed-tenure communities) are being declared obsolete and fit only for demolition (see Figure 3.1).

Incorporating the 'Community'

Regeneration of physical structures to suit business interests is twinned with and facilitated by the changes in the organisation of local government discussed in Chapter 2. Like the physical changes, this organisational restructuring is purported to be regenerative and in the interests of the local 'community', which is presented as taking on a greater role; however, the real beneficiaries are the unelected business 'partners' and the target-setters of central government. Far from giving real power to local people, structures erected in the name of neighbourhood renewal and community-led regeneration and other partnership forms of local governance, tend to increase the democratic deficit and are biased towards the needs of capital. Mike Geddes, discussing their use in England, has described how scope for real political debate is restricted and how the state is able to 'maintain tight control over local institutions and actors who might challenge the hegemony of neoliberalism':[36]

> ... acceptance of the rules of the game by local residents commits them to structures and processes which often both disadvantage them ... and which incorporate them within the apparatus of the state as much, and maybe more than they open up the state to citizens.[37]

The charade of community involvement and consultation wastes creative energies and causes divisions between those who want to resist developments and those who argue that the pragmatic approach is to accept the changes as inevitable and work with them. And when, despite all the forums and discussion groups, people discover their lack of real power to influence events, the result can be an increased fatalism and detachment. This is only increased further when it is realised that traditional labour organisations, who could previously have been turned to for help, have themselves gone so far down the pragmatism route as to become apologists for many elements of neoliberalism.

Chik Collins argues that current practices of 'community' participation and partnership were first conceived as a way of delivering an unpopular Thatcherite agenda, which was piloted through New Life for Urban Scotland, launched in 1988. This regeneration programme was designed to provide a model that could be written up as a success and rolled out elsewhere; however, what was portrayed as community planning actually marginalised and eliminated genuine local organisations. In one instance, the destruction of existing community structures was so thorough that drug-dealers and moneylenders were able to move into the vacuum.[38]

In examining the Scottish Executive's more recent use of 'community engagement', Collins noted that the very term 'is itself an import from the corporate world', where it is used to describe a 'hearts-and-minds' approach to carrying out business in a hostile environment. He also identified a new twist to the incorporation of community groups. Using the example of the centrally organised 'Community Voices Network', Collins showed how years of frustration and anger at the running-down of public services are being harnessed and redirected at the local authorities in order to help break down their resistance to the new changes, and he identified a new willingness to encourage protest in order to exploit it.[39]

Increasing numbers of people have become involved in the regeneration of their area, genuinely hoping to play their part, only to find themselves tied down in bureaucratic detail while the important decisions are made elsewhere. These decisions may even exclude them from any future in the area at all. Few of the original tenants will end up in the regenerated Greenwich estate mentioned above, despite being invited to choose the windows for their new homes.[40] Elizabeth Pascoe, who has made news headlines fighting the compulsory purchase order on her Liverpool house (see Chapter 4), had earlier reorganised her work so that she could play an active part in what was being represented as community regeneration.

Chris Allen's account of this Liverpool regeneration provides a clear exposé of the mechanics of neoliberal governance.[41] Housing Market Renewal is being carried out by a partnership of private developers, housing associations and the city council, co-ordinated through a specially set up management organisation. Allen shows how the lead proponents of the regeneration have used research selectively to support the desired outcomes, how they have repeated their preferred interpretations until they become accepted facts, and how these 'facts' are adopted by those who give contradictory views in less guarded moments. He describes how forums that were ostensibly set up for community decision making were regarded by official institutions as opportunities for one-way communication, and how those institutions were so wedded to their ideology that any resistance was interpreted as a problem of communication failure.[42] He records how locally controlled groups were replaced by groups chaired by a member of the Housing Market Renewal Partnership, how resident representatives were hand-picked by the authorities and swamped with meeting minutes the size of telephone directories, and how all protest was dismissed as invalid, mischievous misinformation, or inappropriately aggressive. And he shows how, consequently, the solutions proposed for those displaced were able to ignore real physical and economic needs and provide no real solution at all. He demonstrates how the branding of Liverpool as 'City of Culture' fed into this process, and he notes how the council was so confident of beating the legal challenge to their compulsory purchase orders that they have no plans for what to do with the now boarded-up homes should they lose.

The dead hand of controlled consultation is used at many levels. Internal party 'reforms' have made this a technique well known to Labour members; and I had direct experience of the process when I co-ordinated an academic response to the SNP (Scottish National Party) government's 'consultation' on Scottish housing. All the responses received from community groups, interested 'stakeholders' and professionals were collated by a private consultancy firm and reduced down into one anodyne report. This document – presumably all most government members will see of the consultation – filtered out our background arguments and supporting references, as well as making no mention of important critical comments, including those on tenure mix and English experiences of arm's-length management organisations.[43]

Out of Sight, Out of Mind

When Engels described 1840s Manchester, he observed how the shops that lined the arterial roads 'conceal from the eyes of the wealthy men and women of strong stomachs and weak nerves the misery and grime which form the complement of their wealth'.[44] In the early twenty-first century, a senior manager for Liverpool's Housing Market Renewal defended the demolition of lower-income homes along a road perceived as a main gateway into Liverpool with the argument that 'people driving into the city must have a more pleasant outlook than is currently there'. And an official commented to the chair of the local residents' association, 'well you wouldn't want people driving past Edge Lane and seeing washing on your line would you?'[45] The local MP has criticised the plans as 'social cleansing'.[46] The less well-off have been squeezed out of the city centres, and those who have replaced them do not wish to be reminded of the other world that complements their prosperity (see Figure 3.2). The economic, and increasingly the physical, marginality of those whom regeneration has displaced is reflected in their absence from public discourse.

But what does regeneration actually mean for those at the receiving end? First, it generally involves a forced move – and sometimes more than one. Moving is always stressful, and these are moves in which households also suffer from uncertainty over what is happening and from lack of choice over where they are going. Some may be lucky and end up in better places, but a great many will not, since housing options for those without much money are contracting. As an area empties out, those who are left are expected to live in decaying surroundings and with growing

Figure 3.2 Housing campaign illustration.

risks of vandalism. Households often end up having to meet higher housing costs and they often receive unrealistically low financial compensation for the actual move. Compulsory purchase orders quote notoriously low valuations and little account is taken of time and labour that tenants have expended on their homes. Local small businesses vanish with their customers. As in past clearances, community links are broken and friends and families find themselves separated. In some cases, this dispersal may even be a deliberate policy aim – as it was for the reformers who attempted to break up the dangerous 'rookeries' of Victorian London, and for the 1960s planner, quoted by Peter Malpass, who described slum dwellers as 'almost a separate race of people'.[47]

Some people do not just disappear from sight, they disappear completely, as regeneration exacts the ultimate price. Elizabeth Pascoe, fighting the demolition of her Liverpool neighbourhood of Kensington, comments:

> I attended 9 funerals in a year of people I knew well … I have been told about a further 25 deaths, 34 from 370 properties sounds a lot, the last two I knew were [aged] 54 and 60. As I have said '34' openly in oral evidence and none of the proponents (LCC officers, etc.) have disputed the figure, I suggest it is in fact higher, possibly a lot higher.[48]

Of course it is impossible to prove that demolition kills, but the stresses that it causes can mean the difference between life and death, especially for the elderly. Bob Dumbleton has collected accounts from residents in two groups of post-war prefabs that are being redeveloped.[49] Most of the residents were elderly and had lived in their homes for a long time. He records stresses around loss of control over life, and not knowing what the authorities might do next, and stresses over the processes of moving and of living through demolition and building work. He notes the particular problems that older people can experience in learning to cope in unfamiliar surroundings – problems that have been the subject of considerable research on care-home patients. And he quotes evidence given him by a doctor:

> For older people in particular moving residence is amongst the highest risk factors for triggering an anxiety response and possible depression. It is only marginally less significant than the death of a spouse.[50]

Dumbleton, who has been a housing activist for decades, is in no doubt that the big slum clearance schemes killed people in the past, that '"Regenerations" are killing them still', and that this is part of the wider social neglect of the elderly.[51]

The Embedded Academic

Academics play an important role in the manufacture of consent and in the positive portrayal of 'regeneration'; and Tom Slater has charted the gradual 'eviction' of critical analysis from gentrification research.[52] Many of the points he makes could also be applied to academic research much more widely. Across the social sciences, postmodern debate has preferred to concentrate on the definition of terms rather than on the processes they are supposed to describe; understanding is obscured by caricaturing arguments and polarising debate, and research on the middle classes has gone from being avant-garde to mainstream, with research on the working classes being concurrently branded as backward looking. All of this weakens the researcher's ability to subject government policy to critical analysis and so to resist the constraints imposed by the neoliberal world-view. Slater shows how arguments for a more 'nuanced' approach to gentrification are used to dismiss more critical understandings, but do not prevent the promotion of positive romantic images. These simply write the working class out of the picture, and talk about 'reurbanisation', as though those who used to live or work in the city centres were not also people. This is all made easier by the fact that those displaced are no longer visible, and are very difficult to count.

Even approaches that in themselves can be seen as progressive, such as acknowledgement of the impacts of racism, and the feminist emphasis on the role of the researcher, are increasingly used to obscure underlying structural forces. So, gentrification by members of an ethnic minority is somehow seen as good for their ethnic 'community' and research becomes an extension of the susceptibilities of the middle-class researcher. Slater even quotes one writer describing how his family mingled with local residents at a yard sale and his wife 'reorganized several residents' display of goods to show them off to better effect, to the delight of the sellers' – a description that could have come straight from the pen of Octavia Hill.[53]

In an increasingly commodified academia, research is expected to justify itself through its policy relevance, even when not directly funded by industry or interested organisations. As well as the more obvious problem of research tending to follow policy, this encourages a sort of self-policing. Academics have become afraid to appear oppositionist and not part of the 'real' (that is, neoliberal) world in which all that is regarded as possible is to record changes and manage them a little better. Allen observes that all but one or two researchers who have looked at Housing Market Renewal (HMR) 'have completely neglected to address issues of power, class and social stratification' and that this, along with 'the academy's embrace of the technocratic discourse' (see

Chapter 2), has resulted in 'the cardinal sin of obscuring what HMR is really doing, thereby facilitating the domination of the dominant over the dominated'.[54]

As if this were not enough, it seems that those who do not police themselves may even find themselves attracting the attention of the regular police force. In 2007, a German sociologist was arrested, and held in solitary confinement in a Berlin jail, for having 'used, in his academic publications, "phrases and key words" also used by a militant group, among them "inequality" and "gentrification"'.[55]

'The New Urban Frontier'[56]

The arrest of the German sociologist is an extreme example of the neoconservative authoritarian complement to neoliberalism, and there is no shortage of examples in the physical process of regeneration itself. Buildings and open spaces in regenerated areas are often guarded by gates, and growing numbers of private security cameras are joining the increasingly sophisticated public ones. Even the old Bryant and May Match Factory, site of the famous match-girls' strike of 1888 that helped establish the unionisation of unskilled workers, is now a picturesque gated community, protected from the wild East End beyond. Those who have been displaced and disenfranchised are physically prevented from returning. Growing inequalities have proved a boon to the security industry,[57] as frontiers between rich and poor demand increasingly sophisticated protection.

While the level of protection is unprecedented, the idea of an urban frontier has always been a conscious part of gentrification. As Neil Smith explained, 'The frontier discourse serves to rationalize and legitimate a process of conquest, whether in the eighteenth- and nineteenth-century West or in the late-twentieth-century inner city.'[58]

In Britain, references are often more colonial, and the idea of the middle classes entering the city's dangerous poor quarters like intrepid colonialists has a long history. The founder of the Salvation Army used the phrase 'in darkest England'[59] when referring to the Victorian slums, and the images that phrase was meant to evoke are still alive today.

Naomi Klein has compared the current expropriations of public wealth more generally to the earlier expropriations of colonialism,[60] and in regeneration, this comparison becomes most explicit. In 2007, in an enlightened interlude from programmes about property investment, the BBC showed a documentary about the conversion of a council tower-block into luxury apartments.[61] The excited frontier talk of the sales staff was cringe-makingly embarrassing; but perhaps even more telling was the footage of a pair of young property speculators poring over a map of the area and marking off the flats they had bought up, like so many territorial conquests.

Further Reading

Allen, Chris (2008) *Housing Market Renewal and Social Class* (London and New York: Routledge).

Cameron, Stuart (2006) 'From Low Demand to Rising Aspirations: Housing Market Renewal within Regional and Neighbourhood Regeneration Policy', *Housing Studies* 21(1): 3–16.

Collins, Chik (2007) '"The Scottish Executive is Open for Business": *People and Place*, The Royal Bank of Scotland, and the Intensification of the Neo-Liberal Agenda in Scotland', in Andy Cumbers and Geoff Whittam (eds), *Reclaiming the Economy: Alternatives to Market Fundamentalism* (Glasgow: Scottish Left Review Press).

Dumbleton, Bob (2006) *'Help us Somebody': The Demolition of the Elderly* (London: The London Press).

Geddes, Mike (2006) 'Partnership and the Limits to Local Governance in England: Institutionalist Analysis and Neoliberalism', *International Journal of Urban and Regional Research* 30(1): 76–97.

Lees, Loretta, Tom Slater and Elvin Wyly (2008) *Gentrification* (Abingdon: Routledge).

Smith, Neil (1996) *The New Urban Frontier: Gentrification and the Revanchist City* (London and New York: Routledge).

Notes

1. Quoted in Stedman Jones, Gareth (1976 [1971]) *Outcast London: A Study in the Relationship Between Classes in Victorian Society* (Harmondsworth: Penguin).

2. Smith, Neil (2002) 'New Globalism, New Urbanism: Gentrification as Global Urban Strategy', *Antipode* 34(3): 446.
3. Gough, Jamie, Aram Eisenschitz and Andrew McCulloch (2006) *Spaces of Social Exclusion* (Abingdon: Routledge), p. 140.
4. Ibid., p. 139.
5. This refers to that part of the labour force in casual employment or out of work. A large pool of available labour can be used to pull down wage levels.
6. Gough and McCulloch, *Spaces of Social Exclusion*, p. 14.
7. Ibid,. p. 3.
8. Slater, Tom (2006) 'The Eviction of Critical Perspectives from Gentrification Research', *International Journal of Urban and Regional Research* 30(4): 753.
9. Cameron, Stuart (2006) 'From Low Demand to Rising Aspirations: Housing Market Renewal within Regional and Neighbourhood Regeneration Policy', *Housing Studies* 21(1): 10.
10. Stedman Jones, *Outcast London*, pp. 183 and 167–8.
11. Quoted in Hewett, Brook and Bill Rashleigh (2008) 'Degeneration Game', *ROOF* September/October: 22.
12. Hackworth, Jason and Neil Smith (2001) 'The Changing State of Gentrification', *Tijdschrift voor Economische en Sociale Geografie* 92(4): 468–9.
13. Collins, Chik (2007) '"The Scottish Executive is Open for Business": *People and Place*, The Royal Bank of Scotland, and the Intensification of the Neo-Liberal Agenda in Scotland', in Andy Cumbers and Geoff Whittam (eds) *Reclaiming the Economy: Alternatives to Market Fundamentalism* (Glasgow: Scottish Left Review Press).
14. Bramley, Glen and Hal Pawson (2002) 'Low Demand for Housing: Incidence, Causes and UK National Policy Implications', *Urban Studies* 39(3): 396.
15. Ibid., p. 408.
16. The survey was carried out between 29 May and 18 June 2007, and got 782 responses.
17. Homeownership in West Germany rose from 39 per cent in 1980 to 45 per cent in 2003 <http://www.iut.nu/EU/HousingStatistics2004.pdf>, p. 50 [accessed 30 August 2008].
18. Bramley and Pawson, 'Low Demand for Housing', p. 413. This article also puts a question mark over Bramley's own estimates of annual surplus, made just four years earlier (see p. 400).
19. Ibid., p 412.
20. DTZ Pieda (2000) *Demolition and New Building on Local Authority Estates*, summary of report commissioned by the Office of the

Deputy Prime Minister, downloaded from <http://odpm.gov.uk> and no longer accessible, p. 1.

21. Ibid., p. 3.
22. Bramley and Pawson, 'Low Demand for Housing', p. 418; Lee, Peter and Brendan Nevin (2003) 'Changing Demand for Housing: Restructuring Markets and the Public Policy Framework', *Housing Studies* 18(1): 72.
23. Quoted in Stedman Jones, *Outcast London*, p. 166.
24. Atkinson, Rowland and Keith Kintrea (2001) 'Disentangling Area Effects: Evidence from Deprived and Non-deprived Neighbourhoods', *Urban Studies* 38(12): 2290.
25. Atkinson, Rowland and Keith Kintrea (2004) '"Opportunities and Despair; It's All in There": Practitioner Experiences and Explanations of Area Effects and Life Chances', *Sociology* 38(3): 451.
26. Butler, Tim and Gary Robson (2001) 'Social Capital, Gentrification and Neighbourhood Change in London: A Comparison of Three South London Neighbourhoods', *Urban Studies* 38(12): 2150 and 2157.
27. Davidson, Mark and Loretta Lees (2005) 'New-build "Gentrification" and London's Riverside Renaissance', *Environment and Planning* A(37): 1165–90.
28. Uitermark, Justus, Jan Willem Duyvendak and Reinout Kleinhans (2007) 'Gentrification as a Governmental Strategy: Social Control and Social Cohesion in Hoogvliet, Rotterdam', *Environment and Planning* A(39): 132 and 137.
29. Gilbert, Pierre (2007) 'Demolitions and Reconstructions in a Large Housing Estate: On Some Social Effects of "Renouvellement Urbain"', conference paper available at <http://www.enhr2007rotterdam.nl/documents/W05_paper_Gilbert.pdf> [accessed 22 August 2008].
30. Doherty J., D. Manley, E. Graham, R. Hiscock and P. Boyle (2006) 'Is Mixed Tenure Good for Social Well Being?' Report for the Joseph Rowntree Foundation <http://ggsrv-cold.st-andrews.ac.uk/chr/mixing-pubs.html> p. 60 [accessed 23 August 2008].
31. Uitermark et al., 'Gentrification as a Governmental Strategy'.
32. <http://www.eyes-and-ears.co.uk/pennine/details.asp?Title=The%20Cutteslowe%20Walls> [accessed 22 August 2008]. John Grayson gives examples of similar walls in Bromley, Cardiff and 1990s Leeds. The Cardiff wall was built by the council: Grayson, John (1996) *Opening the Window* (Salford: TPAS and Northern College), pp. 30 and 39.
33. While there has been some discussion in Britain of opening up social housing to lower-priority groups in areas of 'low demand', there is a danger that this will be used as a ploy to raise social rents and

bring this housing into the market system. Bramley and Pawson, 'Low Demand for Housing', p. 414, note that 'This change will reinforce any policy push towards social rents moving towards a more market-like structure.'

34. Lynne Jones, Labour MP for Birmingham, Selly Oak, in the debate on council housing held on 29 June 2005; Hansard, 29 June 2005, Column 427WH.

35. Cameron, 'From Low Demand to Rising Aspirations', pp. 5–6.

36. Geddes, Mike (2006) 'Partnership and the Limits to Local Governance in England: Institutionalist Analysis and Neoliberalism', *International Journal of Urban and Regional Research* 30(1): 93.

37. Ibid., p. 89.

38. Paper given to Scottish Trade Union Congress conference on 'Communities, Regeneration and Democracy', 5 September 2008. More recently, a private planning consultant was heard to comment at a regeneration meeting in Aberdeen that the area 'has a very strong tenants' association and may give us some trouble'.

39. Collins, '"The Scottish Executive is Open for Business"', pp. 164–5.

40. Hewett and Rashleigh, 'Degeneration Game', p. 20.

41. Allen, Chris (2008) *Housing Market Renewal and Social Class* (London and New York: Routledge).

42. Observers of the way New Labour has refused to understand why it has been deserted by core Labour voters will see similarities here.

43. Our report can be seen at <http://www.publicinterest.ac.uk/component/option,com_docman/task,cat_view/gid,48/Itemid,49/>; the official analysis of the responses is on <http://cci.scot.nhs.uk/Publications/2008/04/02094036/7> [accessed 23 August 2008].

44. Engels, Friedrich (1845) *The Condition of the Working Class in England*, Chapter 4 <http://www.marxists.org/archive/marx/works/1845/condition-working-class/ch04.htm> [accessed 22 August 2008].

45. Quoted in Allen, *Housing Market Renewal*, p. 149. As the redevelopment has not been done in time for Liverpool's year as City of Culture, the boarded-up windows lining Edge Lane have been painted with colour-co-ordinated cartoons. The effect is surreally sinister.

46. Jane Kennedy (Labour) at the public inquiry into the compulsory purchase orders (*Daily Telegraph*, 17 October 2005)

47. Wilfred Burns, who became chief planner at the Department of the Environment, quoted in Malpass, Peter (2005) *Housing and the Welfare State: The Development of Housing Policy in Britain* (Basingstoke: Palgrave Macmillan), p. 86.

48. Email to author and others, sent 26 July 2008.
49. Dumbleton, Bob (2006) *'Help us Somebody': The Demolition of the Elderly* (London: The London Press).
50. Ibid., p. 39.
51. Ibid., p. 112.
52. Slater, 'The Eviction of Critical Perspectives', and Slater, Tom (2008) '"A Literal Necessity to be Re-Placed": A Rejoinder to the Gentrification Debate', *International Journal of Urban and Regional Research* 32(1): 212–23.
53. Peter Byrne quoted in Slater, 'The Eviction of Critical Perspectives', p. 742.
54. Allen, *Housing Market Renewal*, p. 197.
55. See Sennett, Richard and Saskia Sassen (2007) 'Guantánamo in Germany: In the Name of the War on Terror, Our Colleagues are Being Persecuted – for the Crime of Sociology', *Guardian*, 21 August.
56. *The New Urban Frontier: Gentrification and the Revanchist City* is the title of Neil Smith's influential study of gentrification as an instrument of policy (London and New York: Routledge, 1996).
57. Klein, Naomi (2007) *The Shock Doctrine* (Harmondsworth: Penguin), pp. 423–42.
58. Smith, *The New Urban Frontier*, p. xv.
59. William Booth's plans for helping the poor were published in 1890 under the title *In Darkest England and the Way Out*.
60. Klein, *The Shock Doctrine*, p. 57.
61. *The Tower*, though properly criticised for being a little too interventionist in its filming for a documentary and for avoiding existing inhabitants who did not suffer from multiple problems, nevertheless gave a horribly fascinating insight into regeneration in practice.

Part II

Case Studies:
Real Lives and Real Estate

4

FROM POPULAR CAPITALISM TO THIRD-WAY MODERNISATION: THE EXAMPLE OF LEEDS, ENGLAND

Stuart Hodkinson

By 1979, more than a century of tenants' struggles had won England the precious asset of some 5.1 million council homes[1] with tenants awarded Security of Tenure – a low-cost rented home for life. Of course, as Cole argues, the quality of England's public housing 'has always been a variable product ... which cannot be put down solely to lack of resources from central government'.[2] Yet, however imperfect, mass public housing was a necessary solution to market failure, and its political and class significance was enormous. Public ownership allowed for a municipal form of collective control, took both the land and housing out of the private property market, boosted the role of elected local councils and provided a decent home at affordable rents for more than a third of the population by the late 1970s, dramatically reducing the social power of capital and the disciplinary role of rents and mortgages in the labour market. It also had egalitarian credentials by raising the necessary finance through redistributive taxes and collective borrowing, and reinvesting surpluses back into local public services. It should therefore come as no surprise that public housing was the first and eventually largest target of privatisation following the election of Margaret Thatcher's Conservative government in 1979, and has been subject to further waves of privatisation, marketisation and corporatisation under the Labour government since 1997.

Thatcherism and the Rolling-back of Public Housing

Although neoliberalism has many different facets, it was first put into practice as a *strategic* capitalist response to the world profit crisis of the 1970s, aimed at dramatically restoring (finance) capital's power *vis-à-vis* labour and opening up valuable public-sector services and assets to private exploitation.[3] As David Harvey argues, neoliberal urban policy was designed to transform local authorities from their post-war 'managerial' role as providers of public goods, to 'urban entrepreneurs', competing with other local territories across the world 'for resources, jobs and capitals'.[4] One major aim was to reclaim prime, central city space for capital accumulation and elite consumption by encouraging mainly speculative investment in narrow real estate developments.[5] Another aim of neoliberal urban policy was the assault on the 'municipal socialism' of Labour-controlled local authorities, featuring the privatisation of public enterprises and assets, the slashing of budgets and the contracting-out of local services.[6] Housing privatisation was central to both goals.

The 1980 Housing Act unveiled the famous 'Right to Buy' policy, which allowed sitting tenants to buy their council house at huge discounts that would reach 70 per cent of market value. This was joined in 1988 by a number of estate-wide privatisation schemes, including Housing Action Trusts (HATs) and Large Scale Voluntary Transfer (known as 'stock transfer'), which induced some local authorities to sell their housing stock to not-for-profit Registered Social Landlord (RSL) companies, known more commonly as 'housing associations'. By 1997, some 2 million of the best council houses had been sold on the cheap, the majority through direct sales to tenants. At the ideological level, Thatcher's vision of a 'property-owning democracy' proved popular among participating tenants and complemented the Conservative government's efforts to widen share ownership, and thus extend market ideology, to the working class.[7] As Thatcher argued at the time:

> ... why shouldn't [council tenants] have a chance to buy and hand something on to their children? Why shouldn't they have the chance to become little

capitalists? ... Look, they have got something to inherit. They have got the basis to start on! That is tremendous. That is popular capitalism.[8]

But housing privatisation was not just based on bourgeois dogma. It was motivated by an austere fiscal policy to enable what Peck and Tickell call the 'rolling back' of the state.[9] The sell-off of public housing aimed to transfer the long-term responsibility of financing repairs to the private sector, while at the same time raising £24.6 billion[10] to help fund the neoliberal tax-cutting agenda for big business, the rich and the middle classes. It also went hand-in-hand with the slashing of housing budgets. Between 1979 and 1994, total public expenditure on housing decreased in real terms by 60 per cent, its share of public expenditure falling from 7.3 per cent to 2 per cent.[11] The Conservatives found innovative ways of starving local authorities of the financial means to invest in and repair their housing stock. They curtailed their ability to borrow or to reinvest the money generated by council house sales (their capital receipts) and tenants' rents. Instead, 75 per cent of capital receipts had to be ring-fenced to repay the so-called 'historic debt' that financed public housing in the first place, 'despite local authorities having enormous problems of repair and modernisation, and despite the housing debt representing only a tiny fraction of the current value of the local-authority housing stock'.[12] Consequently, the annual number of new council homes built fell from 74,835 in 1980 to just 290 in 1997,[13] while the majority of what remained publicly owned was crumbling under a repair backlog valued at £23 billion by the Chartered Institute of Housing.[14]

Privatisation was accompanied by the deregulation of protections and controls in the private rental sector and the liberalisation of mortgage lending for buy-to-let investment in order to reinsert housing into the private market as a key focus for capital accumulation and driver of labour market reforms. The intention was to allow private landlordism to flourish once more and provide the 'primitive accumulation' necessary for the development of major property companies, agencies and estate agents as part of a booming private housing industry. At the urban scale, the assault on council housing was a major government weapon against local authorities, which lost their best and most valuable housing assets and better-off tenants; meanwhile, once-popular inner-city mixed working-class communities increasingly became by-words for poor quality housing, unemployment, social ills and welfare dependency. This enabled both the government and their free-market supporters in industry and the media to represent inner cities as dangerous places to live, thus justifying the city-centre gentrification agenda.[15]

New Labour, New Privatisation

Far from reviving the public housing sector, as some in the tenants' and labour movements had naïvely hoped for, since its election in 1997, the New Labour government has continued to 'roll back' public housing, hiving off a further 860,000 council homes to RSLs and another 400,000 to former tenants.[16] Not only has social housing become residualised as a tenure of last resort for those in dire need, but it has also been steadily corporatised, with RSLs now the main constructors and providers of social rented housing. Athough they are currently barred from floating on the stock exchange, RSLs are very much private companies with greater freedoms to charge market rents, evict tenants and build private housing. Tenants elected to an RSL board are bound by company law to support the RSL, while recent mergers mean that 95 per cent of RSL activity is controlled by just a third of the sector,[17] removing landlord accountability further from the local community.

Nevertheless, under New Labour, the rate of privatisation has been gradually slowing, with the remaining poor-quality stock both unattractive and unaffordable for most tenants, and stock transfer has been increasingly blocked by tenant 'no' votes in statutory ballots.[18] This has resulted in a gradual evolution in New Labour's housing policy, set out most clearly in the 2003 Sustainable Communities Plan, that brings together existing 'roll-back' policies with new 'roll-out' tools that open up new privatisation opportunities and prime what remains of public housing for future disposal. This urban policy approach has focused on creating 'decent homes in decent places' through three main policies: the Housing Market Renewal Pathfinder, the National Strategy for Neighbourhood Renewal and the Decent Homes Programme. Underpinning all these is the intention to create so-called 'mixed communities' in deprived areas, principally through housing market interventions that imply large-scale demolition of working-class housing, both public and private, in order to create new private housing developments with greater tenure (and thus wealth and household) diversification.[19] The 'social mix' approach, euphemistically labelled by its champions as about 'deconcentrating deprivation'[20] is nothing less than 'state-sponsored gentrification'.[21]

Council housing has been mainly affected by the Decent Homes Programme, which compels all local authorities and RSLs to bring their social housing stock up to a (very) minimum 'decent' standard by 2010.[22] While on paper this appears as an overdue corrective to the decades of Thatcherite cuts and disrepair, most local authorities cannot meet 'decency' from their own resources. Government will only make available 'additional funding' (which actually comes from the central pot of tenants' rents retained by government) to support local borrowing requirements if local authorities first implement one (or more) of three marketisation options. The first option is to set up 'arm's-length management organisations' (ALMOs) to take over the day-to-day management of the local authority's housing stock. While the local authority remains the sole landlord and shareholder in the ALMO, the arm's-length body is run as a not-for-profit business with a significant degree of operational independence to procure its own goods and services. Tenants were told that the ALMO route was the only way to access extra investment for their homes, only to then discover that this additional funding was dependent on their ALMO receiving a 'two-star' rating from inspectors, which some have failed to achieve. While ALMOs have not yet been promoted in Scotland, the experience from England (the only place they have been introduced thus far) indicates that, with very few exceptions, ALMOs have created yet another layer of bureaucracy between landlord and tenant, introducing some of the worst aspects of corporate behaviour, eroding service accountability to tenants and elected councillors through their subservience to company law, and undermining employee morale and trade union rights. Significantly, as separate companies, ALMOs can be fully privatised 'at a stroke'[23] and there is growing pressure from within the ALMO sector to set them free from local authority control.[24]

The second option for local authorities is to privatise directly some or all of their council housing through stock transfer to a housing association. The housing association will be able to secure the necessary investment through a mix of private borrowing and government grants, while the local authority will be rewarded by having its historic housing debts written off by the government. However, due to the increasing resistance to this route, a third option exists – the Private Finance Initiative (PFI) – in which local authorities retain ownership and their landlord status (possibly under ALMOs), but award a private consortium a long-term contract to take on the regeneration and management of a specific housing estate that requires a large amount of capital investment to meet the 'decency' standard.[25] Under PFI, the entire process of financing and carrying out the design, construction and operation of public infrastructure (that is, the *physical* facilities, not the actual *frontline* service itself) is packaged into a lucrative long-term contract (normally 20–30 years). These are then bid for by *private* consortia (each typically comprising a construction firm, a facilities management company and a bank to finance the scheme). The winning PFI consortium will receive regular performance-related payments that cover the entire cost of the scheme and include a large profit for the companies involved, estimated at between 7 per cent and 20 per cent of the total payment.[26] Due to its complexity and the government's initial prohibition on including *new-build* council housing in such schemes, PFI has so far played a relatively small role in public housing. At the time of writing, 23 schemes had been selected, with twelve having signed contracts for a total of £963.41 million in capital investment alone, and a further eight schemes currently in procurement.[27]

There is now a wealth of documented evidence exposing the controversies and problems of PFIs across the public sector, particularly in hospitals and IT systems: PFIs are on average 30 per cent more expensive than publicly financed projects because of the higher cost of commercial borrowing, and are notorious for escalating project costs and delays, poor-quality building work, service failure, worker exploitation, a lack of accountability and corporate profiteering.[28] Despite this, public authorities continue to opt for PFI schemes, first, because PFI is often the only source of large-scale capital investment made available by government, and secondly, because the government's Public Sector Comparator model used to compare 'value for money' between proposed PFI schemes and conventional procurement approaches is inherently biased towards the PFI route.[29] However, while the costs and risks of the PFI are of major concern, its real significance lies in the wider social restructuring processes it unleashes.[30] These, as we shall see later in relation to housing regeneration in Leeds, include gentrification, the reduction of both the amount and proportion of council housing in favour of the private market, and a wider framework of marketisation across the local public sector.

The Affordability Crisis: A New Era for Social Housing?

The turn to neoliberalism has devastated people's hard-won right to decent, affordable and secure housing and is recreating the precarious private market system of the nineteenth century. Since 1981, private housing, both in absolute and relative terms, has grown at the expense of social rented housing, which has declined steadily from 7 million to under 5 million dwellings.[31] The deregulation of the money supply, the growth of home purchase lending and increases to the ratio of credit to income on offer have combined with insufficient supply[32] to produce unprecedented rises in house prices that have made homeownership three-and-a-half times more 'inaccessible' for first-time buyers since 1996, according to the Royal Institute of Chartered Surveyors.[33] This has led to higher private rents (which have more than doubled since 1994) and also higher social-housing rents due to the government's 2002 'rent restructuring formula', that includes property valuation. Overall, council housing waiting lists have nearly doubled since 1997 to 4 million people, with warnings from councils that this could rapidly reach 5 million by 2010.[34] The number of homeless households living in temporary accommodation more than doubled between March 1997 and March 2004 to nearly 100,000[35] and a million children now live in overcrowded housing.[36] All of this has been exacerbated by the global financial crash, sparked by the meltdown of the US subprime mortgage market. In 2008, average British house prices fell by 16.2 per cent, trapping many in negative equity and sparking a surge in home repossessions and homelessness. Yet the housing market slump has had little impact on affordability, due to the simultaneous squeeze on credit availability in the banking sector and the onset of recession.

The housing crisis has placed New Labour under growing and contradictory pressures. On the one hand, we find a sizeable lobby of consultants led by the neoliberal Smith Institute[37] imploring government to sell off, or at least marketise, the remaining public housing stock. On the other are dynamic opponents such as Defend Council Housing (see Chapter 12) arguing for the restoration of council housing as a legitimate tenure in the public's eyes and finding a resonance in what remains of the Labour Party's old grass-roots. This prompted a comprehensive review of the 'future of social housing' during 2006 and 2007;[38] the resulting Housing and Regeneration Act promises 100,000 new social rented homes by 2011 and 50,000 a year from then on, a huge increase on current rates. Local authorities have also been promised that they will once again be empowered to build council housing themselves. Beneath the headlines, however, New Labour appears to have simply tightened the existing neoliberal straitjacket on council housing. While Right to Buy, stock transfer, ALMOs and PFI all remain in place, profit-making companies will now be allowed to register as social landlords under a new, lighter burden of regulation, and there are proposals to replace the current Social Housing Grant (that is, government subsidies given to help RSLs build social housing) with a risk-based model seeking returns on investment. The fear is that RSLs will be forced to compete with large corporations and further encouraged to become developers in their own right[39] – which many already are, although they must keep separate the profit and non-profit sides of the business. This could lead to even greater centralisation of the social rented sector into larger and fewer mega-companies that have no accountability to tenants or communities. Above all, the new era of council-house building is not quite what it seems. In order to receive financial assistance, local authorities must set up either ALMOs or Local Housing Companies, which are joint ventures where local authorities are partnered with a private developer or RSL. The local authority invests 'surplus public sector land' into the company and shares the rising land values with its partner. Only 50 per cent of the new homes built by these companies will be required to be earmarked for social rent, and these will be let at the higher RSL rents and will not be on 'secure' tenancies. This is not council housing. Councils that want to build housing directly must bear all the cost themselves, and this is likely to yield only 2,500 homes a year.[40] The government has indicated that changes to housing finance rules might allow all councils to be able to bid for Social Housing Grants, but anticipates that PFIs are the more likely route.[41] As the remainder of this chapter demonstrates, a future for council housing under PFIs is no future at all.

Housing Regeneration in Leeds: The Role of the Private Finance Initiative

Once a world manufacturing and trading centre for textiles and engineering, the northern English city of Leeds has a strong industrial working-class heritage that led to important pre-war developments such as the Quarry Hill council flats,[42] and pushed the Labour Party into power for much of the post-war era. This resulted in a huge council-house-building programme that by 1981 had produced nearly 100,000 homes, one of the largest local authority stocks in the country.[43] Faced with the Conservatives' assault on 'municipal socialism', the city's pragmatic leaders reluctantly adopted what we might call a 'progressive urban entre-preneurialism'. This opened up the city to private developers, while trying to redistribute resources to zones of entrenched deprivation in the inner city and outer urban council estates that had fallen victim to deindustrialisation.[44] The Labour-run councils of the 1980s and 1990s did resist many of the Conservative government's housing privatisation initiatives, but were powerless to stop the Right to Buy programme, which has so far accounted for the loss of nearly 40,000 council homes, or to do anything about the slashing of central housing budgets that left over 50 per cent of council housing at an 'indecent' standard by the late 1990s.[45] Leeds built its last 18 council homes in 1992;[46] in that same year, 941 council houses were sold under the Right to Buy and 1,114 homeless people waited to be rehoused, the highest number for decades.[47]

The only investment in social rented housing came from the innovative Leeds Partnership Homes, a joint venture company between Leeds City Council and five local housing associations, which built 4,000 homes for social rent and so-called 'low-cost ownership' in the mid-1990s, thanks to the transfer of £33 million of mainly brownfield public land sites to various housing associations.[48] This initiative was successful in pooling resources to build social rented housing at a time of open warfare by central government against the public sector and local authority housing; however, it also contributed in some ways to the privatisation agenda by pioneering a model of delivering affordable housing based primarily on the gifting of public land to the private sector. This public-private partnership ethos has continued apace under New Labour. In 1999, Leeds was one of the first eight local authorities in England and Wales to be selected onto the housing PFI Pathfinder Programme for its Swarcliffe regeneration scheme. Since then, the council has successfully bid for similar PFI schemes for the Little London (see below), Beeston Hill and Holbeck neigh-bourhoods, despite opposition from local tenants and residents. In 2003, following the government's Decent Homes agenda, Leeds City Council spent almost £2 million convincing tenants to welcome the creation of six ALMOs to manage the city's housing services. The result has been a 30 per cent cut in the number of local housing offices, the increased subcontracting of services to private firms, and 18 new senior managers and new head offices for the six companies.[49] After just three years, Leeds ALMOs were projecting a collective £11.8 million deficit by 2009/10, and they were consequently merged into three 'super-ALMOs' in 2007 in order to cut senior management costs.[50] Since then, however, at least one ALMO has focused on cutting its caretaking staff, and is now attempting to alter Joint Consultation arrangements with trade union representatives at the same time as reneging on overtime and pay grading agreements with staff.

One disastrous consequence is the affordable housing crisis gripping the city. Leeds is now the most expensive local authority area in West Yorkshire for buying a house: only four out of Leeds' 102 postcode sectors (3.9 per cent) have prices affordable to those on below-average single incomes,[51] with the recent housing market slowdown making little difference due to the impact of the credit crunch on first-time buyers. This is reflected in the number of people on the city's housing register waiting for a social rented home, which in recent years has risen by almost a third to around 31,000. They face a long wait: currently 6,000 people 'bid' for only 500 empty council properties per month.[52] Rising house prices in turn have pushed up land values, which has encouraged Leeds City Council to allow some 9,500 private flats to be built in the city centre and approve a further 6,000[53] – despite estimates of one-third to a half lying empty.[54] At the same time, it is planning to demolish at least 6,000 council homes over the next decade[55] as part of its 'regeneration strategy' aimed at 'narrowing the gap between the most disadvantaged people and communities and the rest of the city'.[56] What follows is the story of arguably the most controversial of these regeneration schemes: the Little London Private Finance Initiative.

The Gentrification of Little London

Sandwiched in between Leeds' booming central zone and its expanding university quarter, on the inner north-east rim of the city, lies Little London, a once-popular modernist public housing estate with imposing high-rise tower blocks, flat-roofed maisonettes, terraced two-up two-downs, and semi-detached housing. By the late 1990s, Little London had become another victim of Thatcherism, gaining notoriety as a 'no-go area', full of drug-dealing, deprivation and physical decay. In the summer of 2001, Leeds City Council officially informed tenants of its intention to 'regenerate' Little London using the government's housing PFI scheme to 'improve the standard of homes, shopping areas and the wider environment' so that 'residents have the quality of life they deserve'.[57] However, when the council unveiled its original £45 million regeneration blueprint for Little London, the plan went far beyond simply *refurbishing* council homes and *improving* the area for the people already living there. The council's vision was to recreate Little London as a desirable 'mixed community' that would both serve the city-centre housing market and bring 'the benefits of the city centre housing boom to Little London'.[58] According to the plan, at least 150 council homes would be demolished on the most lucrative development land nearest to the city centre; the cleared sites would then be sold to developers to build private housing for market sale. Three high-rise blocks towards the city centre, containing 297 (mainly council) flats, would also be sold off to developers to be refurbished as 'middle-market' homes for rent or sale. The rest of the estate would be given a radical facelift to fit in with the urban form of the city. In concrete terms, hundreds of poor families and individuals would be forced to leave their homes and community, with limited rehousing options and a derisory compensation package. Armed with 'evidence' from international property consultants Kings Sturge, Leeds City Council justified its strategy on the basis that the estate's social problems were linked to 'specific property types', such as the high-rise tower blocks and maisonettes, which had high turnover, low demand and problem tenants (in the shape of mainly young people with 'challenging' and 'anti-social behaviour' requiring welfare support[59]). PFI would provide the 'higher than average investment' required to deal with the flats' physical disrepair, and tenure diversification through private development would solve the social problems by helping to 'maximise the market potential of the area', maintaining 'demand for flats from a diverse customer group where *applicants needing support do not predominate*'.[60] This gentrification blueprint was also about reconstructing the local housing market to enable house prices and rents to rise in line with city averages and reflect the true market value of their prime city-centre location, while replacing a large number of the poor with a more economically desirable population.

Despite the council's bombardment of the local community with pro-PFI propaganda and thinly veiled threats to vote 'yes' or be cut adrift, the local community rejected the PFI scheme by 54 per cent to 46 per cent in the official ballot. The strength of feeling was reflected in the turnout – 67 per cent – that dwarfed the average of 20 per cent in local and general elections. Leeds City Council, however, had no intention of allowing such large amounts of investment to be lost. It refused to accept the ballot result, blaming the 'misleading' propaganda of the anti-PFI campaign, and held a 'fresh' ballot just two months later on what it called a 'new' PFI scheme that no longer proposed to demolish two tower blocks (100 flats) as originally planned. Just to be sure, the council redrew the boundaries of the proposed PFI scheme so that sufficient numbers of 'no' voters identified on the edge of Little London were eliminated from the ballot.[61] Inevitably, the result this time produced a 'yes' vote for PFI, with 56.7 per cent in favour but on a much-reduced turnout (46 per cent). The progress of the Little London PFI scheme was then delayed again for three years due to the government's doubts about the affordability and manageability of the scheme, requiring a fresh consultation exercise in February 2006. This time, however, the council did *not* offer tenants a ballot, and rebranded its preferred scheme as the 'Comprehensive Regeneration Option' with mention of PFI deliberately avoided where possible.[62] The two towers previously 'saved' were once again earmarked for demolition, but a new carrot was put forward: 125 new council homes would now be built to replace them. The catch was a reduction in both the number of council homes to be refurbished and maintained, and the frequency of major renewal, with the contract length reduced from 30 to 20 years. Surprisingly, in March 2008, the council confirmed that, due to the 'global credit crunch' and 'housing market slowdown', it had abandoned its plans to sell off three tower blocks containing 297 flats to a developer and would instead retain and refurbish them as council homes. This decision was also undoubtedly influenced by local resistance, which included a (failed) legal challenge and the emergence of a new tenants' and residents' group for the condemned blocks. At the time of writing, the PFI scheme, which was put out to tender in July 2007, is currently in the procurement phase with physical regeneration work not expected to begin until early 2010, a full nine years after Leeds City Council first applied to the housing PFI scheme.

Unpacking the Neoliberal Urban Enclosures in Little London

In order to understand the shabby way in which the people of Little London have been treated, we have to understand the neoliberal straitjacket that PFI imposes on local authorities. This has three main components in housing. The first is a very deliberate menu of market-friendly *policy* guidelines to be obeyed by local authorities, including the creation of 'mixed communities' (read: 'gentrification') and 'tenure diversification' (read: 'demolition/privatisation of council housing').[63] Leeds City Council has willingly followed these guidelines to the letter in its matrix of refurbishment, selective demolition, privatisation and new private housing development that reduces both the amount and proportion of public rented housing in favour of private housing tenures.

Secondly, local authorities are obliged to use a complex *financial model* to pay for their housing PFI scheme. This incentivises local authorities to demolish public housing and create development sites that can be sold on to part-finance the proposed improvements to the PFI regeneration zone. In Little London, four such development sites have been put forward to be sold for mainly private housing or mixed development. Moreover, any rising or unforeseen costs become the responsibility of the local authority, placing it under constant pressure to 'transfer resources from other parts of the housing budget to pay for its

PFI obligations'.[64] Once that revenue stream dries up, the local authority may look to cut other budgets or outsource services to the private or voluntary sector. The potentially devastating impact of this financial straitjacket on Leeds City Council emerged in November 2006, when leaked confidential documents revealed that an 'affordability gap' had appeared in the Little London scheme due to a two-month delay in the latest project timetable. This had given the council no choice but to increase its own contribution by some £192,000 a year (£3.833 million over 20 years) and to brace itself for other possible scenarios that could hike up the council's long-term liabilities even further.[65] In the worst-case scenario outlined, the council's contribution could rise by 25 per cent over 20 years – a huge £12 million.[66]

The third component is the 'locking-in' of *market forces* and *interests* into the eventual PFI scheme through the exposure of the public sector throughout the design and procurement phase to the overcrowded (and thus very competitive) sellers' market for PFI contracts. When the future uncertainties of economic growth and financial markets are added in, this environment usually allows the scheme to evolve in such a way as to generate opportunities for greater profitability for PFI contractors, at the expense of social provision, high-quality service performance and workers' pay and conditions. 'Carrots' to the private sector usually involve what Whitfield calls the 'privatization of the development process' through land and property deals that enable capital to gain control of 'surplus land and buildings such as school playing fields, vacant land, empty hospital buildings and so on for property development'.[67] Confidential council documents reveal just how far the council has gone in internalising market logic into its regeneration plan. In 2005, following a disappointing round of market testing in which the council put forward a range of new options to private-sector actors, Council officers argued for the need to refocus the PFI scheme to 'create a more favourable investment opportunity'.[68] The constant exposure to market forces has so far seen the Little London regeneration plan change eight times since it was first initiated in 2001, as council planners and housing officers have been forced to come up with increasingly 'bolder proposals to create mixed tenure; larger development sites to create "critical mass"'.[69] Documents released under the Freedom of Information Act show that the council also had a radical 'Plan B' if the private sector was eventually not satisfied with the stock condition of the remaining housing: to demolish up to six more tower blocks on the estate.[70] This threat has since been rescinded and the council has promised that no more flats will be demolished, but the scale of gentrification could be expanded as, in July 2008, Leeds City Council submitted an outline planning application for an enormous 807 new homes for sale on the estate, over 700 more than initially promised.

Wider Implications

The Little London PFI story demonstrates the extent to which the PFI is a purposely designed framework of disciplinary neoliberalism: its rules of access and use by local authorities come with in-built mechanisms that unlock public revenues and assets for capital accumulation. By entering into long-term, legally binding contractual commitments to make regular profitable payments to capital, the local authority is forced to adopt an increasingly entrepreneurial and commercial understanding of its entire portfolio of services, land and property holdings. All local public services and buildings thus become at risk of being sold off, creating strong incentives for the public authority to enter into yet more PFI contracts in order to raise short-term finance for vital public investment, and so strengthening and speeding up the vicious circle. Eventually, Whitfield foresees that the many PFI and other public-private partnership schemes across a city will become centralised under a small number of parent companies through buy-outs and mergers, leading to contract rationalisation and job losses, and, ultimately, a publicly financed but unaccountable 'company town':

> ... the company town is reemerging, not dominated by one industry or family, but by business elites through their involvement in regeneration, partnerships, outsourcing and sponsorship of arts and culture. The local

state transfers assets and defers to the needs of and interests of the business sector first and foremost.[71]

Cities such as Leeds rely heavily on PFI schemes to finance street lighting, new schools and leisure centres, social housing, joint services and waste management.[72] In an already austere fiscal environment for local authorities, councils must shoulder the rising costs of PFI schemes as they occur, regardless of other commitments or local needs, by transferring revenues from other budgets and selling assets from elsewhere in their portfolio. The implications of these huge future commitments in a context of growing fiscal austerity under neoliberalism could be catastrophic for the local public sector in Leeds. The council could be forced to raid other budgets or sell off more public assets to ensure that all of its PFI schemes are financially solvent. This may start with service cuts and property sales from within the physical PFI zone, spread out to general budgets and assets associated with the particular service (for example, housing), then go on to wider cuts in grants for non-statutory services (for example, arts and culture) and then gradually the closure and sale of community centres, schools, libraries, art exhibition premises, museums, leisure centres, prestigious listed buildings, and so on, in order to create development or investment opportunities for developers and real estate corporations. Far from being a future dystopian scenario, this is already happening across many British cities and towns.[73]

Yet, in the gloom, there is still hope. The very material processes of enclosure – school closures, housing demolitions, the erosion of public space – provoke very real material responses in the form of popular opposition and resistance seeking to 'reclaim social spaces ... and turn them into spaces of commons'.[74] In Little London, a small but committed group of tenants has questioned and fought the council's PFI scheme since it was first unveiled in 2001 (see Figures 4.1, 4.2).

While the campaigners have narrowly failed to stop the PFI scheme, their resistance has forced the council to make decisive concessions, such as the like-for-like replacement of demolished

Figure 4.1 Campaigners take over the window of Little London's disused betting shop (*photo: Stuart Hodkinson*).

Figure 4.2 A tenant opposed to the PFI scheme hangs a banner from his threatened tower block flat (*photo: Stuart Hodkinson*).

council homes with social rented housing, and the retention of 300 flats originally scheduled for privatisation. In other words, they have saved some 430 public housing units having been previously fobbed off with Thatcher's favourite phrase 'There Is No Alternative'. Moreover, their dogged resistance has sparked the formation of a growing city-wide housing movement, supported by local academics and trade unionists, that aims to learn from the Little London experience and fight the planned demolitions, privatisations and gentrification policies across Leeds.[75] While these struggles remain marginal and marginalised for the time being (and it will require a major and sustained organising and educational drive by progressive forces to reverse the current trends), there is hope that neoliberal housing policy in Leeds can be decisively challenged at last.

Acknowledgements

The author is grateful to the ESRC (RES-000-23-0957) and the British Academy (PDF/2007/75) for funding the research that went into the chapter. I would also like to thank Huw Jones for his patient help, and Jenny Pickerill, Sara Gonzalez, Paul Waley, Andy Jonas and Sarah Glynn for advice on earlier drafts of this paper. Above all, my respect and admiration to the tenants of Little London, Leeds, for their dogged resistance and their input and ongoing collaboration. The chapter is a substantially revised and updated version of a journal article submitted to *Urban Studies* in May 2008.

Further Reading

Allen, C. (2008) *Housing Market Renewal and Social Class* (London and New York: Routledge).

De Angelis, M. (2007) *The Beginning of History: Value Struggles and Global Capital* (London: Pluto Press).

Whitfield, D. (2001) *Public Services or Corporate Welfare: Rethinking the Nation State in the Global Economy* (London: Pluto Press).

Zacchaeus 2000 Trust (2005) *Memorandum to the Prime Minister on Unaffordable Housing* (London: Zacchaeus 2000 Trust).

Websites

Autonomous Geographies Project <http://www.autonomousgeographies.
org/>
Leeds Hands Off Our Homes <http://www.handsoffourhomes.org.uk/>

Notes

1. Department of Communities and Local Government (DCLG), 'Live
   Tables, Table 101 Dwelling Stock: By Tenure, United Kingdom
   (Historical Series)' (published online, last updated 25 September
   2007) <http://www.communities.gov.uk/documents/housing/xls/
   table-101.xls> [accessed 27 May 2008].
2. Cole, I. (2007) 'What Future for Social Housing in England?', *People,
   Place and Policy Online* 1(1): 3–12 <http://extra.shu.ac.uk/ppp-
   online/issue_1_220507/article_1.html>, pp. 7, 9 [accessed 3 May
   2008].
3. Gough, J. (2002) 'Neoliberalism and Socialisation in the
   Contemporary City: Opposites, Complements and Instabilities',
   Antipode 34(3): 405–26.
4. Harvey, D. (1989) 'From Managerialism to Entrepreneurialism:
   The Transformation in Urban Governance in Late Capitalism',
   Geografiska Annaler 71(B): 3, 5.
5. Barnekov, T., R. Boyle and D. Rich (1989) *Privatism and Urban
   Policy in Britain and the United States* (Oxford: Oxford University
   Press).
6. Whitfield, D. (1992) *The Welfare State* (London: Pluto Press).
7. Stevens, R. (2004) 'The Evolution of Privatisation as an Electoral
   Policy, c.1970–90', *Contemporary British History*, 18(2): 47–75.
8. Walpole, A. (n.d.) 'Margaret Thatcher: Reggae, Royalty and Riots',
   in *Harold Hill: A People's History*, <http://www.haroldhill.org/>
   [accessed 10 September 2007].
9. Peck, J. and A. Tickell (2002) 'Neoliberalizing Space', *Antipode*
   34(3): 380–404.
10. Hansard, 'Council House Sales', Written Answers to Questions,
    Environment, Transport and the Regions, 24 July 1997 <http://www.
    publications.parliament.uk/pa/cm199798/cmhansrd/vo970724/
    index/70724-x.htm> [accessed November 2007].
11. Balchin, P.N. (1996) 'The United Kingdom', in P.N. Balchin (ed.)
    Housing Policy in Europe (London and New York: Routledge),
    p. 211.
12. Ibid., p. 218.

13. DCLG, 'Table 244 House Building: Permanent Dwellings Completed, by Tenure, England, Historical Calendar Year Series' <http://www. communities.gov.uk/documents/housing/xls/140912.xls> [accessed May 2008].
14. Moody, G. (1998) *Council Housing – Financing the Future* (Coventry: Chartered Institute of Housing).
15. Smith, N. (1996) *The New Urban Frontier: Gentrification and the Revanchist City* (London: Routledge).
16. DCLG, 'Live Tables on Social Housing Sales, Table 670 Social Housing Sales: Local Authority Stock Sold Through the Right-to-Buy Scheme, by Region' <http://www.communities.gov.uk/documents/ housing/xls/table-670.xls> [accessed 30 June 2008]; DCLG, 'Completed LSVTs' <http://www.communities.gov.uk/documents/ housing/xls/completedlsvts.xls> [accessed June 2008].
17. Day, K. (2007) 'Social Housing: Opening Doors', *Financial Director* (published online, 26 April) <http://www.financialdirector.co.uk/ financial-director/features/2188466/openingdoors>.
18. Ginsburg, N. (2005) 'The Privatisation of Council Housing', *Critical Social Policy* 25: 115–35.
19. Allen, C. (2008) *Housing Market Renewal and Social Class* (London and New York: Routledge).
20. Cowans, J. (2006) 'Cities and Regions of Sustainable Communities – New Strategies', *Town and Country Planning*, Tomorrow Series Paper 4.
21. Lees, L. (2003) 'Visions of "Urban Renaissance": The Urban Task Force Report and the Urban White Paper', in R. Imrie and M. Raco (eds) *Urban Renaissance? New Labour, Community, and Urban Policy* (Bristol: Policy Press, 2003), pp. 61–82.
22. Department of Environment, Transport and the Regions (DETR) (2000) *Quality and Choice: A Decent Home for All. The Housing Green Paper* (London: The Stationary Office).
23. Whitfield, D. (2003) *ALMOs – The Issues Explained* (Sheffield: Centre for Public Services).
24. National Federation of ALMOs, Chartered Institute of Housing and HouseMark (2005) *ALMOs – A New Future for Council Housing* (Coventry: Chartered Institute of Housing).
25. Spoehr, J., D. Whitfield, C. Sheil, J. Quiggin and K. Davidson (2002) *Partnerships, Privatisation and the Public Interest: Public Private Partnerships and the Financing of Infrastructure Development in South Australia* (Adelaide: University of Adelaide & The Public Service Association of South Australia).
26. See ibid.; Unison (2002) 'PFI: Failing Our Future – A Unison Audit of the Private Finance Initiative' (published online) <http://www. unison.org.uk/acrobat/B537.pdf>.

27. HM Treasury (2008) 'PFI Signed Projects List' (published online, October) <http://www.hm-treasury.gov.uk/media/B/E/pfi_signeddeals_231007.xls> [accessed 14 February 2008]; DCLG website, 'Private Finance Initiative (Housing PFI)', DCLG homepage <http://www.communities.gov.uk/housing/decenthomes/delivering-decenthomes/housingpfiprivate/> [accessed 14 February 2008].

28. Beckett, F. (2007) *The Great City Academy Fraud* (London and New York: Continuum); Monbiot, G. (2000) *Captive State: The Corporate Takeover of Britain* (London: Pan Books); Pollock, A. (2004) *NHS Plc: The Privatisation of Our Health Care* (London: Verso).

29. Coulson, A. (2008) 'Value for Money in PFI Proposals: A Commentary on the UK Treasury Guidelines for Public Sector Comparators', *Public Administration* 36.

30. Kerr, D. (1998) 'The Private Finance Initiative and the Changing Governance of the Built Environment', *Urban Studies* 35(12): 2277–301.

31. DCLG, 'Live Tables, Table 101 Dwelling Stock'.

32. Zacchaeus 2000 Trust (2005) *Memorandum to the Prime Minister on Unaffordable Housing* (London: Zacchaeus 2000 Trust).

33. Royal Institute of Chartered Surveyors (2008) 'Access to the Housing Market 351 per cent Worse than 1996' (published online, 30 January) <http://www.rics.org/Newsroom/Economiccommentary/affordability_q42007_rn_300108.html>.

34. Local Government Association (2008) *Councils and the Housing Crisis: The Potential Impacts and Knock-on Effects of the Credit Crunch on Councils and their Housing Role* (published online, May), Local Government Association website <http://www.lga.gov.uk/lga/core/page.do?pageId=566381>.

35. Office for National Statistics (2005) 'Housing Highlights', *Social Trends* [website version] <http://www.statistics.gov.uk/cci/nugget.asp?id=1052> [accessed 5 March 2008].

36. Shelter (2007) 'Overcrowding Blights Lives of a Million Children' (published online, 18 May) <http://england.shelter.org.uk/home/home-8130.cfm>

37. Dwelly, T., and J. Cowans (eds) (2006) *Rethinking Social Housing* (London: Smith Institute).

38. Cave, M. (2007) *Every Tenant Matters: A Review of Social Housing Regulation* (Wetherby: Department for Communities and Local Government); Hills, J. (2007) *Ends and Means: The Future Roles of Social Housing in England. CASE Report 34* (London: London School of Economics).

39. Social Housing (2007), 'RSLs Face Long-term Profit-seeking Approach From New Homes & Communities Agency', *Social Housing* 19(11): 5 (published online, November) <http://www.socialhousing.co.uk/downloads/nov2007.pdf>.

40. DCLG (2007) *Housing and Regeneration Bill – Impact Assessment* (London: The Stationary Office), p. 58.

41. Ibid.

42. Once an overcrowded and unsanitary inner-city area of back-to-back housing, Quarry Hill was cleared and redeveloped as 'revolutionary' council flats in the early twentieth century. According to Thornton, the flats were the largest block of council flats in Europe and based on the Karl-Marx-Hof flats in Vienna, 'which included homes and public facilities combined on a single site' (p. 192). On the 26-acre site, 938 flats for over 3,000 people were built, and a Garchey waste disposal system was included in every flat. However, the steel frame and concrete-clad construction eventually failed and, in 1978, the whole complex was demolished: Thornton, D. (2002) *Leeds: The Story of a City* (Ayr: Fort Publishing Ltd).

43. Jones, H. (n.d.) 'The Need for Affordable Rented Housing in Leeds', Presentation to Leeds Tenants Federation <http://www.leedstenants.org.uk/Affordable per cent20rented per cent20homes.htm> [accessed 10 August 2006].

44. Haughton, G., and C. Williams (eds) (1996) *Corporate City? Partnership, Participation and Partition in Urban Development in Leeds* (Aldershot: Avebury).

45. Leeds City Council (2002) *HRA Business Plan. Department of Housing and Environmental Health Services* (Leeds: Leeds City Council).

46. Leeds is set to build council houses again – approximately 500 under a number of PFI schemes. However, this relatively tiny number is certainly not what was implied by the council's high-profile announcement in December 2007, which talked of 1,000 homes a year until 2020. It now appears that Leeds City Council did not understand the difference between 'council housing' – built and managed by the local authority – and 'social housing' more generally, which includes housing associations and housing for sale under so-called 'affordable schemes'.

47. Interview with Huw Jones, Strategy and Intelligence Director, Re'new, June 2007.

48. Moran, C. (1996) 'Social Inequalities, Housing Needs and the Targeting of Housing Investment in Leeds', in Haughton and Williams, *Corporate City*, pp. 277–92.

49. House of Commons Council Housing Group (2005) *Support for the Fourth Option for Council Housing: Report on the Inquiry into the Future Funding of Council Housing 2004–2005* <http://www.support4councilhousing.org.uk/report/> [accessed 3 March 2008].

50. Leeds City Council (2006) 'Report of the Director of Neighbourhoods and Housing Department to the Executive Board, Subject: The Future of Arms Length Management Organisations for Housing in Leeds' (Leeds: Leeds City Council, 5 July).

51. Jones, 'The Need for Affordable Rented Housing in Leeds'.

52. Ibid.

53. Unsworth, R. (2007) *City Living in Leeds – 2007* (Leeds: University of Leeds).

54. Hencke, D. (2008) 'MPs to Call for Big Increase in Number of Rented Homes', *Guardian* 21 May <http://www.guardian.co.uk/politics/2008/may/21/planning.housing> [accessed 11 August 2008]; Wright, G. (2008) 'There Seems to be an Empty Feeling about Living in the City', *Yorkshire Post*, 8 July <http://www.yorkshirepost.co.uk/business-comment/Greg-Wright-There-seems-to.4264609.jp> [accessed 11 August 2008].

55. Outside Research and Development (2007) *Leeds Strategic Housing Market Assessment 2007 – Executive Summary* (Leeds: Leeds City Council), p. 18.

56. Leeds Initiative (2004) *Vision for Leeds, 2004–2010* (Leeds: Leeds Initiative), p. 21.

57. Leeds City Council (2001) 'Little London and Woodhouse Newsletter', Summer (Leeds: Leeds City Council), p. 2.

58. Leeds City Council (2001) 'Private Finance Initiative for Housing Revenue Account, Round 2. Expression of Interest, Little London, Leeds, February 2001' (Leeds: Leeds City Council), p. 12.

59. Ibid.

60. Ibid., p. 11, emphasis added.

61. Interview with Dave Smethurst, Independent Tenant Advisor during the first Little London PFI consultation (2001–02), in October 2007.

62. For a full account of the consultation process, see Hodkinson, S. (2007) 'The Regeneration of Little London, Leeds, under the Private Finance Initiative: A Complaint to the Local Government Ombudsman about the Process of Community Consultation, 2001–2006, on Behalf of the Little London Tenants and Residents Association' (ESRC Autonomous Geographies Project, 2007) <http://www.autonomousgeographies.org/files/Hodkinson_Ombudsman_2007.pdf>.

63. ODPM (2003) *Delivering Decent Homes – Option Appraisal Guidance for Local Authorities* (London: The Stationery Office).

64. Hodges, R., and S. Grubnic (2005) 'Public Policy Transfer: The Case of PFI in Housing', *International Journal of Public Policy* 1(1/2): 58–77, p. 63.
65. Leeds City Council (2006) 'Report of the Director of Neighbourhoods and Housing to Executive Board, 15 November, Subject: Little London Housing Private Finance Initiative – Outline Business Case Update' (Leeds: Leeds City Council).
66. Ibid.
67. Whitfield, D. (2001) *Public Services or Corporate Welfare: Rethinking the Nation State in the Global Economy* (London: Pluto Press), p. 99.
68. Leeds City Council (2005) 'Report of Chief Regeneration Officer to Neighbourhood and Housing's Departmental Management Team, Little London Project Update', 12 April, Appendix 14.4 (Leeds: Leeds City Council), p. 3, 4.
69. Ibid.
70. Leeds City Council (2006) 'Little London Private Finance Initiative: Outline Business Case' (Leeds: Leeds City Council).
71. Whitfield, *Public Services or Corporate Welfare*, p. 164.
72. Leeds City Council (2007) 'Progress Report on the PPP/PFI Programme in Leeds', Report of the Deputy Chief Executive to Executive Board, 17 October (Leeds: Leeds City Council).
73. See Minton, A. (2006) *The Privatisation of Public Space* (London: Royal Institute of Chartered Surveyors); Kingsnorth, P. (2008) *Real England: The Battle against the Bland* (London: Portobello Books).
74. De Angelis, M. (2007) *The Beginning of History: Value Struggles and Global Capital* (London: Pluto Press), p. 139.
75. See Hands Off Our Homes website <http://www.handsoffourhomes.org.uk>; Leeds Gentrification Watch <http://savecornexchange.blogspot.com/>; Leeds Tenants Federation website <http://www.leedstenants.org.uk>; Save Little London website http://www.savelittlelondon.org.uk>.

5

GETTING RID OF THE UGLY BITS: THE MYTH AND REALITY OF REGENERATION IN DUNDEE, SCOTLAND

Sarah Glynn

This chapter presents a case study of processes that are changing the physical and social fabric of Dundee, concentrating on the proposed demolition of the multi-storey flats that, for over 30 years, have dominated the city's skyline. It provides a detailed example of regeneration in action; of the misuse of resources, the failures of local democracy and the destructive impact of current policies on those with the least economic and political leverage.

'A Smart Successful Scotland'[1]

For a working-class family in late 1970s Scotland, home was generally in public housing, which was predominantly developed, owned and run by the local council.[2] In the post-war years, council estates had become an established part of working-class life, and had developed into busy neighbourhoods where new generations were being brought up in an increasingly affluent working class. Scotland had previously suffered from particularly bad housing conditions, and public housing now provided homes for over half the country.[3] The focus of Scottish housing programmes had been on numbers and speed,[4] and as elsewhere in Britain, much of the housing could have been planned better, built and maintained on more generous budgets, and managed more sensitively. There were some spectacular failures, but most homes and estates, rather less spectacularly, were fulfilling the job they were built to do.

As in the rest of Britain, the turning-point for Scotland's public housing came with the election of Margaret Thatcher and the two-pronged attack of the 1980 Housing Acts,[5] which combined reductions in public investment with the subsidised sell-off of the best homes to their tenants. By the end of 2007, around 467,000 of the 974,000 publicly owned homes recorded in the 1981 Scottish census had been sold under Right to Buy and over 200,000 had been transferred to housing associations.[6] In addition, as we saw in Chapter 3, public housing is under threat not only of privatisation, but also of destruction. Cash-strapped councils, unable to maintain decaying homes, have frequently resorted to demolition; however, the debts do not vanish with the buildings, and councils are left having to pay them off from a smaller rental income, which often compounds the problem and leads to a destructive spiral of under-investment, decay and more demolition.[7] Between 1990 and 2006, inclusive, over 77,000 Scottish homes were demolished.[8] Government statistics do not give tenure prior to 1998, but the great majority will have been public rented, or former public rented, housing.

Current Scottish housing policy is based around the idea that social housing (both public and housing association) should be no more than a safety-net service for those who absolutely cannot afford any other option. To achieve this, the Scottish Executive has commissioned a group of academics to calculate social housing 'need'. The aim has clearly been to produce a figure that is as low as possible and use it as the basis for future planning. The *Local Housing Need and Affordability Model for Scotland*[9] includes a daunting number of tables and equations, which can be expected to put most people off looking beyond the headline figures; but it is not necessary to work through these to have serious concerns about the assumptions on which they are all based. Social housing need is calculated, for the most part, by combining the needs of new households with the existing backlog. (There are also some people moving from owner-occupation and variations due to migration.)[10] In estimating the need from new households, the model assumes that there will be no need to provide social housing for any family who can afford to buy or rent in the private market, and that this may reasonably involve a mortgage of three-and-a-half times the household salary, or rents of up to 30 per cent of income, and a *residual income after housing costs only just above benefit level.*[11]

The other most worrying assumption concerns the backlog of people inadequately housed. While those families who make up the 'backlog' might be forgiven for thinking that they should be recognised as having an immediate housing need, the model allows this need to be met in annual instalments of 10 per cent. The authors explain that they are following government guidelines that say that local authorities should not plan to exhaust the backlog. The British government recommends an already severely low maximum quota of 20 per cent per annum, and in choosing to reduce this figure even further, the authors hope that families will be driven to find other sources of housing.[12]

As elsewhere, demolition is frequently promoted under the guise of 'regeneration', and cities are expected to compete through their gentrification projects to attract wealthier residents. Bringing in international middle-class incomers – or 'Fresh Talent' – is official Scottish policy.[13] It is this marketisation through regeneration that forms the subject of this chapter. This is looked at through a case study of Dundee, where in 1981, 41,500 homes – 62 per cent of the city's total housing stock – were publicly owned.[14] Sales under Right to Buy, small-scale stock transfers and demolitions – over 9,000 homes were demolished between 1990 and 2006 – have now reduced this figure to 14,000, or 20 per cent of homes, and a further 8,000, or 11 per cent, are rented by housing associations.[15] Despite these losses, and growing recognition of a housing crisis in the city,[16] the *Local Housing Need ... Model* does not recognise Dundee as having a social housing problem. It acknowledges that the city has a backlog need for 6,061 homes – almost half due to overcrowding and sharing – but this is translated into a backlog quota of 605 homes a year; which allows its authors to claim that Dundee has a net *surplus* of social housing relets of 700 homes a year, and the council to conclude that there is no need to increase its production of new social housing from 200 homes a year.[17] This is less than the number of homes currently being lost to the public sector under Right to Buy, and so cannot even begin to compensate for homes being lost through demolition.

But that is the point. This once-generic industrial city, whose council used to boast of having a higher proportion of public housing than Warsaw, is trying to reinvent itself in a new image, and it is doing this in part through seismic changes in housing patterns. This chapter concludes by looking at what this means for the large portion of the population who, whether or not they have a waged job, still make up Dundee's working-class core.

'Dundee – A City Vision'[18]

In the summer of 2005, Dundee's chief planner told a public meeting about his vision for the city. He began by describing the city as viewed by a visitor arriving over the Tay Bridge from Fife, and the positive impact there would be on that view when the ugly multi-storey blocks were demolished and the largely barren riverside area was redeveloped. The demolition of the 'multis' is hugely unpopular with the people who live in them, and any new housing in the riverside development will be focused on attracting a new layer of middle-class professionals. He could hardly have picked a better example if he had set out to demonstrate how the regeneration planning of a city can increase polarisation and consign whole sections of its population quite literally to the margins.[19]

Chapter 3 has looked at some of the theories that have been put forward to justify what is happening, and investigated the rationalisation behind the much-used concepts of 'low demand', 'tenure mix' and 'modernisation', and what these really mean in practice. It has also looked at how new forms of local governance are being used to push through market-led policies while purporting to give a greater role to local communities. This case study demonstrates all this in action.

Dundee is not – for the present at least – facing large-scale housing stock transfer. We have had partial transfers, but a citywide tenants' consultation in 2004 voted 2 to 1 against proceeding with the full transfer process – despite the efforts of the Dundee Federation of Tenants' Associations, who had organised the consultation on behalf of the council. Their council-funded glossy magazine, delivered to all council houses, presented transfer as the only practical alternative, but the federation has little connection to the majority of tenants.

However, almost as soon as the council had acknowledged the result of this consultation, it announced the next stage in its plans for the transformation of the city's homes. This involves the demolition of thousands of council houses – initially nearly 2,000, including multis in the Hilltown in central Dundee, and Menzieshill in the west end. According to council documents, the decision to demolish is founded on three good reasons: the housing is surplus – there is no demand for so much social housing; the homes being demolished are unpopular, and demolition makes economic sense, freeing up money for improving other homes.[20] The trouble is that none of these statements is supported by the evidence, which suggests that the opposite is the case every time.

The council defends its housing strategy by reference to a report it commissioned from the private consultants, DTZ Pieda. When tenants in some of the homes scheduled for demolition, together with housing activists, requested to see that report under the Freedom of Information Act, they were refused on the grounds that disclosure of the methodology used would harm the commercial interests of the consultants.[21] We finally had to extract it by appealing to the commissioners. So what does the report tell us about the three good reasons for demolition?[22]

'An Objective and Thorough Appraisal'[23]

First, let us look at demand. The report gives no data or arguments to support its claim that the 'most likely' scenario for Dundee is 'population decline and social rent residualisation'.[24] We know that Dundee has seen a fall in population,[25] and also a decrease in average household size; but under this scenario the report predicts (without supporting evidence) that between 2002 and 2012 the total number of households in the city will fall by just 200 (from 66,600 to 66,400), and that the number of households living in socially rented housing will fall dramatically, and precisely, by 5,386 (from 24,642 to 19,256).[26] The logic behind this claim needs to be made publicly available. Even before the recession, this was a city with large numbers of residents on low wages and on benefits, and an ageing population, which would suggest the need for the provision of more, rather than less, social rented housing.

It is also noteworthy that the report simply 'assumes' that the number of housing association homes will rise from 6,400 to 7,700 (in 2008), and that the overall reduction in social housing will be made entirely from council housing stock.[27] There is no basis given for this assumption.

The report also tells us that across the city only half the people applying for a council house were actually allotted one.[28] The number of people withdrawing their names from the list was increasing,[29] but this could reflect frustration with a system that is not delivering, rather than falling demand. And the report acknowledges that 'the Council is currently experiencing problems finding alternative accommodation for tenants living in properties that are likely to be scheduled for demolition'.[30]

Some areas and some homes are, of course, much more popular than others. But the report does not consider the option of improving the less popular areas and housing so as to decrease the pressure on over-subscribed areas.[31] It is also significant that, as less popular areas are often more neglected and allotted to 'problem' tenants, low demand can become an increasingly self-fulfilling label.

Further, the report notes that younger tenants are dispro-portionately renting in the private sector rather than the social rented sector.[32] Our own surveys in the Hilltown and Menzieshill showed very significant dislike of the private rented sector (which is generally a more expensive and insecure option), so we need to ask why younger tenants do not appear to be looking for social rented housing, and whether this reflects actual preferences, or difficulties in getting suitable homes in the social housing sector within a reasonable time-frame. Is there, in fact, a potential demand here that is being missed?

Crucially – and this point is so often forgotten – demand for council housing, or social rented housing more generally, is not a fixed number waiting to be discovered, but will increase if this housing is improved or otherwise made more desirable.

So much for lack of demand; what, then, about popularity? Those who, for whatever reason, wish to dismiss the anti-demolition campaigns that have been taking place in Dundee, are quick to characterise them as condemning tenants to poor-quality housing that no one wants to inhabit. This is, of course, the opposite of the case. No one is arguing for keeping the status quo, or for council tenants to make do with second-rate housing. Clearly, too, it is not appropriate to put families with young children in high flats; however, the high-rise boom in the private market demonstrates that multi-storey buildings are often regarded as very desirable homes if they are well maintained and looked after.

The DTZ Pieda report explains the method used to determine which homes should be demolished so as to reduce the total number of homes roughly in line with the report's projected scenario. The less popular housing areas were identified through letting records and through more subjective assessment by council officers, and this information was combined with the maintenance costs of different types of building, and various other factors. Although the council tends to refer to all the homes scheduled for demolition as 'unpopular', popularity was only one factor in the equation.

The council's claims of 'unpopularity' were backed up through the use of surveys. Partnership rhetoric demands the demonstrable involvement of local people to legitimise changes in the eyes of the wider public, and to reduce the potential for dissent among those affected. For the final decisions to demolish the various groups of buildings, the council's housing officers presented the housing committee with a brief document that quoted both the DTZ Pieda report, and also, importantly, feedback from what was termed tenant 'consultation'. The consultation process had been carried out very quickly, shortly after the possibility of demolition was announced. Tenants were asked to vote in a postal survey for or against demolition, without being given any background information about the reasons for the proposal, or any realistic idea what they would be offered instead – though they were told they would get £1,500 for moving. Council documents officially described the buildings as 'at risk',[33] a term that naturally led to assumptions that there must be structural problems; and although many people were sceptical, others assumed that they were being moved to be given 'braw wee hoosis'.[34] No time was allowed for proper discussion or investigation of alternatives. This rushed process produced the desired majorities in favour of demolition, and councillors were able to agree unanimously to proceed. Despite an impassioned plea from tenants' representatives and a packed gallery of protesters, the Hilltown demolitions were given the go-ahead with hardly a murmur of dissent from among the councillors, and six months later, the fate of the Menzieshill multis was confirmed in just five minutes.[35]

These decisions were followed by growing unease and anger among tenants, and in two of the areas I worked with other housing activists alongside tenant campaigners to produce alternative independent surveys.[36] These gave a more realistic assessment of tenants' views after anti-demolition campaigns had generated discussion of the issues in the media and in the blocks concerned, and there had been time for people to understand what was involved and the other options available to them.

The picture that emerged was very different from that portrayed by the council – and I think that the tenants involved in carrying out the surveys were themselves surprised at the extent of the opposition to demolition. Our surveys show that in the two Derby Street multis at the top of the Hilltown, 71 per cent of respondents wanted to remain in the buildings. Only 18 per cent wanted to leave – and several of those told us that they needed to find somewhere without stairs for medical reasons, or somewhere cheaper. Only 9 per cent supported the idea of demolition. (We also found that 30 per cent of responding households said they had not received the council ballot paper on demolition.) In the five multis in Menzieshill, the results, though strong, were not quite so dramatic. This is probably due in a large part to three problems that all have implications for planning a future for buildings of this kind, and could all be solved with better maintenance and management. First, unlike in the Hilltown, these buildings do not have a 24-hour concierge system, and this had major implications for security and for problems with neighbours. Secondly, these buildings housed several families with young children, who, unsurprisingly, wanted to move somewhere with access to a garden, and thirdly, some of the flats have damp problems and there are, of course, no plans to over-clad the building, which would remedy this. In addition, several people were living in the multis while working on temporary contracts at nearby Ninewells Hospital. Nevertheless, we found that 47 per cent of respondents wanted to stay in the multis, compared to 43 per cent who wanted to move, and that 64 per cent were opposed to the idea of demolition, compared to 22 per cent who supported it (with support for demolition dropping to 11 per cent if the buildings were properly repaired and maintained). And, importantly, 77 per cent wanted, whatever happened, to remain in the area. This is unsurprising as around half the people surveyed had other family members with homes in Menzieshill, but they will not be able to stay because there is so little housing available.

The two sets of buildings surveyed were both reasonably well maintained, but even in an estate that is less well sited and has become palpably run-down and neglected, such as the four 30-flat multis in Foggyley Gardens in Lochee, it is difficult to talk about unpopular buildings *per se*. Few residents objected to being moved out to allow the recent demolition of these buildings, but similar flats in nearby Dryburgh Gardens, which had been improved some years back and are well looked after, provide much-sought-after homes.[37]

In all the areas targeted for demolition, some people have, of course, been glad to move – especially those who had previously been turned down for a transfer and now found themselves near the head of the housing queue – and there were others for whom it was of no great importance. But in both of the areas surveyed, we found a core group of tenants who did not want to leave their homes. The surveys demonstrate how widely held that feeling was, and the depth of attachment felt by many was clear at the first public meetings, when anger at what was happening made it difficult to hear what was being said. Some of these people had been in the buildings for many years, such as Betty and Mike who moved into a top flat in the Menzieshill multis when they were first built.[38] Betty told the Menzieshill meeting that when she left 'it would be in a wooden box'. But it has not only been long-term residents who have been reluctant to give up their homes. Liz, who was a member of the group who organised the Hilltown survey, explains that she and others just love living there:

> Are we going to greet [cry] when they knock this down? Yeh. I'm going to be oot the country ... Cos I think it would break my heart if I drove past it when they were knocking this down ... I think a lot of people that's in this multi would feel that way, ken?

And there are good reasons for her passion: 'It's quiet, peaceful, beautiful view, you've everything at your feet when you walk out of the door there. What else could you ask for?'[39]

So much for unpopularity. Perhaps, then, despite all the fine talk, it is simply a case of money. When DTZ Pieda combined different factors to choose which buildings to demolish, it seems that for the multis it was maintenance costs that were the deciding issue. Their report quotes an earlier consultants' assessment of the multis as in 'good condition' with a likely *minimum* life of 30 years,[40] but DTZ Pieda go on to note that 'Very high costs are associated with the mechanical and electrical aspects of the multi-storeys and this includes lift replacement twice throughout the projected 30-year life.'[41] They do not, however, consider the many savings in areas such as road maintenance, public transport and street lighting that are associated with high-density vertical living, and which could significantly outweigh the cost of replacing the lift. These costs may come out of different sections of the council's budget, but all, eventually, will come from the same pot. Similarly, the costs of the concierge and security systems need to be set against substantial savings in maintenance, as well as the less easily measured benefits of reducing 'anti-social behaviour'.

The council claims that demolition makes economic sense, freeing up money for improving other homes in accordance with new housing standards – and, as noted in Chapter 3, it is well recognised that the introduction of new standards without substantial extra funding will encourage councils to demolish large amounts of their stock. However, figures given by DTZ Pieda show that demolition is, in fact, an extremely expensive option. The 'bottom line' is quite startling – though in tune with other huge public subsidies involved in privatisation.

DTZ Pieda have calculated the public subsidies that would be needed to balance the books, and ensure all housing is brought up to the new Scottish standards, under different scenarios. Their baseline figure, with no demolition, is £89 million. If the council were to demolish 4,630 homes this would *rise* to £121 million, and on top of that, there would be another £60 million of grant subsidy for 1,350 new housing association homes subsidised at 60 per cent of construction costs – giving a staggering total of £181 million (and a net loss of 3,280 social rented houses). If demolitions were increased to 7,390 homes, the costs rise to £128 million, with a £185 million grant for 4,100 new homes, or a grand total of £313 million.[42]

Demolition, according to the figures used by the council, is a hugely more expensive option than repair and improvement. *But*, these vast sums of money would not be required to come from council funds; the expectation was that they would be paid by the Scottish Executive – now the Scottish Government – which has already granted the council £3.4 million from its regeneration fund to go towards immediate demolition costs.[43]

In other words, a critical examination of a report that we were not meant to see, demonstrates that public money is being used to subsidise extravagant and unpopular policies on the basis of groundless assumptions.

Every possible argument has been recruited in the cause of justifying the demolitions. They are even presented as 'green' because the existing buildings do not comply with new insulation standards. However, recladding to the new standards would be a much greener solution than the waste of wholesale destruction

– and of much more significance than the recycling of bottles and newspapers. There are also, of course, strong sustainability arguments in favour of a 'compact city' with minimal travel distances.

The way in which housing expenditure is geared towards government subsidy has made it unnecessary for improvements that would not attract subsidy even to be properly considered and costed. When tenants in the Derby Street multis were told that their homes did not comply with the new housing standards, the only significant problem that most were aware of was the poorly conceived heating system. Tom Black, in Butterburn Court, challenged the council to say what was needed. In reply, he was sent heat-loss measurements from other multis of different construction, and told that insulated cladding would cost 'up to £2 million per block'.[44] Besides new heating, he was informed that the building needed rewiring (which is relatively inexpensive) and new bathrooms and kitchens (for which there seems to be no pressing demand from the tenants). The council claims that improvements to the multi-storey flats would cost, on average, £30,000 per unit – as opposed to an average cost of £11,000 per unit for the homes it intends to retain[45] – but it is difficult to account for these figures. The biggest cost for the multis would indeed be recladding, assuming this is always necessary; however, the experience of Glasgow suggests this would average at around £1.3 million per multi,[46] or £11,600 a flat.[47] It is also worth noting that the estimated cost of demolition and site reinstatement, combined with the relocation payment, averages at £6,317 per flat.[48]

The short-term policies that arise from the council's need to divest itself of all property requiring expenditure, are demonstrated, on a much smaller scale, by the fate of a walk-up block in Douglas (East Dundee) following a fire in one of the twelve flats. This building was one of a row of ten identical blocks, and there was no suggestion of any problem with the others; however, the cost of repairs was estimated at £116,600, with a further £156,720 for bringing the building up to the new standards. The council voted to demolish the building at a cost of £71,500, rather than pay a further £16,818 per flat and end up with twelve good-quality homes.[49] The wasteful demolition of 84 four-in-a-block houses in Charleston (West Dundee) was even condemned by a local developer, who had wanted to take them on as a commercial proposition.[50]

The council's housing strategy for 2004–09 gave a short-term (five-year) target of just 98 new social-rented units in the Hilltown, rising to 250 units by 2034.[51] On the sites where over a thousand council houses in the multis and adjacent buildings now stand, the regeneration strategy document proposes to increase the percentage of 'affordable' private housing, through mixed-tenure developments of around 420 new homes, of which less than a quarter would be socially rented. And the plans to remove a large section of the area's current population are disguised under the usual mission statements about consulting with 'community groups', creating 'a place where people would want to live' and 'planning for strong and stable communities'.[52] No account is taken of the views of existing tenants being forced to leave their homes, for whom these developments are 'fancy houses for somebody else to buy on my plot'.[53] In Menzieshill, the short-term target for social rented housing is 90 units. The council 'would welcome proposals for social rented development following demolition of [the] existing buildings' provided housing associations 'can fund [the] land value'[54] – but this is prime land close to the hospital. It was always clear that if demolition is allowed to go ahead in the Hilltown and Menzieshill, only a fraction of those tenants forced to leave their homes will be able to be accommodated in low-rise buildings in the area: these plans demonstrate a willingness to allow that fraction to be even smaller.

An internal council discussion document on 'affordable housing', leaked to housing activists in the summer of 2006, clearly shows how closely events in Dundee conform to the patterns of gentrification and marketisation discussed in Chapter 3. The document presents the development of private housing on the demolition sites in the Hilltown and Menzieshill as improving the quality and choice of *private* housing in the city, and as bringing 'regeneration benefits through encouraging more balanced communities with more diversity of tenure'; and it points out that it will generate more income for the council. The document also notes that registered social landlords (RSLs) are 'reporting difficulties in competing with private developers to acquire land ... for new housing development' and that '[t]here is a danger that RSLs are only able to secure land in locations that are least attractive to the private sector'.[55] This leaves little hope for new social housing in Menzieshill, and suggests that those who require such housing will increasingly be pushed to the margins of the city. Finally, the document notes a rise in buy-to-let and private renting in the city – making nonsense of the council's claims (which the paper repeats) of falling demand for social rented homes. We can expect to see more tenants having to rely on the private rented sector, which, of course, is itself heavily subsidised through housing benefit.

Collateral Damage[56]

To make sense of all this, I have attempted to draw up a balance sheet for the different players involved, beginning with the Scottish Government – or what used to be called, prior to the Scottish National Party administration, the Scottish Executive. Housing-led regeneration forms a major plank in the government's privatising agenda and an important boost to what are thought of as key players in the Scottish development and finance industries. Investment in construction can be seen as beneficial at many levels, but for the same amount of government money, this privatised system produces fewer homes, and bigger profits for the developers.

For the city council, demolition means saving on the cost of refurbishment, which would be greater than the loss of rent, and it releases valuable city-centre and west-end sites that can be sold to private developers to raise revenue. They expect demolition costs to be subsidised by the Scottish Government, and any new social housing built by housing associations to replace the demolished homes would also receive government subsidies not offered to the council. It is also hoped that new private houses built on these sites would contribute to attracting a new middle class to the city, boosting the economy and tax base, but in this

Dundee is competing with other cities following similar policies. The plans being pushed forward would also result in a huge net loss of social rented housing and an even greater loss of housing under direct council control. Good-value decent housing would no longer be available for a sizeable section of the electorate, and a hugely valuable asset, built up over generations, would be dissipated. The council may find itself presiding over an even more geographically divided city, with those on low incomes banished to the periphery.

And what about the tenants? What is happening affects not only tenants in the buildings scheduled for demolition, but many other existing and would-be tenants, as the number of houses available decreases and people whose homes are to be demolished move to the head of the housing queue. To compensate for the loss of rent on empty flats, the council has raised rents for all its tenants.[57] The loss of flats must also have knock-on effects on the private rental market; and the credit crunch will only have increased these pressures.

By 2006, the casework for Dundee's political representatives (Members of Parliament and Members of the Scottish Parliament) was exposing the crisis in Dundee's housing, with examples of incredible overcrowding and people being stuck for months in temporary accommodation because there was nowhere for them to relocate.[58] For those with particular housing requirements, the wait could be as long as 18 months.[59] The city's homeless unit was becoming increasingly overwhelmed, not only because Scottish homelessness legislation is relaxing the rules that restricted who local authorities had to find accommodation for, but also because many people were no longer being housed through the mainstream waiting list. Families staying with friends and relations, but looking for their own home, lose out in competition with those being rehoused from temporary accommodation and from buildings threatened with demolition, until worsening circumstances or desperation force them to declare themselves also potentially homeless.[60]

The shortage of homes for those with limited mobility is already severe, and people are stuck in upper-floor tenements while level-entry multi flats stand empty, awaiting demolition. The case of Gladys Storrier made newspaper headlines.[61] Gladys and William Storrier and their daughter and grandchildren lived in a council-owned tenement not far from Derby Street. They were moved temporarily into a ground-floor flat when their second-floor flat next door was rewired, and, for the first time in years, Mrs Storrier, who can only walk with a frame, was able to go out of the house. The difference this made to her life and her health was enormous, and the family asked to stay in their 'decant'. Their request was refused, and after months of legal wrangling, which appeared to take no account of public petitions or her doctor's warnings, the family was evicted, and Mrs Storrier, bedridden with worry, was physically carried out into the close.[62] More recently, the local paper highlighted the council's failure to rehouse a wounded soldier and his family.[63] The council's hard-line stance can be explained by a fear that there are many others for whom a move to ground-floor accommodation would make a vital difference – if they were seen to be responding once they would be inundated with similar requests.

Some of those forced to move from the buildings scheduled for demolition will find themselves in better homes, or grow to like new areas, but often they will also end up paying higher housing association, or even private, rents and service charges. Service charges are not covered by housing benefit, and if benefits are being given to cover high rents, then that can put tenants into a poverty trap where they cannot afford to risk losing their benefits to take on a, generally low paid, job. Others have gone to other multis in the city, and several people have a housing history of moving from flat to flat ahead of different regeneration schemes. People are being put under a lot of pressure, which encourages them to accept places they may not be happy with, in areas where they have no links, for fear of something worse. There are many stories of people who regret having moved and who miss their multi – the security, location, friends, generous-sized rooms and, of course, the views.

The sense of security in a multi with a full-time concierge, as in the Hilltown, is frequently commented on – not least by the council, whose website still extolled the advantage of this system even as it was dismantling it (including the comment that 'there is now a waiting list for some of these blocks, when once they had empty properties'[64]). A good concierge system is able to deal with problems quickly and in a low-key manner. One of the Hilltown concierges commented, 'It's like you could be a social worker, financial advisor, you name it, you are it … It's a combination of everything. 'Cos you build a relationship with the tenants, you see.'[65] This could be a model for the kind of community policing that is often proposed for troubled housing estates, but the system is being run down as the buildings empty out, and tenants will find nothing similar elsewhere.

Although new social-rented homes are being built in the Hilltown, it is a slow process, and, as we have seen, there will be never be anywhere near as many houses as are being demolished. This means that many people will be forced to move to other areas – away from a place that is walking distance from the city centre, with many services on the doorstep and others just a bus ride away. It would be hard to replicate this anywhere else. Liz's description sounds almost poetic:

> You've got the doctors, dentists, chiropodists, supermarkets, pubs – if you want to go there – and hairdressers. There's butchers, bakers, candlestick-makers, and you cross the road and there's even undertakers.[66]

At Menzieshill, where there is no sign of any new social housing, a busy community centre can be found just at the foot of the blocks, where activities range from youth groups to the modern sequence dancing classes at which Betty is a regular attendee. And, of course, the flats are very convenient for anyone who works at the adjacent Ninewells Hospital. The demolitions will mean a substantial reduction in low-cost rented housing in the centre of the city and in the west end, so that many existing tenants, and also new tenants looking for social housing, will find themselves isolated in peripheral estates, away from the services they are used to, and often with few services altogether, dependent on the bus for everything.

At the time the multis were built, slum clearance schemes were accused of destroying communities. Now another generation of linkages is being pulled apart. In most places today, community ties are not seen to be as strong as they were at that earlier time, but that does not mean that they are not there, or not important. There are several families in which two or even three generations live in different flats in the same multi; and many people, as our Menzieshill survey demonstrated, have other family members in the area. There are also people who have maintained long-term friendships. The Hilltown concierge quoted earlier was especially concerned about those who lived on their own and relied on each other for company:

> There is life-long pals in the multi ... There was a clique of sort of alcoholics, like bachelors that have maybe gone on hard times ... there has been three or four of them where I work have voiced concerns about when the multi comes down they're frightened about being split up and what. The sort of last 20, 25, 30 years they've lived together, visited each other's flats ... like a big community. Now they're wondering what's going to happen.[67]

And there are examples of more traditional community organisation: before the building started to empty out, one of the Menzieshill multis held such a boisterous pensioners' Christmas party that complaints were made to the police about the noise.

The condemned buildings were designed to more generous space standards than many homes built today, as people have realised when they have had to sell their larger furniture on moving out. And the views from many of the flats would make an estate agent drool. One of the tenants in Alexander Street, in the middle of the Hilltown, described the view from her windows as something 'money couldn't buy', but in a time when high flats are increasingly being built as luxury homes, perhaps she is wrong. The only disagreement among the tenants about the views, is whose is the best.

The consultative vote organised by the Tenants' Federation indicated that a substantial majority of Dundee tenants are opposed to stock transfer, which recent ballots in other areas have shown to be a deeply unpopular policy. However, the proposed

Figure 5.1 A view from the Derby Street multis – showing small local shops in the foreground, two of the four Alexander Street multis and the River Tay beyond (*photo: Sarah Glynn*).

demolitions will result in a substantial reduction in the city's council housing, without the chance of a vote. As a local trade unionist put it, it's not even privatisation by the back door, it's by the front door.[68]

Those who thought that moving would take them away from 'anti-social' neighbours may be in for a shock. They may have simply exchanged one anti-social neighbour for another; and, of course, their old neighbours have moved as well, and taken their problems with them. In fact, those with few ties and responsibilities have often been the first to accept the money and go. Households relocated to the award-winning, regenerated Ardler 'Village' have found their new location the subject of frustrated letters in the local evening paper chronicling violence and drug abuse;[69] and one of the respondents to the Menzieshill survey noted that the flat they had been offered 'is upstairs from [a] drug dealer'. Demolition does not erase entrenched and structural social problems.

Although £1,500 for moving can seem a lot to someone with few possessions and no investment in their home,[70] many people have spent significant sums and many hours of their own labour on improvements (see Figure 5.2). Flats can be in a depressing state when they are first let. Like anywhere, some people decorate and care for them better than others, but, to quote the concierge again, some tenants have made their flats 'like five-star hotels'.[71] To reproduce what they had in the multi costs such tenants large amounts of time and money, for which there was no compensation beyond a derisory £150 decoration voucher (which had to be spent in one transaction).

Figure 5.2   A much-loved flat in the Derby Street multis
(*photo: Sarah Glynn*).

The buildings are emptying only slowly. The lack of alternative housing makes this inevitable, but many people intend to stay as long as possible. While, at first, the relative quiet may be welcomed, other problems materialise. As the buildings empty out, repairs are kept to a minimum and there are growing concerns about vandalism. People are finding themselves the only ones left on an otherwise empty landing (see Figure 5.3). The vital concierge system is being cut to the bone, and the four multis in the middle of the Hilltown now rely on a single concierge station in place of the previous two.[72] There are no longer landing checks and tenants try not to think what would happen if someone were to light a fire in an empty flat.[73] Flats where all the surrounding tenants have left can become unbearably cold and damp – and expensive to heat. A disproportionate number of old people lived in the multis, for whom both a forced move and a decaying environment can be particularly stressful. Quite early on, we were already being told of older people being made ill with worry.

Figure 5.3   October 2008: The remaining tenants in Menzieshill are surrounded by cold, boarded-up flats, while the empty corridors attract vandalism (*photo: Sarah Glynn*).

In the longer term, others living in these areas may also suffer. The people who live in the multis form a large proportion of those who use local shops, schools, health centres, bus services and community organisations. If large numbers are forced to move out of an area, many of these amenities, which are at the heart of a healthy community, may no longer be viable. The council is already concerned about commercial decline in the Hilltown.[74]

The multis may not be pretty, and many of their inhabitants may not fit the new image of the 'City of Discovery',[75] but Dundee is their city. The new Dundee that is planned to greet visitors coming over the Tay Bridge will conceal a very different world, out of sight on its peripheral estates. This transformation is not happening without protest, but the angry defiance of the first months is increasingly being replaced by a bitter resignation as tenants, facing a long war of attrition, come to realise that no one with the power to influence events appears to be listening.

Since the decision was made to demolish the multis, the housing situation in Dundee has deteriorated significantly, to the extent that in the spring of 2008, the local evening paper was able to run features on the city's housing crisis – and the council's denial of its existence – for over two weeks.[76] In response to this, I worked with other activists to organise a public meeting and street stalls. No member of the council administration (a Labour/Liberal/Tory alliance) accepted our invitation to the meeting and the 'official' Federation of Tenants' Associations refused too, on the grounds that such a meeting was 'political'. We were also told, as noted in Chapter 2, that we could not have permission to hold a stall in the city square since we did not have public liability insurance and someone might injure themselves by, for example, tripping over the table.[77]

Our political establishment, at various levels, is doing all it can to suppress dissent, but at the same time, understanding of what is happening is growing. In the aftermath of the credit crunch, pressures on low-cost housing are increasing and so is anger towards policies that forgot that housing is for living in. Now, more than ever, investment in improving and investing in our council housing stock makes sense, while plans for large private developments seem to belong to a past age, and major policy u-turns might be presented as imaginative responses to new situations. Although many households have already suffered, it is not too late to halt the juggernaut of Dundee's housing-led regeneration. Already it looks as though some of Glasgow's multis may be given a reprieve.[78] But market-centred ways of thinking have become deeply ingrained into the political system and alternatives will not be accepted without pressure.

Acknowledgements

With thanks to the tenants of Butterburn and Bucklemaker Courts and the Menzieshill Multis. (An account of this research has been previously published in *Urban Research and Practice* – see below.)

Further Reading

Glendinning, Miles and Stefan Muthesius (1994) *Tower Block: Modern Public Housing in England, Scotland, Wales and Northern Ireland* (New Haven, CT and London: Yale University Press).

Glynn, Sarah (2008) 'Soft-selling Gentrification?', *Urban Research and Practice* 1(2): 164–80.

Scottish Executive (2003) *A Review of Scotland's Cities – The Analysis* <http://www.scotland.gov.uk/Publications/2003/01/15950/15144>.

Websites

Glasgow Community Health and Wellbeing Research and Learning Programme – ongoing research project into regeneration in Glasgow <http://www.gowellonline.com>.

Public Interest Research Network, Housing and Regeneration Working Group – including the Dundee Tenants' Surveys and analysis of the DTZ Pieda report <http://www.publicinterest.ac.uk/content/section/17/72>.

Notes

1. This was the title given by the Scottish Executive to its economic strategy document drawn up in 2001 and revised in 2004.
2. There were also significant proportions owned by the central government's Scottish Special Housing Association (which became Scottish Homes), and by the New Town Development Corporations.

3. Nearly 55 per cent of homes in the 1981 census.
4. Glendinning, Miles and Stefan Muthesius (1994) *Tower Block: Modern Public Housing in England, Scotland, Wales and Northern Ireland* (New Haven, CT and London: Yale University Press).
5. Scotland had its own Act and slightly different systems of finance.
6. For Right to Buy sales see <http://openscotland.gov.uk/Resource/ Doc/933/0060113.xls>. It is surprisingly difficult to find the figures for stock transfer. This total has been put together using information from Audit Scotland (2006) *Council Housing Transfers* (Edinburgh: Audit Scotland) <http://www.audit-scotland.gov.uk/docs/central/2005/ nr_060324_council_housing_transfers.pdf>; Berry, Kate (2006) 'Housing Stock Transfers', Scottish Parliament Information Centre (SPICe) Briefing 06/55 <http://www.scottish.parliament.uk/business/ research/briefings-06/SB06-55.pdf> (omitting figures for Stirling, the Highlands and Renfrewshire, which all voted against transfer); Pawson, Hal and Cathie Fancy (2003) *Maturing Assets: The Evolution of Stock Transfer Housing Associations* (Bristol: Policy Press), pp. 1, 2; Taylor, Mary (2004) 'Policy Emergence: Learning Lessons From Stock Transfer', in Duncan Sim (ed.) *Housing and Public Policy in Post-devolution Scotland* (Coventry: Chartered Institute of Housing). The figure for transfer to housing associations comprises some 117,700 transferred from local authorities in whole stock transfers, 24,600 in smaller transfers, 54,000 transferred from the government-owned Scottish Homes and 4,000 from New Town Corporations. Some of the sales were of homes previously transferred [all websites accessed 9 October 2008].
7. 'Too often physical housing decay has been followed by demolition and demolition by unpaid housing debt. Unpaid debt with capital and interest to be repaid, with fewer tenants left to pay, means either rising rents, with no service increase, or reduced services, that is curtailing management and maintenance. But reduced management and maintenance then means higher vacancy rates, more abandonment and more demolitions' (Scottish Executive (2003) *A Review of Scotland's Cities – The Analysis*, Section 4.3.8 <http://www.scotland.gov.uk/Publications/2003/01/15950/15144> [accessed 9 October 2008]).
8. <http://www.scotland.gov.uk/Resource/Doc/933/0056544.xls> [accessed 16 May 2008].
9. Bramley, Glen, Noah Kofi Karley and David Watkins (2006) *Local Housing Need and Affordability Model for Scotland – Update (2005 Based)* (Edinburgh: Communities Scotland). Glen Bramley is also one of the main proponents of the idea, discussed in Chapter 3, that 'low-demand' housing is a cause of area decline.

10. Ibid., p. 11.
11. Ibid., p. 87. (This assumption about the mortgage predates the credit crunch.)
12. Ibid., p. 89.
13. <http://www.scotland.gov.uk/Publications/2004/02/18984/33666> [accessed 9 October 2008].
14. Just less than the 63 per cent figure for Glasgow (1981 census).
15. Figures supplied to the author by Dundee City Council in March 2007 gave 14,476 council houses and 8,054 housing association houses. The number of houses on the council tax register in September 2007 was 72,736.
16. 'Get Your Housing Facts; Dundee City', downloaded from <http://scotland.shelter.org.uk>, 27 March 2007; *Evening Telegraph*, March–April 2008.
17. Bramley et al., *Local Housing Need*, pp. 117, 11 and 8; note AN 90-2007 to Dundee City Council Housing Committee Agenda for 19 March 2007. In Glasgow, a backlog need for 29,603 homes is translated into a backlog quota of 2,960 homes a year and a claimed 'surplus' of 'social housing' relets of 4,590 homes a year. And the scale of demolition is vast.
18. Title of the (undated) 'community plan' produced by Dundee Partnership. Each Scottish city is expected to produce such a document. Dundee claims a pioneering role in the development of 'community partnerships', with the first Whitfield regeneration being carried out under the New Life for Urban Scotland programme.
19. It could be added that the current examples of developer-driven new building – which include plans for a 15-storey tower – do not leave much room for optimism about improved aesthetics either.
20. See report by the Director of Housing to Dundee City Council Housing Committee, 21 June 2004, 'Building Stronger Communities – Physical Regeneration in the Council Sector'. It was on the basis of this report that the council voted to consider the demolition of the multis discussed in this chapter and to declare them 'at risk'. Similar arguments are still being repeated: see the response of housing convenor Councillor George Regan to my critical analysis of the DTZ Pieda report discussed below, as printed in the *Courier*, 28 April 2006, and the letter from the director of housing reproduced in Glynn, Sarah (2008) 'Soft-selling Gentrification?', *Urban Research and Practice* 1(2): 168.
21. Letter from the council's legal manager, 15 February 2005.
22. Glynn, Sarah (2006) 'The Report They Didn't Want Us to See: An Analysis of DTZ Pieda's Report on Dundee's Council Housing' for Defend Dundee Council Housing <http://www.publicinterest.ac.uk/content/section/17/72> [accessed 9 October 2008].

23. 'The overall aim of the study was … to undertake an objective and thorough appraisal of the financial and operational issues that are likely to impinge on the Council as it looks to the long-term ownership and management of its stock': DTZ Pieda (2005) *Dundee City Council – Financial Viability Study Phase 2: Final Report*, para 1.4.
24. Ibid., paras 2.18–19.
25. Between 1991 and 2004, the population fell every year bar one, declining in total by 8.8 per cent over the period (*About Dundee 2005*, Dundee City Council).
26. DTZ Pieda, *Dundee City Council*, para 2.18.
27. Ibid., para 2.19.
28. Each year the council allotted around 2,500 houses, of which around two-thirds were new lets and one-third transfers from other council houses (ibid., paras 1.12–2.13).
29. Ibid., para 1.15.
30. Ibid., para 3.49.
31. Recent research carried out for Angus Council has found that rural areas north of the city are also over-subscribed, with a clear need for more social rented housing (Angus Council (2006) Report no. 1154/06: Sidlaws Housing Needs Research – Research Project Report, p. 2).
32. DTZ Pieda, *Dundee City Council*, para 2.9.
33. On 21 June 2004, 1,898 homes had been declared 'At Risk' by the Council Housing Committee.
34. 'fine little houses'.
35. The council meetings were held on 18 October 2004 and 18 April 2005.
36. Glynn, Sarah (ed.) (2005) 'More Time for Butterburn and Bucklemaker Courts? The Tenants' Survey'; Glynn, Sarah (ed.) (2006) 'Views from the Menzieshill Multis: The Tenants' Survey', both available on <http://www.publicinterest.ac.uk/content/section/17/72> [accessed 9 October 2008].
37. Dryburgh Gardens is now owned by a housing association, but the difference is due to the investment in the buildings rather than the tenure.
38. These names have been changed.
39. Interviewed 28 July 2006 (the name has been changed).
40. DTZ Pieda, *Dundee City Council*, paras 2.23 and 2.25.
41. Ibid., para 2.23.
42. Ibid., para 4.27.
43. They have had to be quite inventive in spending this as they have not been able to empty the buildings as quickly as planned (*Courier*, 11 January 2007 and 19 February 2008).

44. Letter from the head of housing to Tom Black, 28 November 2005.

45. Letter from the Chief Executive of Dundee City Council to the author, 1 September 2005.

46. This is the cost that was given for recladding the 120-flat Yoker multi (Glasgow Housing Association press release, 5 September 2006). The eleven multis in the Hilltown and Menzieshill have an average size of 112 flats.

47. This is not very different from the cost of cladding other homes, which the council has done for an average of £10,000 each (Dundee City Council, Home Energy Conservation Act Fourth Progress Report 2003–05). Although multis have obvious problems of access, they also have smaller wall areas per home and economies of scale.

48. Letter from the Chief Executive of Dundee City Council to the author, 1 September 2005.

49. Dundee City Council Housing Committee, 18 April 2005.

50. *Courier*, 5 September 2006. Buildings combining two upper and two lower flats are a standard Scottish council-housing pattern.

51. Dundee City Council, *Local Housing Strategy*, p. 27.

52. Dundee City Council (2008) *The Hilltown Physical Regeneration Framework*, pp. 8, 12, 10 and 7.

53. Interview with Liz, 28 July 2006.

54. Dundee City Council, *Local Housing Strategy*, p. 25.

55. Dundee City Council (2006) 'Affordable Housing and Housing Choice Issues in Dundee', consultation paper.

56. 'Unintentional or incidental injury or damage to persons or objects that would not be lawful military targets in the circumstances ruling at the time. Such damage is not unlawful so long as it is not excessive in light of the overall military advantage anticipated from the attack', US Department of Defense, *Dictionary of Military and Associated Terms*, JP 3-60.

57. Rents were raised by around 4 per cent in 2006, 2007 and 2008, and on each occasion the director of housing commented on the fall in rental income due to council house sales and demolitions (*Courier*, 17 January 2006 and 2007 and 22 January 2008).

58. Meeting with Shona Robison MSP and Stuart Hosie MP (both Dundee East, and SNP), 6 October 2006.

59. Interview with director of the council's homeless unit, 31 October 2006.

60. Ibid.

61. For example, *Evening Telegraph*, 17 November 2005.

62. The open passageway that gives access to a group of tenements.

63. *Courier*, 28 June, and 2 and 3 October 2007.

64. <http://www.dundeecity.gov.uk>, downloaded 20 October 2006.
65. Interviewed 18 August 2006. He also emphasised that they did not take on responsibilities for which they were not trained.
66. Interviewed 28 July 2006.
67. Interviewed 18 August 2006.
68. At a meeting of Defend Dundee Council Housing in 2004.
69. *Evening Telegraph*, 18 August 2006 and 27 September 2006.
70. This is the statutory minimum, and lower than anywhere else we have heard of. It has not gone up in very many years.
71. Interviewed 18 August 2006.
72. Housing Committee Minutes, 20 February 2006. A similar arrangement seems to be about to be instituted in Derby Street (February 2009).
73. This point was raised in my discussion with the MP and MSP. When I took the photograph in Menzieshill (Figure 5.3), I found the remains of a fire in one of the storerooms.
74. *Courier*, 9 January 2007.
75. This is how the city is branded in its promotional literature, taking its cue from the name of the ship used by 'Scott of the Antarctic'. The *Discovery* was built in Dundee and is now moored in the otherwise rather inactive harbour.
76. *Evening Telegraph*, March–April 2008.
77. When the Dundee and Angus Scots Guards Association protested the council's failure to rehouse their wounded comrade, they had also been refused official permission (*Courier*, 2 October 2007).
78. Talks are under way (October 2008) about the remaining multis in Sighthill, though the first demolitions there have already taken place.

6

THE POLITICS OF HOUSING UNDER FRANCE'S NEW RIGHT

Corinne Nativel

With its high levels of taxation, 'social expenditure', and numerous tenured civil servants, France is often believed to represent the antithesis of the Anglo-American neoliberal model. It is true that, since the mid-1970s, welfare 'reforms' have been less radical and the attachment to state regulation has been stronger than in Britain or in the US. None the less, France has undergone several 'neoliberal moments', with significant privatisation programmes that have considerably reduced the role of the state in various sectors of the economy, including housing. According to Prasad, France has embraced a kind of 'neoliberal pragmatism', driven by economic growth objectives and consideration for the well-being of the middle and upper classes, which makes its apparent concern for egalitarianism and social redistribution something of a myth.[1] In addition, drawing on the work of Peck and Tickell about the process of neoliberalism, Blanc argues that in France, the changing role of the central state in housing provision (from a 'provider' to an 'enabler') in response to neoliberal imperatives, reflects the 'rolling-out' of a new regulatory framework but without the kind of prior destructive 'roll-back' experienced by other countries in the 1980s.[2] In this chapter, I argue that this 'soft' image may have become an understatement to describe the country's latest neoliberal 'moment' under a forceful New Right, whose style of politics combines American-inspired 'Bushism' with Euro-Mediterranean 'Berlusconism'.[3] Nicolas Sarkozy, the former home secretary who was elected president in May 2007, seems to have been seduced by the free market and enterprising values of liberalism, and clearly reveres state authoritarianism. He excels at using the media to pursue an agenda of reactionary and repressive politics, particularly towards the dispossessed, such as immigrants and young people. His government has promoted sharp state downsizing, with the privatisation of utilities, attacks on the status and recruitment of public service workers and significant devolution of central state responsibilities. In other words, while previous governments, of both the 'left' and right, had already rolled out neoliberal policies in the 1980s and 1990s, the roll-back process has undoubtedly unfolded in the current decade. It reflects a political willingness to catch up with the 'role models' of the North Atlantic zone.

In 2008, 15 million French people owned their homes, that is, 56 per cent of the population (with around 35 per cent outright owners), compared to 70 per cent in Britain. Two surveys conducted in 2006 and 2007 respectively by Ipsos and TNS-Sofres, the two largest opinion polling institutes in France, showed that 89 per cent of the population viewed homeownership as their preferred tenure, while a similar proportion (87 per cent) found that accessing adequate and affordable housing was very difficult.[4] The fears and aspirations of ordinary citizens have provided Sarkozy with ammunition for his repeated claims that France must 'catch up' with Spain and the US to become 'a country of homeowners' (deliberately ignoring that these two countries have been profoundly affected by the recent subprime crisis). Government officials, from former Urban Renovation and Social Cohesion Minister Jean-Louis Borloo to Housing Minister Christine Boutin, have produced multiple statements, including such hackneyed phrases as 'property equals individual empowerment, responsibility, security and peaceful neighbourly relationships'. These statements are clearly out of step with the urgent (re)housing needs facing millions of homeless or poorly housed residents. The government's fiscal goodies to the middle class, introduced in September 2007 in the form of tax-deductible interest rates for the purchase of their main residence, and its commitment to sell 1 per cent of the social housing stock to its tenants every year (which will amount to 40,000 units instead of the current 6,000), are equally ill-suited to respond to the pressing needs of those million people excluded from work or in insecure employment. For them, home purchase is beyond reach since, according to the old adage, 'banks only lend to the rich',[5] that is, to those who own capital and draw a steady income.

While government and media attention is increasingly focused on middle-class families priced out of city centres and on the inevitability of traffic congestion and urban sprawl, the crisis is much wider and deeper: above all, it hits the unemployed, the working poor, students who struggle to find a room to rent, and immigrant populations forced to live in derelict homes and ghettoised housing estates. The segmentation of the housing market has, unsurprisingly, created significant backlash, one of the most reported events being the outburst of urban unrest that emanated from the Paris suburbs of Clichy-sous-Bois and Villiers-le-Bel in the autumn of 2005. Advocacy work has long been carried out by well-known civil society actors such as the Abbé Pierre Foundation (named after the charismatic clergyman who made a famous call for the homeless in the winter of 1954 and whose death in February 2007 was mourned across France) and DAL (Droit au Logement – Right to Housing, an organisation created in 1990 and led by the energetic figure of Jean-Baptiste Eyraud since 2006). More recently, this has been boosted by new, and less mainstream, direct action groups, which have engaged in small-scale, carefully targeted actions.[6] However, despite the media coverage of these actions, their overall impact remains limited. The chapter will end with a look at the campaign for the right to housing, which, whilst responding to the imperative of bringing justice and democracy into housing, has so far not made any real breakthrough. France, like many other wealthy countries, will eventually be obliged to face the housing consequences of neoliberal choices.

To understand the gulf between governmental positions and the actual housing needs of the French population, we must start with a brief historical detour through the features that underpin the French housing framework, and then examine how the latest crisis has mounted in the past decade of housing speculation and inflation.

Understanding French Housing Provision and Regulation: A Brief Historical Detour

The housing crisis facing France in the immediate aftermath of the Second World War was due not solely to the consequences of the bombing, but also to the insufficiency and inadequacy of pre-war housing stock. In response to this crisis, in 1947 and 1948, policymakers funded the development of the social housing sector, known as HLM (*habitation à loyer modéré* – housing with moderate rent), and also introduced the first system of individual assistance, the family housing allowance.[7] The HLM were newly built or renovated homes, owned and managed by a range of public- or private-sector providers across France (see below). In 1953, housing was declared a national priority and state intervention became more significant, notably with a series of slum clearance policies in the city centres. It was also in that year that a ring-fenced tax for social housing, amounting to 1 per cent of their payroll, was introduced for companies with more than ten employees, thereby generating extra resources for new homes. The home construction policy that followed was supported by a diversity of public finance mechanisms, including loans from the (then) state-owned Crédit Foncier, which was the main state-owned financial institution in the position to collect and manage private savings.

Because they offered cheap land, the so-called 'ZUP' areas (*zones à urbaniser en priorité* – priority zones for urbanisation) saw the emergence of mass construction programmes financed by the state, with tower blocks and high-rise housing estates known as the *grands ensembles*. Nine million new homes were created on these peripheral estates from the mid-1950s to the mid-1970s. But 1977 marked a major shift, when public authorities, in the belief that the housing crisis had been eradicated, turned their attention from 'bricks-and-mortar' supply-side policies (called '*aide à la pierre*') to financial assistance to individuals (called '*aide personnalisée au logement'*). In other words, housing policy moved from the realm of urban planning to that of social redistribution, which encouraged both the development of homeownership and the continued existence of substandard housing. This radical reform proved particularly ill-timed given that the page of the prosperous *Trente Glorieuses* era (or post-war boom) was already being turned.

It is often pointed out that France's social housing sector has not undergone the kind of ferocious residualisation that other European countries, such as Portugal or Spain, have experienced. France still has a stock of 4.5 million homes, housing 11 million residents and representing 17 per cent of main residences. The stock is managed by some 863 social housing providers, which may be established as either public or private entities. These providers – known as '*organismes HLM*' – are grouped under the umbrella of the Union Sociale pour l'Habitat (Social Union for Housing). Public HLM organisations act either on behalf of the central state, or on behalf of local authorities, and are known as Offices Publics de l'Habitat (Public Housing Offices). Private HLM organisations may be co-operatives, foundations, or private limited companies. However, the picture is far from rosy, since the housing stock has suffered from severe under-investment. In the era of 'modernity', when the majority of people enjoyed stable employment, social housing was commonly seen as a temporary platform for upward mobility, and not as permanent accommodation. The classical path (and aspiration) was for people to start off in private rented accommodation, and then move into social housing as the family expanded until they could buy a house of their own. Those residents who could move out did so in the 1970s and 1980s and were gradually replaced by families originating from North Africa who were encouraged to settle. However, with the breakdown of traditional career and family trajectories, the turnover in social housing has decreased, with fewer exits and more applicants for entry.[8] Currently, over 1.3 million people are on housing waiting lists, including 330,000 for the Île-de-France region alone (the figures have doubled since the mid-1980s). With a stagnating stock and reduced in- and outflows, the social housing sector has come to be seen as a trap for immigrants and people on low incomes. The government's tactic is to blame the HLM organisations for mismanagement. A Green Paper to restructure the sector and subject it to performance criteria was presented by Housing Minister Christine Boutin in May 2008.[9]

Between Exclusion and Euphoria

The annual report of the Abbé Pierre Foundation provides a snapshot analysis of the housing situation at a national level.[10] The picture is alarming. In 2008, over 3 million people were reported to be experiencing severe housing problems: 1 million people were classed as homeless (that is, living in temporary hostel accommodation, living in campsites, being accommodated by friends and family, or other such arrangements); another 100,000 were estimated to be sleeping rough, while 2.2 million were poorly housed (in homes lacking basic amenities or in overcrowded conditions). In addition, 6 million people were at risk of losing their homes for a variety of reasons, such as rent arrears or those homes being in urgent need of refurbishment.

The problem of unfit homes was brought to public attention in the summer of 2005, when a series of derelict hostels that housed migrant families caught fire in Paris, Lyon and Marseille. It was not surprising that the Paris fires took place predominantly in the northern and southern districts and that they affected families of African immigrants living in overcrowded conditions. The fire of 25 August 2006, which engulfed an entire building located on Auriol Boulevard in a southern district of Paris, caused 17 deaths, including 13 children. The mayor of the district later admitted that there had been warning that the building was unfit for decent accommodation. It is estimated that in the capital city, around 40 per cent of furnished hostel rooms are rented by the government to provide subsidised housing for poor and/ or migrant people.[11] Another striking statistic is that around a third of homeless people actually have a job. Work is no longer a protection against homelessness: in the absence of rent control, the gap between wages and rent levels in the private sector has increased exponentially, particularly in large cities, and there are long waiting lists for public-sector housing.

According to the National Statistical Office,[12] between 1997 and 2007, property prices rose by 146 per cent. Extreme difficulties accessing overpriced dwellings in the private-rented sector boosted the demand for homeownership and contributed to this inflationary 'euphoria'. Other factors included the changing demography, state support in the form of 'zero-interest' loans (*prêts à taux zéro*), a sustained period of 'cheap credit' (which came to an end in 2007), and the extension of mortgage repayment from 20 to 25 (and sometimes even 30) years. Between 1965 and 2001, the acquisition of their home represented approximately two-and-a-half years of a household's income. Since 2005, it has been the equivalent of four years' income. In the mid-1980s, households used to spend less than one-fifth of their total income (18.6 per cent) on housing. Two decades later, the share amounted to 25 per cent. Of course, there is no doubt that speculation has been a significant driver: in 1999, 54 per cent of French people's wealth was in property. In 2008, the figure has gone up to two-thirds. While it is true that there is a shortage of homes, it is striking that, on average, one in ten dwellings is vacant in several conurbations – such as Lille, Nice, Bordeaux, Lyon and Paris – where property, often owned by wealthy French or foreign individuals or financial institutions, is left empty for speculative purposes.

Government Responses

Sarkozy's team likes to point out the steps they have taken to address the housing shortage – and figures clearly show that since 2004 the volume of house construction has risen again. Four hundred thousand new homes have been built each year since 2005, compared with 300,000 in the two previous decades; the government's target for 2009 is 500,000, including 120,000 social homes. But these figures mask the fact that the housing crisis is less about the total volume of homes than about who gets them and at what price. To see the problems here, one simply needs to look at the distribution of the three major financial mechanisms, based on a mix of subsidies and fiscal deductions that are granted to local actors for the construction of social homes. France has three categories of social housing that correspond to varying degrees of 'affordability' (from low-quality/low-cost to the higher end of the spectrum), which inevitably leads to a segmentation of resident categories. The share of the most affordable category amounted to a third of the total in the early 1990s, but only 13 per cent in 2005.[13] The great majority of recently built homes are found in the least affordable category, which is only accessible to the most affluent people on the waiting lists. Social housing, in the true sense, is not on the top of the government's list of priorities. There are, in fact, many signs that it is being abandoned to market rules.

The Changing Face of Land-use Planning

In the last decade, one obvious area in which to look for signs of 'rolling back' and increasing housing inequalities, is in the field of urban planning. The implementation of the Law of December 2000 on Solidarity and Urban Renewal is a striking example. The law stipulates that each locality with more than 3,500 inhabitants (1,500 in the Île-de-France region) and belonging to a wider agglomeration of at least 50,000 inhabitants must have 20 per cent of its housing stock classed as 'HLM' by 2020. Its stated objective is to promote mixed communities (what the French call '*mixité sociale*'), fostering a better balance between those localities that have a high proportion of social housing and those that have none or hardly any.[14] At the end of his presidential mandate, and following riots in the *banlieues* (peripheral housing estates[15]), Jacques Chirac, looking to increase his popularity, stated that the law need to be applied more strictly; but, predictably, wealthy white neighbourhoods prefer to pay financial sanctions rather than see social-housing tenants move nearby. Residents are, in fact, very astute at using various forms of political pressure and lobbying on local mayors to help implement 'avoidance tactics'. The most blatant mockery of the law comes from the locality of

Neuilly-sur-Seine, an affluent suburb to the west of Paris, of which Sarkozy himself was long mayor, and which, in 2008, had less than 3.5 per cent social housing. In this locality, vacant land for property development has been sold to large private developers, such as Cogedim or Kaufman & Broad, who build luxury 'yuppie' flats at prices averaging between €8,500 and €10,000 per square metre. (In 2008, price per square metre for Paris flats averaged €6,430, and for the 110 largest cities, €2,500.)

A further significant urban scheme is the National Programme for Urban Renewal (Programme National de Rénovation Urbaine) launched by Minister Jean-Louis Borloo in 2003. This focuses on depressed neighbourhoods, where it is proposed that by 2011 250,000 dwellings will be demolished and another 400,000 renovated. The programme is being implemented via a government agency, which selects the projects in competition and allocates funds to chosen local authorities. However, from the evidence so far, it is clear that demolition programmes have taken precedence over rehabilitation and also over the rehousing of tenants under similar or better conditions. Instead, local politicians have used the programme as a tactic to gentrify their constituencies and disperse unwanted residents, who despite the trumpeting of consultation and participative democracy, have hardly been informed let alone asked how they felt about decisions that directly concern their daily lives.

In 2005, residents from the northern Parisian suburbs of La Coudraie and Genevilliers set up an anti-demolition coalition network that now co-ordinates struggles against evictions and demolitions across France (see Figure 6.1). On the most contested sites, discussions have revolved around the flawed timing and the ways in which the authorities handled the operations. Some tenants were particularly shocked that decisions were taken to demolish buildings that only very recently had been rehabilitated. Others felt pressured and disempowered by the tactics used by the social landlords, who simply stopped the daily maintenance of the site and started to board up the buildings, making the environment very unpleasant to live in.[16]

Figure 6.1   Josseline Bruneau, the last of some hundred protesters, makes a final stand to save her flat in Bourges, January 2008 (*photo: Jean-Claude Dubois*).

The Silent Privatisation: Dismantling a French Symbol

A silent attack on social housing comes through the reform of the finance mechanism at the heart of the French system that is being carried out in the name of 'economic modernisation'.[17] Savings made through so-called 'Livret A' accounts (non-taxable savings accounts) have traditionally been tightly regulated by the central state. These savings accounts are managed by three lending institutions: the Post Office, the Caisse d'Epargne and the Crédit Mutuel. While they have all recently undergone privatisation, the state still holds a major stake in them. However, significant deregulation of the Livret A is under way. From January 2009, this product can also be offered by private banks. The Livret A is a very popular way of saving for lower-income households: 46 million French people own one. In 2008, it offered an attractive interest rate of 4 per cent, which banks were finding difficult to compete with. Why is the Livret A worth mentioning in relation to housing deregulation? The reason is that the €140 billion yielded by the Livret A savings are entirely controlled by the state-owned Banque des Dépôts et Consignations (BDC), which transfers the funds to local authorities and HLM organisations to help them build or renovate social housing; and now, the rules of the game are about to be overhauled. In the future, only 70 per cent of the funds will go to the BDC (thus reducing the sums available to social housing). In the longer term, this percentage could be even further reduced, and the Livret A allowed to disappear altogether.

Resisting: Social Movements and Action Groups

Since 2006, actions of various kinds have sought to fight back against 'roll-back neoliberalism' in housing. The commonality between these actions is their strong local rootedness and their intense media coverage.

A first noteworthy example is the squat of Cachan, which was no doubt the largest squat in recent French social history. The squat, located in the Paris suburb of Cachan, was established in a tower block and, since 2003, housed around 700 people who could find nowhere else to stay. The squatters were of different ethnic backgrounds and nationalities, and the great majority were *sans-papiers* immigrants.[18] In August 2006, the regional authorities announced that the building was unfit for housing and sent hundreds of armed officers to brutally evict the squatters. The socialist mayor of the locality intervened, transferring the squatters to a nearby sports centre, where an important social movement lasted for two months. Demonstrations, hunger strikes and support from celebrities and the wider community meant that Cachan soon became a national issue. It led to an agreement signed on 5 October, with mixed results. A handful of families were rehoused, others were put in hostel accommodation or expelled from France.

Les Enfants de Don Quichotte ('Don Quixote's Children'), a movement initiated by the Legrand brothers, is devoted to increasing the visibility and restoring the dignity of the homeless (the '*Sans Domicile Fixe*', 'SDF' in common parlance). The movement was astutely named after Cervantes' famous fictional hero, personified by the actor Augustin Legrand who leads the movement. He explained:

> We chose Don Quixote for the doomed dimension of the character. But we have added the word 'children' to say that we don't make the same mistakes as mummy and daddy. Don Quixote was fighting for lost causes. We fight against unacceptable issues.[19]

These activists use a simple yet effective tool: hundreds of tents are set up in urban locations at times when the weather makes it very difficult to be out on the streets. This was inspired by the sanitary and humanitarian action of the health organisation Médecins sans Frontières (MSF), which distributed tents to help homeless people shelter from extreme weather conditions. However, MSF's action had not gained significant media impact. Taking up the idea in the winter of 2006–07, Les Enfants de Don Quichotte set up an encampment of 200 tents alongside the Canal Saint-Martin in central Paris, while further encampments mushroomed in other cities such as Lyon, Lille, Toulouse and Rennes (see Figure 6.2). The actions were repeated the following winter, ending with the eviction of the tents by the police. The hours of film footage assembled by the Legrand brothers resulted in a film entitled *Poudre aux yeux* (*Throwing Dust in Our Eyes*), which was screened at the 61st Cannes Film Festival in May 2008. Taking on board the criticism spurred by the initial internet version (downloaded 600,000 times), the final version of the film works hard at highlighting the discrepancies between official government statements and the actual voices of the homeless.

Figure 6.2   Tents along the Canal Saint-Martin, December 2006 (*photo: Sarah Glynn*).

Despite the brutality of the police, the success of the Don Quichotte movement in drawing attention to this issue is undeniable. Meanwhile, symbolic events have been conducted, such as a 'sleepless solidarity night' on the Place de la République on 21 February 2008. This initiative, organised by 28 organisations, brought together 1,800 people with sleeping bags and blankets to protest against the government's housing measures and lack of funding. (€250,000 million have been allotted to implement the new Law on Defensible Rights to Housing – to which we will return at the end of this chapter – though it is estimated that €1.5 billion would in fact be necessary.)[20]

Another important direct action group, known as Jeudi Noir, came to life in October 2006 to 'fight with confetti for a regulation of the property market'. Translated into English, 'Jeudi Noir' means 'Black Thursday' and refers to the release, each Thursday, of the weekly magazine *de Particulier à Particulier* in which private-sector lettings are advertised. In Paris especially, studio flats attract hundreds of applicants – generally students and young professionals who are made to compete with each other in an extremely tight market. Spoiled for choice, landlords have allowed their expectations to go through the roof, fuelling a speculative boom based on the increasing value of land in Paris. Besides the indecent monthly rentals asked for, unscrupulous landlords have been formulating expectations about the 'ideal tenant' background. Like cattle queuing to be slaughtered, prospective tenants are all invited at the same time, bringing their credentials (salary slips, employers' references, parental financial guarantee, four months' deposit, and so on), into a tense competitive atmosphere. Drawing on an increasingly popular and effective repertoire, Jeudi Noir developed festive gatherings. They have turned up unexpectedly to landlords' 'interviews' in fancy dress, bringing bottles of champagne, a DJ to play music for the crowds and cameras to film the landlords' response. More recent actions have revolved around squatting in large empty buildings, and have necessitated a rigorous selection of recruits to find those prepared to engage with the group's spirit and tactics. For the action to be successful, the squat must be highly discreet and go unnoticed for more than five days, following which the proprietors have no other resort but the judiciary route, which can take months to lead to an eviction. However, many of these actions have not managed the initial five days, resulting in violent evictions by the police.[21]

In early 2007, together with DAL and other direct action groups (such as Macaq, another urban youth movement) and members of the International Alliance of Inhabitants (IAI), Jeudi Noir established the 'Ministry of the Housing Crisis' (Ministère de la Crise du Logement). This served as a co-ordinating centre, used to exchange experiences, build solidarity, construct strategies for the requisition of empty dwellings, and provide *sans-papiers* with emergency housing.

The headquarters of the 'Ministry' are in the very heart of Paris, ironically situated in front of the stock exchange at number 24 Rue de la Banque. The indulgence of the Green mayor of this Parisian district has enabled activists to stay put and to make plans to convert the building into social housing. Again, these developments were highly publicised in the media, using a logo akin to that of the real Housing Ministry (see Figure 6.3).

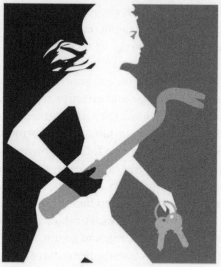

Figure 6.3 Logo of the
Ministère de la Crise du Logement.

At the time of writing, the 'Ministry of the Housing Crisis' was preparing a book to collect activists' experiences and reflect on several years of struggle. There is no doubt that these actions have helped to bring about the new law on the right to housing (see below), and also to raise awareness of the problem of vacant buildings and put pressure on the authorities to apply for the requisition of such buildings held by wealthy private landlords: a process enshrined in the law of 1945, but never previously enacted.

(Since this chapter was first written, a Paris court has demanded that DAL pay a substantial fine of €12,000 for obstructing the pavements of the Rue de la Banque; and tents put up by DAL and Don Quichotte to house 374 families, which formed that obstruction, have been permanently confiscated. However, this has not stopped these organisations from continuing to campaign on behalf of the homeless and against the imposition of new pro-business housing laws.)

The Difficult Path Towards an Effective Right to Housing

The reference to the right to housing is not new in French legislation, as exemplified by the 'Besson Act' of May 1990 and the July 1998 Act on the fight against social exclusion, which made this right explicit. But so far, the right to housing has remained no more than a statement of good intentions. The latest important development is the adoption by Parliament on 5 March 2007 of the Law on Defensible Rights to Housing (Loi sur le Droit au Logement Opposable – or 'Loi Dalo'). The law, which became applicable in January 2008, allows people falling within five defined 'priority groups'[22] who have filed a demand for social housing with the local council (or *préfecture*) to take the housing commission to the *tribunal administratif* (the court in charge of settling disputes between citizens and state administrations) if their claim has been dealt with inappropriately or rejected arbitrarily. The first court case was won by a 26-year-old single mother of two on 20 May 2008, when the judge of the Paris *tribunal administratif* pronounced that she had been unfairly treated by the *préfecture*'s housing commission, which had rejected her claim for housing on the grounds that the family lived in a centre for the social inclusion of the homeless[23] and was thus not 'truly homeless'. Following on from the court's decision, if the family is not housed within six months, the state will be liable to pay financial compensation. This first court victory is no doubt going to spur more cases, which, ironically, could land the state with higher costs than if it had provided housing in the first place; especially since, by 2012, the Loi Dalo will be extended to all those experiencing unusually long waits for their claim to be processed. The introduction of the law is something of a gamble. As in other countries with similar legislation, such as Scotland with its 2003 Homelessness Act, it is becoming increasingly clear that legislation is of little value if it is not combined with adequate housing provision. A major problem lies in the multiplication of governance layers that are disconnected from each other. Housing actors intervene at five different levels (state, region, county (*préfecture*), district (*commune*), and district agglomeration (*intercommunalité*). At state level, Parliament can keep on passing new legislation, but, in effect, land planning and construction permits are delivered at the local level where protectionism can be fierce. Funding remains by and large provided by the central state. Inevitably, then, questions of housing will be more and more fought out in the courts.

Concluding Perspectives

This brief overview of the housing crisis in France reveals a huge paradox: while the right to housing has been firmly established in national legislation, it is far from being implemented effectively on the ground. The list of conditions that would make it possible to resolve the crisis is very plain: rent control, mass construction of affordable housing, ending demolitions without prior replacement housing, and the requisition of empty dwellings are amongst some of the most obvious solutions. But these measures are not amongst those favoured by the French New Right.

Now, in 2009, the housing bubble has burst. There are many signs of the housing market cooling down. House sales are taking longer to complete and the volume in the first quarter of 2008 was already down by almost 9 per cent over the same period in 2007.[24] Some estate agencies (the number of which doubled in the past decade) have been closing down, while several private developers, unable to find clients, have been offering some of their housing projects at discount prices to social landlords, though the impact of these changes is geographically uneven. Despite the gathering crisis, New Right partisans have continued to make proposals that demonstrate disrespect for the social, environmental and architectural fabric of cities. The chairman of the National Property Union (Union nationale de la propriété immobilière), for example, has suggested that the best way to end the housing crisis is to get rid of social housing altogether, on the grounds that private actors are best placed to provide housing with 'social features'.[25] Meanwhile a group of right-wing local councillors from the Union pour un Mouvement Populaire (the party in power), argued that it was time to turn the 'Haussmanian page' and make way for the building of skyscrapers in Paris by getting the best architects in the world to compete for large-scale projects. This, they argued would reflect what a real capitalist metropolis should look like in the global cities competition of the twenty-first century.[26] Well, that's the point.

Further Reading

Damon, J. (2002) *La question SDF: Critique d'une action publique* [The Homeless Issue: A Critique of Public Action] (Paris: Presses Universitaires de France).

Driant, J.-C. (2008) (ed.) *Problèmes de l'habitat et crises du logement* [Poor Living Conditions and Housing Crises], Problèmes politiques et sociaux Series, No. 944 (Paris: La Documentation Française).

Fée, D. and C. Nativel (2008) (eds) *Crises et politiques du logement en France et au Royaume-Uni* [Housing Crises and Policies in France and in the United Kingdom] (Paris: Presses Sorbonne Nouvelle).

Lienemann, M.-J. (2005) *Le scandale du logement* [The Housing Scandal] (Paris: Jean-Claude Gawsewitch Éditeur).

Péchu, C. (2006) *Droit au logement, genèse et sociologie d'une mobilisation* [The Right to Housing: The Genesis and Sociology of a Mobilisation] (Paris: Dalloz).

Vanoni, D. and C. Robert (2007) *Logement et cohésion sociale. Le mal-logement au cœur des inégalités* [Housing and Social Cohesion. Poor Housing at the Heart of Inequalities] (Paris: La Découverte).

For activist websites see end of Chapter 12.

Notes

1. Prasad, M. (2005) 'Why is France so French? Culture, Institutions and Neoliberalism', *American Journal of Sociology* 111(2): 357–407.

2. Blanc, M. (2004) 'The Changing Role of the State in French Housing Policies: A Roll-out without Roll-back?', *European Journal of Housing Policy* 4(3): 283–302; Peck, J. and A. Tickell (2002) 'Neo-liberalising Space', *Antipode* 34(3): 380–404.

3. Musso, P. (2008) *Le Sarkoberlusconisme* (La Tour D'aigues: Éditions de l'Aube).

4. Ipsos survey cited by Bissuel, B. and I. Rey-Lefebvre (2007) 'Une France de propriétaires', *Le Monde*, 4 July 2007. TNS Sofres survey conducted in January 2007 on behalf of private builder Nexity (see <http://www.tns-sofres.com/etudes/pol/141107_logement.pdf>).

5. This statement still holds true in France where credit has traditionally been tightly regulated in an attempt to avoid the kind of subprime loan crisis recently experienced in the US and Spain. In France, mortgage applications are examined very carefully by credit institutions. It is thus not uncommon for mortgage applications to be rejected, particularly if the borrower cannot prove that they hold a permanent employment contract. In addition, mortgages rarely exceed 20 years and the monthly instalment must not exceed one-third of the individual's net salary.

6. See the 'nouveaux militants' website <http://nouveauxmilitants.net/>.

7. Of course, housing regulation and social housing have a longer history. The first law against unfit homes goes back to 1850. In 1894, the Siegfried law led to the habitations à bon marché (affordable homes), making it possible for local authorities to support the social housing sector. The HBM were replaced by the HLM in 1949.

8. In six years, between 2000 and 2006, the percentage of social housing residents with less than three years of tenure decreased from 33 to 28 per cent: Fondation Abbé Pierre (2008), *L'État du mal-logement en France* [The State of Poor Housing in France] (13th annual report), Paris, p. 17 <http://www.fondation-abbe-pierre.fr/rml.html>.

9. *Logement – Un projet de loi présenté au début de l'été: Mme Boutin veut soumettre les HLM à des indicateurs de performance* [Housing – Green Paper Presented at the Beginning of the Summer: Mme Boutin Wants HLMs to be Subjected to Performance Criteria], *Le Monde*, 27 May 2008.

10. Fondation Abbé Pierre, *L'État du mal-logement en France*.

11. Lévy-Vroelant, C. (2005) 'Retour sur une catastrophe annoncée: le logement précaire en Île-de-France' [Looking Back onto a Predictable Catastrophe: Precarious Housing in the Île-de-France], *Mouvements* 42: 84–9.

12. Institut National de la Statistique et des Études Économiques, or INSEE.

13. Subra, P. (2006) 'Heurts et malheurs d'une loi anti-ségrégation: les enjeux géopolitiques de la loi Solidarité et Renouvellement Urbain' [Sufferings and Misfortunes of an Anti-segregation Law: The Geopolitics of the Law on Solidarity and Urban Renewal], *Hérodote* 122: 138–70.

14. Ibid.

15. Although the literal translation of *banlieue* is 'suburb', the term tends to be associated with the deprived and isolated mass-housing schemes.

16. Deboulet, A. (2006) 'Le résident vulnérable. Questions autour de la démolition' [The Vulnerable Resident: Questions Surrounding Demolition], *Mouvements* 47–8: 174–81.

17. The Law on the Modernisation of the Economy (Loi sur la modernisation de l'économie) was adopted by Parliament in June 2008. See Mauduit, L. (2008) 'Modernisation de l'économie: le texte du projet de loi', *Mediapart*, 31 March; Mathieu, M. (2008) 'Banalisation du Livret A: les députés PS dénoncent un péril sur le logement social', 12 June <http://www.mediapart.fr>.

18. '*Sans-papiers*' literally means 'paperless', the expression referring to people who are considered illegal immigrants because they do not hold a valid residence permit. They may be clandestine refugees or their initial permit may have expired. As a result, they cannot access fundamental social rights such as the right to work.

19. 'Augustin Legrand dans le rôle de sa vie' ('Augustin Legrand in the Role of a Lifetime'), *Le Figaro*, 15 October 2007.

20. Highlights can be seen on video: <http://www.dailymotion.com/video/x4guq7_republique-nuit-solidaire-du-logeme_news>.

21. See film footage of Jeudi Noir's action on <http://www.jeudi-noir.org>.

22. Priority groups are people: (1) who are homeless, (2) who live in housing unfit for accommodation, (3) who are about to be evicted following a court's decision, (4) who have been housed in social centres for the homeless for over six months, (5) who are disabled or looking after a disabled person or a child and residing in unfit accommodation or accommodation of a floor area below 16 square metres. It is estimated that the priority groups amount to a total of 600,000 households, which must be compared to the 60,000 units being provided by county councils each year: a ratio of 1 to 10 ... .

23. These centres (managed by local authorities) provide emergency accommodation as well as medical and social care to single people and families (often headed by single mothers) in severe distress. Practices vary from one centre to another, depending on housing capacity and resources (some only provide day care). The initial

period of accommodation is six months and this can be renewed upon the condition that the beneficiary follows an education and training plan.

24. Rey-Lefebvre, I. and M. Picouët (2008) 'Le marché de l'immobilier se retourne dans le neuf et l'ancien', *Le Monde*, 1 July.

25. Fondation Abbé Pierre, *L'État du mal-logement en France*, p. 51.

26. Alphand, D. et al. (2008) 'Vive les gratte-ciel à Paris', *Le Monde*, 3 July.

7

CIRCUMVENTING CIRCUMSCRIBED NEOLIBERALISM: THE 'SYSTEM SWITCH' IN SWEDISH HOUSING

Eric Clark and Karin Johnson

> Sweden is an example of what might be called 'circumscribed neoliberalization', and its generally superior social condition reflects that fact.
>
> David Harvey, 2005[1]

During the middle decades of the twentieth century, the social democratic welfare state in Sweden succeeded in institutionalising the redistribution of prosperity, while maintaining a market economy, to a greater extent than perhaps any other country. Often considered the most generous social welfare system in the world, the 'Swedish model' ensures general access to basic human needs such as health care, education and housing. Or rather, it used to. Since the early 1990s, the housing sector has been radically reformed in accordance with neoliberal ideology, with far-reaching consequences for the increasingly polarised poor and rich. This chapter provides a brief historical background to Swedish housing before outlining how the neoliberalisation of the housing sector in Sweden has radically changed housing conditions, circumventing hindrances to the otherwise relatively circumscribed neoliberalism of the Swedish welfare state.

Housing in Sweden: A Brief Historical Overview

Historically, Sweden has been at one extreme of the housing policy spectrum, emphasising interest-rate subsidies to investment, neutrality between tenures, generous overall benefits to housing both in the form of general subsidy and income-related benefits, and low risks to financiers, investors and households alike.

Bengt Turner and Christine Whitehead, 2002[2]

The complex social system of housing provision in Sweden, sometimes referred to as a socialist market system, was politically constructed in the 1930s and 1940s and came to be a pillar of the Swedish social democratic welfare state. Continuously modified to overcome challenges and problems – some of which were generated by its own successes and failures – and with considerable variation between municipalities across Sweden, the system was part and parcel of Social Democratic popularity and dominance in Swedish politics since the 1930s, catering as it did to the basic needs of the broad working and middle classes. In many international comparative analyses, Sweden's post-war housing policies and programmes have been deemed 'phenomenally successful both qualitatively and quantitatively'.[3] The historical and political contexts and the genesis of the system have been described and analysed in considerable detail in the voluminous literature on housing in Sweden. Here, only the very broad strokes can be outlined.

Housing conditions among the working population in Sweden during the first decades of the twentieth century were miserable – indeed, among the worst in Europe. An early effort at regulation focused on land policy to curtail speculation, with legislation in 1907 providing for municipal right of site leasehold, encouraging municipal ownership of housing land and control over land development.[4] The First World War brought housing construction to a standstill. Following the war, the most severe housing problems were addressed with rapidly built, poor-quality and short-lived housing for the most deprived, constructed under municipal or state programmes; rent control was instated to combat post-war inflation, and a temporary system of subsidies and credits was established that ran from 1917 to 1922.

The labour movement, consolidating in strong unions, took an active interest in housing issues. The National Organisation of

Housing Tenants (Hyresgästernas Riksförbund) was established in 1923, as was the Tenants' Savings Bank and Building Society (Hyresgästernas Sparkasse och Byggnadsförening – HSB). Both came to be central agents in the construction of Swedish housing policies.

Brief periods of Social Democratic-led coalition governments in the 1920s were followed by a 44-year-long era of Social Democratic governments, from 1932 to 1976. Gunnar and Alva Myrdal's book *Kris i befolkningsfrågan* (*Crisis in the Population Question*), published in 1934, drew attention to the impact of poor housing conditions on fertility and family formation. Another highly influential work was Lubbe (Ludvig) Nordström's popular series of reports on Swedish national public radio in the autumn of 1938, *Lort-Sverige* (*Dirt-Sweden*), which documented the very low standards of living and housing in the Swedish countryside.[5] The housing question rose to prominence on the political scene.

A cornerstone of 'the Swedish model' established at this time was the 'historical compromise' between the Swedish Trade Union Confederation (LO) and the Confederation of Swedish Enterprise (SAF), reached in the Saltsjöbad agreement in 1938. Sweden was characterised by strong centralised labour unions and well-organised private enterprise dominated by a few large owners of capital. Put simply, the agreement involved effective co-operation between labour, capital and the state. Capital accepted LO as its legitimate counterpart in central wage negotiations and labour's influence through the state on far-reaching policies for distribution of welfare. In return, they gained labour peace and state investments in housing and infrastructure that facilitated labour mobility to wherever capital found it profitable to invest. Labour accepted the control of capital over work organisation and rationalisation – with the argument that increased competitiveness could secure high employment – in return for central wage negotiations. The agreement was a watershed event, as decades of conflicts and strikes were succeeded by decades of relative peace between labour and capital.

The Social Democratic government authorised a Commission on Housing and Redevelopment (Bostadssociala utredningen) in 1934 to analyse housing issues and propose legislation and institutional reform, with the aim of establishing long-term solutions to the organisation of housing provision. Key members of the commission were Alf Johansson and Gunnar Myrdal, both professors of economics. Their work was strongly supported by Minister of Finance Ernst Wigforss, who anticipated Keynes in regarding housing construction as vital to stabilising full employment and economic growth. During the 14 years of its work, the commission published a series of reports upon which legislation and policy formation came to be based.

Early legislation provided improvement grants and loans to farmers, home loans to rural workers, and financial support to municipalities to build housing for 'child-rich' families in towns. Though more than marginally successful in their limited aims, these measures were directed primarily towards the weakest households, and their results came to be stigmatised. Work in the Commission on Housing and Redevelopment turned towards greater ambitions: state housing policy was to constitute a framework for national and local institutions engaged in provision of high-quality housing for the general population, and not be limited to provision of low standard housing for those most in need. Low-income households were to be able to afford a decent standard of housing in the common housing stock, rather than be confined to a special category of housing. Public housing (*allmännyttiga bostäder*) was to be a common ground, not a marginal element (see Figure 7.1).

The commission's final report, published in 1945, laid the foundation for legislation and a system of housing finance that remained largely in place until 1991.[6] Rather than dismantle wartime regulatory legislation and institutions guiding housing provision, Sweden continued to develop legislative programmes, planning apparatus and financial controls in the housing sector. These included laws on housing provision, housing allowance, housing loans, regulation of rents and powerful land policy instruments. After a century of housing shortage, the market was deemed incapable of providing adequate stimulus to housing production. Stimulus was to come from broad

Figure 7.1   Youth theatre and housing in the
Stockholm suburb of Tensta (*photo: Karin Johnson*).

programmes of subsidies guided by the social aims of improved housing quality and of equality between forms of tenure, and the economic aims of full employment and of adequate infrastructure in the sphere of labour reproduction.

The objectives set out in the commission's final report can be summarised: eliminate the housing shortage through a 15-year programme, after which housing production would stabilise; raise space and equipment standards; control rent levels so that the average wage-earner can afford spacious and modern family housing (that is, rent for a modern two-room and kitchen flat should not exceed 20 per cent of the average wage); establish programmes for the public financing of housing production; encourage the housing activities of local authorities, and discourage speculative building through favourable loans to individuals, housing associations and local authorities. While the means came to be continuously adjusted and reformed to match changing contexts, the goals remained the same: the provision of good-quality housing at a cost that everyone could afford.

Housing production remained at high levels, by international comparison, over the following three decades, both in terms of quantity and standard. Massive urbanisation in the 1960s spurred the so-called '1 Million Programme': the construction of over 1 million dwellings, in a country with a population of 8 million, over the ten-year period from 1965 to 1974. In 1945, over 30 per cent of the population lived in crowded housing conditions according to 'Norm 1' – that is, more than two persons per room, not including the kitchen. By 1960, this figure had fallen to 13 per cent. In 1965, a new 'Norm 2' for overcrowding was established: more than two persons per room, not including the kitchen and living room. Overcrowding according to this norm fell from 33 per cent in 1965 to 4 per cent in 1985.

Figure 7.2 Tensta, January 2006: Million Programme housing included homes for low-cost ownership, such as these, and similar flats for rent – all built to keep out the cold of the Swedish winter (*photo: Hugh Rodwell*).

Since the introduction of 'Norm 3' in the mid-1980s – more than one person per room, not including the kitchen and living room (and single-occupancy households in one room and kitchen or less), overcrowding according to this new norm has remained constant at about 15 per cent. However, an increase in population means that the number of crowded households has increased, and is presently estimated to include over 1 million adults and 500,000 children.[7]

This is just one indication (among many) that the so-called 'system switch' in Swedish housing policy – carried out by the Conservative government in 1991 to 1994 and subsequently maintained by Social Democratic governments – has reversed the long-standing trends toward equality in housing conditions and toward improved housing conditions for the lower echelons of Swedish society. From Chicago and Washington via Santiago, New York and London,[8] the concerted neoliberal restoration of class power had reached Sweden.

The Neoliberal 'System Switch' in Housing Policy

Probably nowhere in the Western world was the power of capital more democratically threatened in the 1970s than in Sweden.

David Harvey, 2005[9]

Harvey refers here to the Rehn-Meidner plan for wage-earner funds proposed by LO, which was based on a 20 per cent tax on corporate profits that would be controlled by the trade unions for reinvestment in the corporations. The plan entailed a gradual shift in ownership from capital to labour. This threat to Sweden's highly concentrated capital-owning class was not taken lightly. The political polarisation that ensued in the decade-long debate over the wage-earner funds upset the 'historical compromise'. Labour had breached the compromise and the SAF reacted by mobilising its membership and resources for a counter-attack on the unions and on what it saw as labour's extended arm, the welfare state. A conservative think-tank, Timbro, initiated a series of reports that mimicked governmental White Papers (Timbro called them 'Citizens' Public Reports' instead of the State's Public Reports). These propagated the signature neoliberal view that the welfare state is the root of economic problems and that the state stands in conflict with individual freedom – notwithstanding that the Social Democratic governments had been democratically elected with mandates to pursue certain goals, and that their successes towards achieving these goals considerably enhanced degrees of freedom for broad swaths of the population. The third report in Timbro's series focused on a critique of the social housing system and on proposals for radical reform: *A Market for Housing for All*.[10] Another private enterprise think-tank, SNS (Centre for Business and Policy Studies), published in the same year (1990) a book called *Power Over the Home*, in which three economists drew on public-choice theory and inspiration from neoliberal 'solutions' in Britain and the US.[11] Both publications called for nothing less than a radical termination of existing housing policies, laying out the road-map for the changes implemented by the new Conservative government.

One of the first things the Conservative government did after coming to power in 1991 – the first government in Sweden led by a Conservative prime minister (Carl Bildt) since 1930[12] – was to close the Department of Housing. Under the new regime, housing was not to be distinguished from any other commodity market.[13] Various functions of the Department of Housing were either discontinued or moved to other departments dealing with finance, environmental issues, integration, and so on. Former housing legislation was nullified, including the housing provision law (*bostadsförsörjningslagen*), the housing assignment law (*bostadsanvisningslagen*), and the land condition law (*markvillkoret*, which required municipal land ownership or transfer for loan subsidies). Subsidies were discontinued or radically reduced. Even subsidies given directly to households most in need – that is, housing allowances according to income and family size – were reduced.[14] The only part of established policy that survived the 'system switch' of Bildt's government was the use-value system of rent regulation.[15]

Remarkably little was done to reconstruct housing legislation and policy administration when the Social Democrats regained power in 1994. Rather, under the leadership of Ingvar Carlsson (1994–96) and Göran Persson (1996–2006), the system switch was tacitly endorsed. This chimed poorly with the heavy criticism it had aroused among Social Democrats while they were in opposition, especially criticism against the symbolically momentous closure of the Department of Housing. Sweden became a member of the European Union in 1995, and agendas across the board were dominated by adaptation to the new supra-national order. The Social Democrats inherited – without noticeable resistance – the neoliberal programme according to which 'deficit reduction, inflation control and balanced budgets rather than full employment and an equitable distribution of income became cornerstones of macroeconomic policy'.[16] Consequently, the housing sector went from being a net burden to state finances of roughly 30 billion Swedish kronor (SEK) in the late 1980s, to providing a net income of roughly SEK 31 billion ten years later.[17]

The Carlsson government did establish a Housing Policy Commission (Bostadspolitiska utredningen, 1995–96), giving it the task of specifying policy goals. The commission's final report, *Housing Policy 2000 – From Production Policy to Dwelling Policy*,[18] suggested elements of a return to traditional Swedish housing policy, but did little to change the actual direction of housing policy as these elements were not included in subsequent government bills. Generating many goals but few means of achieving them, the report was criticised by the National Board of Housing, Building and Planning for 'lowering the level of ambition in housing policy' and for not providing guidance from word to action.[19] Neoliberalism now came in shades of Social Democracy, Liberal and Conservative, providing reason for the expression 'we are all neoliberal now'.

Campaigning as the 'new labour party' against a lame Social Democratic party, Fredrik Reinfeldt's Conservatives won the election in late 2006, and, in coalition with centre-right parties, swiftly pursued privatisation schemes and renewed the roll-back of long-established welfare systems. In housing, this roll-back has taken a variety of forms. Already on 1 January 2007, the Department of Environment and Built Environment was reduced to the Department of Environment, and housing issues were moved to the Department of Finance. At the same time, restrictions on municipal sales of public rental housing were removed.[20] In July 2007, restrictions on tenure transformation from public rental to co-operative ownership (*bostadsrätt*) were lifted.[21]

In May 2007, the government intervened in the work of a commission on public housing, in progress since 2005, and rewrote its directives:

> According to the original directive, public housing companies should follow the long-term principle of self-cost [non-profit]. This puts limits on the commission's possibilities to present recommendations compatible with EU law. This restriction is to be removed.[22]

The background to this revision is a case brought to the EU by the Swedish Property Federation, which argued that state subsidies to non-profit municipal housing companies constitute a breach of the EU law against state support that impacts on conditions of competition. The EU Commission's conclusion (in July 2005) was that this general prohibition does not apply to subsidies to social services of general societal interest, and consequently subsidies to 'social housing providing housing for disadvantaged citizens or socially less advantaged groups, which due to solvability constraints are unable to obtain housing at market conditions' were not in conflict with EU law.[23] When the Swedish commission's report – *EU, Public Housing and Rents* – came out in April 2008, it juxtaposed two models: one in which municipal housing companies were to operate according to strict business criteria for profit, and another in which municipal housing companies were to continue in accordance with principles and practices of non-profit firms. About the former, the report stated: 'There is no doubt that this model is compatible with EU law.' About the latter, the report stated: 'It is uncertain – though not precluded – that this model would be accepted by an EU judicial trial.'[24] Bluff or not, adaptation to EU law is invoked to reach domestic reform. The issue remains contested, as critics claim that Sweden's non-profit public housing is not in conflict with EU law.[25] The recent EU reform treaty and subsequent EU court decisions, they claim, provide greater freedom for member states to formulate national policy concerning social services of general societal interest.

In the budget proposition for 2008, the Reinfeldt government rewrote the goal for housing policy in a time-warp of pre-welfare-state ambition: 'The goal for housing issues is a long-term well-functioning housing market where consumers' demands meet a supply of housing which corresponds to their needs.'[26] Long-standing formulations including ambitious goals of equality, social responsibility, high standards, reasonable cost and good living conditions were erased.

In March 2008, despite the lessons of the US subprime crisis, a programme to stimulate owner-occupation was introduced, involving credit guarantees to first-time buyers who would not otherwise be eligible for loans.[27] These credit guarantees have been met with severe criticism from the National Bank of Sweden, the Swedish Consumer Agency and the National Board of Health and Welfare, who argue that they increase the risk of disadvantaged groups ending up in a debt trap and eventually losing their homes.

Property taxation was also reformed in 2008. Previously a progressive national tax, property tax is now a regressive municipal tax with a flat rate of SEK 6,000[28] per year for all properties with a taxation value above SEK 800,000,[29] or 0.75 per cent of assessed taxation value if below SEK 800,000[30] (roughly half of all owner-occupied homes have assessed taxation values over SEK 800,000).[31]

The old idea of filtering and trickle-down, a blast from the past, has been dusted off and seriously forwarded as a strategy of housing provision for weak households. Filtering and chains of moves are frequently invoked to legitimate the increasing shares of housing production catering to the upper segment of the market. Through residential mobility, as the old story goes, quality housing trickles down to lower segments: 'chains of moves arise – which benefit economically weak groups such as younger people'.[32] Never mind that over 60 years of research into residential mobility consistently shows that policies based on filtering have never more than very marginally improved housing for low-income households.[33]

The term 'system switch' is evidently no exaggeration. What, then, have the consequences been?

Consequences of Neoliberal Housing Reforms

A considerable number of households must reduce their consumption of housing in order to make ends meet.

Bengt Turner, 2001[34]

Since the 1980s, Swedish society has experienced marked social and economic polarisation.[35] The geographical concentration of low-income and high-income groups is even more striking than the overall measure of polarisation.[36] It is impossible to isolate, precisely, the impact of housing policies on these and other manifestations of neoliberal reforms, from the impact of changes in other areas of the welfare state – and from broader forces such as the economic crisis of the early 1990s. But the nature and direction of their impact can be ascertained analytically and estimated empirically. However complex the specific historical geographical context – for example, Swedish housing in recent decades – the types of relations, tensions, mechanisms and issues involved are not entirely new phenomena.

The following (by no means exhaustive) list of highly interrelated consequences captures the main findings of housing researchers regarding the impact of the 'system switch' in Swedish housing policy since 1991:

- Decline in new production and rise in vacancies
- Municipalities closing housing agencies and abandoning social housing commitments
- Public housing companies operating increasingly on market terms: increased exclusion of the very poor
- Segregation: super-gentrification and slum formation

- Segmentation: differential effects on different forms of tenure
- Privatisation and out-sourcing of planning.

Fall in Production, Rise in Vacancies

The rapid increase in relative housing costs, directly caused by the subsidy-cutting reforms of the early 1990s, resulted in reduced supply (in terms of new production) and reduced demand (manifested in increased vacancies). Production of new dwellings collapsed from around 70,000 a year in 1990 to just over 10,000 in 1997, lower than any time since the Second World War.[37] The minor reintroductions of subsidies during the Social Democratic governments, combined with recovery from the economic crisis, brought production up again to nearly 40,000 in 2006, but with the new round of reforms under Reinfeldt, production has again declined sharply.[38] During the same period (1990–97), vacancies in housing owned by municipal housing companies rose from a few thousand to 45,000, to which can be added over 10,000 vacancies in private rental housing and housing co-operatives.[39] Sweden's population rose by over 250,000 during this period, so the vacancies do not reflect a decline in need, but rather a decline in effective demand and (as we have seen) increasing overcrowding, with considerable regional variation. The impact of reduced subsidies on production and demand is magnified as risks increase for firms, credit institutions and households to invest in housing.

Municipal Abandonment of Social Housing Responsibilities, Public Housing for Profit and Increased Exclusion of the Very Poor

In the early 1990s, with the abrogation of broad swaths of the legal structure whereby the central state determined the rules for the municipalities' engagement with the planning and provision of housing, many municipalities swiftly closed their local housing agencies and authorities. Municipal housing queues became history.

Many years ago, Gunnar Myrdal noted that solidarity commonly assumes more committed and durable expressions when channelled through higher democratic governmental bodies than through more local ones. Once the central state removed financial support and concise directives on the forms of commitment expected of municipalities, local organisational structures collapsed like a house of cards. With the municipalities abandoning their role in housing provision, the responsibility for helping disadvantaged households who cannot get into the housing market is turned over to the social welfare offices. As central government reduced subsidies to public housing and increased taxation on all rental property, municipal and public housing companies came under severe pressure to operate in accordance with strict principles of profit, or suffer harsh economic consequences. In an increasing number of municipalities, as Ingrid Sahlin notes, 'public housing is no longer open to all, but only for those with sound economy and good references'.[40] The poor who are unable to gain access to the housing market are referred to the municipal office of social welfare, which provides temporary shelter without rights of tenancy until the household can find a dwelling or move elsewhere.

Increased Segregation, Super-gentrification and Slum Formation

A number of studies have shown marked increases in ethnic segregation in Swedish cities over the last couple of decades.[41] Segregation by income in Sweden's three largest cities – Stockholm, Gothenburg and Malmö – increased dramatically between 1986 and 2001. A clear image of the social geography of polarisation is displayed in maps of super-gentrification – where residents of rich areas are replaced by the super-rich – and of low-income filtering (a euphemism for slum formation) – where the poor are replaced by the super-poor. Seven per cent of high-income areas in these cities experienced super-gentrification between 1986 and 1991, 14 per cent between 1991 and 1996, and 22 per cent between

1996 and 2001. Corresponding figures for filtering in low-income areas were 12 per cent, 33 per cent and 16 per cent.[42]

Segmentation: The Move Away from Tenure Neutrality

Between 1986 and 2005, rents increased by 122 per cent, costs of living in owner-occupancy increased by 41 per cent, while general inflation was 49 per cent.[43] In a detailed empirical analysis of the composition of the increase in rents between 1989 and 1997, Bengt Turner showed that 90 per cent of the increase was a direct consequence of reduced subsidies and increased taxation on rental properties. Shares of disposable income spent on housing increased more among low-income earners and households in rental housing than among the better-off in other tenure forms, even as the latter displayed extravagance in the mushrooming geography of super-gentrification. Single adults, with or without children, in rental housing paid nearly 40 per cent of their income on rent in 1997.[44] However, owner-occupation was favoured, as interest payments on home loans remained subsidised. The Housing Policy Commission observed in 1996 that 'in practice, the state subsidises housing for economically strong households', that is, in the owner-occupied and co-operative tenures.[45] These differences in impact on different forms of tenure have led to segmentation: increased differences in welfare between residents of rental housing and residents of owner-occupied housing. Between 1986 and 2003, the welfare gap between tenures increased in terms of income, housing standard, employment and material resources.[46]

Privatisation of Planning

Under near-total silence from political parties, national and local authorities, media, researchers and the public, power over planning has shifted towards private corporations. Sweden has a long history of public-private partnerships, since long before those three Ps became a planning concept. But whereas earlier, 'planners were firmly in charge of the planning process', now 'contemporary neo-liberal planners are confined to negotiating urban design schemes originating from developers' officers'.[47] Increasingly, urban development projects originate from private planning consultancies and large development firms. Largely under-researched, this dimension of neoliberal urbanism essentially involves handing over urban planning to private capital interests.

Why Housing? Why so Little Resistance?

Why then, did the far-reaching 'system switch' in Swedish housing and all its consequences meet with so little public resistance? Anders Lindbom argues that this is largely due to relative lack of transparency in a very complex system of regulation into which few have much insight, combined with a time-lag between reform and the impact of that reform.[48] This translates into an easily disguised chain of responsibility (for example, rents, it is easily claimed, are set on the 'market', even if increases are due to political decisions), leaving greater political room for manoeuvre in the housing sector than in other areas of welfare politics.

Programmes relatively susceptible to non-transparent reforms, he argues, have suffered greater cutbacks than more transparent programmes. Comparing the effects on households of housing policy cutbacks with those of cutbacks in other policy areas, Lindbom observes that:

> The lowered ... unemployment benefit cost an unemployed industrial worker about 880 crowns per month after taxes. The lowered ... sickness benefit cost a long-term sick industrial worker 1,062 crowns after taxes. By comparison, the rent of an average two-room apartment rose 1,613 crowns per month between 1990 and 1998 ... Thus, the rising rents were *more* important, even for the unemployed or long-term sick industrial worker, than the lowered replacement rates.[49]

This clearly suggests that the relative weight of neoliberal housing reform – *vis-à-vis* other cutbacks – on the healthy and employed work-force is even greater.

Conclusion

Sweden has gradually become one of the most liberal market-governed housing markets in the Western world. State engagement is substantially less in Sweden than in the homelands of market liberalism, Great Britain and the United States.

Hans Lind and Stellan Lundström, 2007[50]

While Sweden remains one of the most equal societies in the EU and in the world, the politics of neoliberalism have rapidly transformed housing policies and the provision of housing in directions conducive to increasing inequality. Over the last twenty years, Sweden has experienced the 'consolidation of a powerful national political shift favouring the interests of the wealthiest households',[51] a 'restoration of class power'.[52] This has generated social and economic polarisation, as evidenced in the geographic concentration and growth of areas of super-gentrification at one end of social geographic space, and of slum formation at the other. This shift has driven a wedge into the long-standing tradition of general housing policies, creating a divide between the financial aspects and the social aspects of housing politics. Bengt Turner complained over the lack of connections between these two dimensions in any of the government bills and commission reports of the 1990s. He argued, very perceptively, that 'When the ties connecting these aspects are severed, the political process of relating economic change on housing markets with political assessment of its social consequences is also discontinued.'[53] This political process needs to be restarted – this wedge needs to be replaced by a bridge.

Though Sweden has been relatively resilient to the most radical transformations of welfare brought on by the tide of neoliberalism – earning Harvey's description as 'circumscribed neoliberalism' – the 'new politics of welfare' has clearly held sway in Sweden. With the ongoing wave of reform under Reinfeldt's 'new workers' party', the circumscription of neoliberalism is being effectively circumvented, especially in housing, with tangible consequences for many in Sweden at both ends of an increasingly polarised society.

While Lind and Lundström's characterisation of Sweden as one of the most liberal market-governed housing markets in the western world may be accurate, it is important to remember that there is nothing natural about governance by the market. Guy Baeten reminds us that 'the neo-liberalisation of the Nordic urban world ... is not so much the result of "market forces" but rather of strictly planned and government-induced interventions in the urban social, economic and political fabric'.[54] There are struggles going on over the unfolding of the geography of housing. If we do not participate in these struggles, we lose them. We need to engage in creating new geographies, which are, after all, 'struggles for power over the entry of entities and events into space and time'.[55]

Further Reading

Headey, Bruce (1978) *Housing Policy in the Developed Economy: The United Kingdom, Sweden and the United States* (London: Croom Helm).

Lindbom, Anders (2001) 'Dismantling Swedish Housing Policy', *Governance: An International Journal of Policy and Administration* 14: 503–26.

Lindbom, Anders (2007) 'Obfuscating Retrenchment: Swedish Welfare Policy in the 1990s', *Journal of Public Policy* 27: 129–50.

Turner, Bengt (1997) 'Municipal Housing Companies in Sweden: On or Off the Market?', *Housing Studies* 12: 477–88.

Turner, Bengt and Christine M.E. Whitehead (2002) 'Reducing Housing Subsidy: Swedish Housing Policy in an International Context', *Urban Studies* 39: 201–17.

Notes

1. Harvey, David (2005) *A Brief History of Neoliberalism* (Oxford: Oxford University Press), p. 115.
2. Turner, Bengt and Christine M.E. Whitehead (2002) 'Reducing Housing Subsidy: Swedish Housing Policy in an International Context', *Urban Studies* 39: 204.
3. Headey, Bruce (1978) *Housing Policy in the Developed Economy: The United Kingdom, Sweden and the United States* (London: Croom Helm), p. 44. Cf. Dickens, Peter, Simon Duncan, Mark Goodwin and Fred Gray (1985) *Housing, States and Localities* (London: Methuen); Heclo, Hugh and Henrik Madsen (1987) *Policy*

and Politics in Sweden: Principled Pragmatism (Philadelphia, PA: Temple University Press).

4. Poorly conceived, municipal site leasehold did not have any significant impact on housing until after it was reformed in 1954. See Clark, Eric, and Lennart Runesson (1996) 'Municipal Site Leasehold in Sweden: A Land Policy Instrument in Decay', *European Planning Studies* 4: 203–216.

5. Myrdal, Gunnar and Alva Myrdal (1934) *Kris i befolkningsfrågan* [Crisis in the Population Question] (Stockholm: Bonniers). Nordström's radio report was also published in book form as Nordström, Ludvig (1938) *Lort-Sverige* [Dirt-Sweden] (Stockholm: Kooperativa förbundet).

6. 'Statens Offentliga Utredningar 1945: 63 Allmänna riktlinjer för framtida bostadspolitiken. Förslag till låne- och bidragsformer. Slutbetänkande av Bostadssociala utredningen, del 1 [General Guidelines for Future Housing Policy. Recommendations for Forms of Loans and Subsidies. Final Report of the Commission on Housing and Redevelopment, Part 1].

7. 'Var finns rum för våra barn? – en rapport om trångboddhet i Sverige' [Where is there Room for Our Children? – A Report on Crowded Housing Conditions in Sweden], *Boverket*, September 2006.

8. Harvey, *A Brief History of Neoliberalism.* ·

9. Ibid., p. 112.

10. Andersson, Knut et al. (1990) *En marknad för bostäder åt alla: ett förslag till ny bostadspolitik* [A Market for Housing for All: A Proposal for New Housing Policies] Medborgarnas Offentliga Utredningar, 1990(3) (Stockholm: Timbro).

11. Meyerson, Per-Martin, Ingemar Ståhl and Kurt Wickman (1990) *Makten över bostaden* [Power Over the Home] (Stockholm: SNS).

12. There had been right coalition governments between 1976 and 1982 led by Centre and Liberal prime ministers.

13. 'We don't have a truck department for truck issues, or a truck minister. Why would we need one for housing?', Minister of Finance Mats Odell, interviewed in *Planera Bygga Bo*, 2007(1), National Board of Housing, Building and Planning (our translation).

14. Bengtsson, Bo (1995) *Bostaden – välfärdsstatens marknadsvara* [Housing – The Welfare State's Market Commodity] (Uppsala: Almqvist and Wiksell); Bengtsson, Bo, and Eva Sandstedt (eds) (1999) *Systemskifte i bostadspolitiken? Boinstitutets årsbok 1999* [System Switch in Housing Policy? Housing Institute Yearbook 1999] (Stockholm: Boinstitutet); Persson, Thomas (2001) 'Sektorn som försvann! Historien om bostadsdepartementets uppgång och fall' [The Sector that Disappeared! The History of the Rise and Fall of the Department of Housing], in Anders Lindbom (ed.) *Den nya bostadspolitiken* [The New Housing Policy] (Umeå: Borea).

15. The main rule of the Swedish use-value system of rent regulation is that 'the reasonableness of the rent in the private sector should be judged by a comparison with rents in similar apartments owned by municipal housing companies. These rents are in turn set after negotiations between the company and the local tenants union. The starting point is often the companies' total costs and the negotiation primarily concerns how these total costs should be distributed between different apartments. No distinction is made between new tenancies and rent reviews for current tenants. In most municipalities the result has been rents that are considerably below market rents in older apartments in attractive areas': Lind, Hans (2001) 'Rent regulation: A Conceptual and Comparative Analysis', *European Journal of Housing Policy* 1: 50.

16. Blyth, Mark (2002) *Great Transformations: Economic Ideas and Institutional Change in the Twentieth Century* (Cambridge: Cambridge University Press), quoted in Harvey, *A Brief History of Neoliberalism*, pp. 114–15.

17. Statens Offentliga Utredningar (1999) 'På de boendes villkor – allmännyttan på 2000-talet' [On the Residents' Conditions – Public Housing in the 21st Century], pp. 33–4.

18. Statens Offentliga Utredningar (1996) 'Bostadspolitik 2000 – från produktions- till boendepolitik' [Housing Policies 2000 – From Production Policy to Dwelling Policy] (1996: 156).

19. Boverket (2005) *Många mål – få medel. Boverkets utredning av statliga stöd till bostadsbyggandet 1993–2004* [National Board of Housing, Building and Planning (2005) Many Goals – Few Means. Report on State Support to Housing Construction 1993–2004].

20. <http://www.regeringen.se/content/1/c6/07/60/76/3a6dcc47.pdf>.

21. '*Bostadsrätt*' is a form of co-operative ownership: a form of tenure between rental and owner-occupied. Prior to 1967, transactions were regulated such that the dwellings, almost always apartments, could not be sold on the market. Legislation since 1967 has meant that *bostadsrätt* more and more resembles a form of owner-occupied tenure for apartments.

22. Dir. 2007:73 Tilläggsdirektiv till Utredningen om allmännyttans villkor (M 2005:04) 31 May 2007 <http://www.regeringen.se/content/1/c6/08/38/80/76019fa3.pdf> (our translation).

23. Quoted in Sahlin, Ingrid (2008) '"Social housing" som bostadspolitiskt spoke' ['Social Housing' as Housing Policy Ghost] *Alba.nu* 6 December <http://www.alba.nu/artikel/artikel.php?id=735>.

24. Statens Offentliga Utredningar (2008) 'EU, allmännyttan och hyrorna' [EU, Public Housing and Rents] (2008: 38) (our translation).

25. Moberg, Carina, Egon Frid and Jan Lindholm (2008) 'Alliansen säljer ut allmännyttan och låter EU diktera bostadspolitiken' [The Alliance Sells Off Public Housing and Allows EU to Dictate Housing

Policy), *Aftonbladet* 18 April. The authors are members of the Swedish Riksdag (Parliament) for the Social Democratic, Left and Green parties.

26. Budget proposition for 2008. Prop. 2007/08:1 expenditure area 18: Planning, Housing Provision, Construction and Consumer Policy, p. 16 <http://www.regeringen.se/content/1/c6/08/81/69/143bb9de. pdf>.

27. Government bill: <http://www.regeringen.se/content/1/c6/08/34/31/ af661408.pdf>.

28. Corresponding to roughly US$800 or €600 in October 2008.

29. Corresponding to roughly US$112,000 or €83,000 in October 2008.

30. Government bill: <http://www.regeringen.se/content/1/c6/09/11/13/ 6bbc8e82.pdf>.

31. Statistics Sweden <http://www.scb.se/templates/tableOrChart____ 30291.asp>.

32. Minister of Finance Mats Odell, interviewed in *Planera Bygga Bo*, 2007(1), National Board of Housing, Building and Planning. (our translation)

33. Ratcliff, Richard (1949) *Urban Land Economics* (New York: McGraw-Hill); Murie, Alan, Paddy Hillyard, Derek Birrell and Dermot Roche (1976) 'New Building and Housing Need: A Study of Chains of Moves in Housing in Northern Ireland', *Progress in Planning* 6(2): 81–186; Clark, Eric (1981) *Housing, Residential Mobility and Studies of Chains of Moves* (Stockholm: ERU); Magnusson-Turner, Lena (2008) 'Who Gets What and Why? Vacancy Chains in Stockholm's Housing Market', *European Journal of Housing Policy* 8: 1–19.

34. Turner, Bengt (2001) 'Bostadspolitik and samhällsekonomi – verkningar av den förda politiken' [Housing Policy and Economics – Effects of the Conducted Policy], in Anders Lindbom (ed.) *Den nya bostadspolitiken* [The New Housing Policy] (Umeå: Borea), p. 185. Cf. Turner, Bengt (1997) 'Municipal Housing Companies in Sweden: On or Off the Market?', *Housing Studies* 12: 477–88.

35. *Social rapport 2001* (Stockholm: Socialstyrelsen) [Social Report 2001. Swedish Board of Social Welfare], p. 10.

36. *Social rapport 2006* (Stockholm: Socialstyrelsen) [Social Report 2006. Swedish Board of Social Welfare], p. 13.

37. Turner, 'Bostadspolitik and samhällsekonomi'.

38. Boverkets indikatorer (2008) 'Utvecklingen på bygg- bostads- och kreditmarknaden' [National Board of Housing, Building and Planning, 'Indicators of Development on the Housing, Construction and Credit Markets'], June.

39. Turner, 'Bostadspolitik and samhällsekonomi'.

40. Sahlin, '"Social housing" som bostadspolitiskt spoke'.

41. *Social rapport 2006* [Social report 2006]. Magnusson, Lena (ed.) (2001) *Den delade staden* [The Divided City] (Umeå: Borea).

42. Clark, Eric, Karin Johnson, Emma Lundholm and Gunnar Malmberg (2008) *Gentrification and Social Mixing in Swedish Cities 1986– 2001*, ESRC Seminar Series, Gentrification and Social Mixing Seminar, 22–23 May 2008, King's College London. These mappings have been done with a database allowing for a spatial resolution of one hectare. Each 'area' is a square hectare, 100 metres on each side. High income is the top quartile; low income the bottom quartile. The change included is only that through residential mobility, not that of the incumbent residents, or 'stayers'. Thresholds for calculating gentrification and filtering, always in some sense arbitrary, are the same for the entire 15-year period of analysis. Thanks to Gunnar Malmberg and Emma Lundholm, who've mastered the skills of data base analysis and GIS.

43. Bergenstråle, Sven (2006) 'Boende och välfärd 1986–2003' [Dwelling and Welfare 1986–2003], Landskrona.

44. Turner, 'Bostadspolitik and samhällsekonomi'.

45. Statens Offentliga Utredningar, 'Bostadspolitik 2000' [Housing Policies 2000], p. 10.

46. Bergenstråle, 'Boende och välfärd 1986–2003'.

47. Baeten, Guy (2008) 'Building the Neo-liberal City on the Ruins of Social-democracy: Malmö, Sweden', paper presented at the Association of American Geographers Annual Meeting, Boston, MA, 15–19 April.

48. Lindbom, Anders (2001) 'Dismantling Swedish Housing Policy', *Governance: An International Journal of Policy and Administration* 14: 503–26.

49. Lindbom, Anders (2007) 'Obfuscating Retrenchment: Swedish Welfare Policy in the 1990s', *Journal of Public Policy* 27: 129–50.

50. Lind, Hans and Stellan Lundström (2007) *Bostäder på marknadens villkor* [Housing on Market Conditions] (Stockholm: SNS), p. 129.

51. Lees, Loretta, Tom Slater and Elvin Wyly (2007) *Gentrification* (London: Routledge), p. 183. Lees, Slater and Wyly are not referring to Sweden here, but to the main causal force behind a 'fourth wave' of gentrification in North American cities.

52. Harvey, David (2006) 'Neoliberalism as Creative Destruction', *Geografiska Annaler* B(88): 145–58.

53. Turner, 'Bostadspolitik and samhällsekonomi', p. 192.

54. Baeten, 'Building the Neo-liberal City'.

55. Hägerstrand, Torsten (1986) 'Den geografiska traditionens kärnområde' [The Core of the Geographical Tradition], *Svensk Geografisk Årsbok* 63: 38–43.

8

MARKET RULES: NEOLIBERAL HOUSING POLICY IN NEW ZEALAND

Laurence Murphy

The 1980s represented a significant turning-point in the political and economic history of New Zealand. The long-held commitment to Keynesian welfare economic policy, centred on full employment and extensive government intervention in productive industries, was abandoned in favour of neoliberal policies. This radical and enthusiastic engagement with neoliberal ideals fundamentally altered the nature of New Zealand's society and economy and produced the internationally recognised 'New Zealand experiment'.[1] The initial phase of reforms centred on the wholesale deregulation of the economy and included a broad programme of privatisation.[2] By the 1990s, the reform process had moved on from 'roll-back' neoliberalism,[3] which involved the dismantling of Keynesian welfare institutions, to 'roll-out' neoliberal policies[4] that centred on the institutionalisation of market processes, competition and consumer sovereignty within new state regulatory and governance structures. From the 1990s, as part of the far-ranging reforms that were instituted, the state withdrew from its traditional role as a key agent in the housing system and adopted a policy stance that emphasised market provision. The neoliberal turn in housing policy resulted in a profound restructuring of the operation of the social rented housing sector and significantly altered the dynamics of the national housing system. While the broad contours of the housing reforms mirrored processes at work elsewhere in the world, the specific character of the reforms were quite radical and, in many ways, unique.

The shift to neoliberal housing policies represented a dramatic break in a long history of government intervention in the New Zealand housing market. Up until the 1980s, the twin pillars of housing policy were support for homeownership and the provision of subsidised rental accommodation. In response to housing need, and as part of the development of the welfare state, the central government provided rental accommodation (state housing) for 'workers' from the 1930s onwards. By 1986, state housing accounted for 5 per cent of the housing stock and represented approximately 25 per cent of the total rental market. Although small by European standards, the state sector played a key role in the housing market. The state's Housing Corporation was the largest landlord in the country and was also the major provider of mortgage funding for low-income homeownership. As the dominant social housing provider, the Housing Corporation allocated houses on a needs basis and operated an 'income-related rents' policy in which tenants paid a maximum of 25 per cent of their income on rent.

The housing reforms of the 1990s included the transfer of state housing to a Crown-owned profit-oriented company, the sale of state housing to sitting tenants and investors and, most significantly, the introduction of market rents in the public housing sector. In addition, the state abandoned traditional supply-side (production) subsidies in favour of demand-side housing assistance through the introduction of an accommodation supplement. The reforms, aligning with neoliberal principles, were designed to encourage 'fairness', 'self reliance', 'efficiency' and 'personal choice', and were described by the then minister of housing as 'the most fundamental redirection in housing policy since the 1930s'.[5]

While the reforms accorded well with the broad ideology of neoliberalism, they did not solve ongoing housing problems centred on issues of affordability and access to quality housing. By the late 1990s, the persistence of housing problems, in conjunction with a broader reaction to the negative consequences of economic and social restructuring, resulted in political pressure for change.

Since 2000, there has been a shift toward more interventionist housing policy and a return to income-related rents in the state housing sector.

This chapter examines the nature and implications of the reform process, paying particular attention to the social and economic impacts of the reforms on state housing tenants, and the increasing housing affordability problems evident throughout the wider housing market. It is argued that while elements of the housing reforms of the 1990s have been abandoned, current housing policies are still shaped 'within neoliberal parameters'[6] that emphasise market provision but include 'soft' institutional arrangements that present the state as a partner for third-sector housing agents.

Housing Policy and the Housing Reforms

Throughout the twentieth century, housing policy in New Zealand strongly favoured the expansion of homeownership. From the 1930s onwards, tax policies, combined with specific housing initiatives and funding programmes, were designed to encourage households to participate in the Kiwi dream of the 'quarter-acre paradise'. Support for homeownership extended beyond market incentivisation as state agencies were, up until the mid-1970s, key providers of mortgage finance. Indeed, during the 1970s, the state was the largest provider of mortgage funding in the market, offering subsidised mortgage rates and supporting the expansion of low-income homeownership. Under the aegis of the state, homeownership became the dominant tenure and by the mid-1980s, New Zealand boasted a homeownership rate of 74 per cent.

In addition to its support for homeownership, the state built and managed a stock of rental accommodation. While state housing was always a residual tenure, never accounting for more than 7 per cent of the stock, it occupied something of an iconic status in the public imagination, being viewed as a 'material manifestation of the country's early and innovative welfare state'.[7] Developed by the first Labour government from the 1930s, state housing was initially characterised by high-quality housing (see Figure 8.1), designed to meet the needs of working-class families.[8] However, in line with international trends, the stock of state housing over time became associated with poorer-quality housing units (see Figure 8.2) and problem housing areas, reflecting the targeting of lettings to households with the greatest social needs.[9]

Figure 8.1   Post-war state housing (*photo: Laurence Murphy*).

Figure 8.2   More recent state housing (*photo: Laurence Murphy*).

In 1974, the state consolidated its various housing activities into one agency, the Housing Corporation. Responsible for the state's mortgage and rental business, the Housing Corporation was a large multifunctional bureaucracy that not only participated in the market but offered policy advice to the government. Notwithstanding the dramatic reorganisation of state agencies, as part of the initial neoliberal 'roll-back' of the state from the 1980s, the Housing Corporation resisted privatisation; however, it increasingly targeted its services to meet 'serious housing needs'. This emphasis on targeting meant that the corporation assumed a more residual role, housing poorer and needier households who had traditionally depended on the private rental market for accommodation. By the late 1980s, the corporation disproportionally housed low-income, lone-parent and female-headed households as well as older and Maori households. In effect, it housed those households that could not access homeownership or the private rental market.

The advent of a National Party government in 1990, with its desire to extend the economic 'reform' process to the welfare sector, ushered in a new era for housing policy. The Housing Corporation, with over 69,000 rental units, revenues in excess of NZ$700 million and assets of over NZ$8,500 million, was targeted for reform.[10]

Within the context of neoliberal orthodoxy, the reforms centred on three areas. First, the rental operations of the corporation were restructured along business lines. This involved the introduction of a profit motive and the transition to market rents in the social rented sector. Secondly, the state significantly reduced its mortgage operation and sold down its mortgage book. In effect, the state withdrew its support for marginal homeowners. Thirdly, following advice from US consultants,[11] the government introduced an accommodation supplement to assist households with their housing costs. In order to effect its reforms, the government introduced the Housing Restructuring Act (1992), which established Housing New Zealand Ltd (HNZ) as the new manager of state housing. These reforms radically altered the nature and character of state housing and had profound implications for the evolution of the sector and the experience of tenants. But the reforms were not confined to state housing and had significant implications for the private rental sector and homeownership.

Social Rented Housing: The Impacts of the 1990s Reforms

Priemus,[12] reflecting on the different characteristics of social rented housing internationally, argues that an essential element of social provision is that rents are set below market levels. In this context, the introduction of market rents in the state sector represented a fundamental shift away from the notion of social provision in New Zealand. This shift was officially justified on the basis that price signals would result in a more 'efficient' allocation of resources and would reduce 'inappropriate over-consumption' on the part of tenants. As rents shifted to markets levels and incorporated locational premiums, it was expected that tenants would exercise their 'consumer sovereignty' and seek accommodation suited to their budget.[13] Notwithstanding the rhetoric of consumer choice, the reforms relied on the coercion of the market, as price signals forced households to move in order to 'defend' their welfare position.[14]

The nature, evolution and impacts of the reforms have been the subject of considerable analysis and critique.[15] For the purpose of this chapter, two key impacts will be examined: the impact of the sale of state housing and the impact of market rents on tenants.

The shift from income-related rents to market rents held significant implications for the operation of the new company. Previous development strategies, including pepper-potting (building state housing in private housing areas), combined with developments in the private market, meant that parts of the HNZ stock had attained over time significant market value. The incorporation of locational premiums into the rent-setting strategy meant that certain parts of the stock were no longer 'suitable' (that is, were too expensive) for the company's target 'customers'. The company's commercial imperative, in conjunction with a broader privatisation programme being pursued by the state, led HNZ to adopt a stock 'reconfiguration' programme. This 'reconfiguration' involved the strategic sale of existing stock in areas of high demand. Between 1992 and 1999, HNZ sold a total of 12,565, or 18 per cent, of its houses.[16] The reconfiguration also involved the company managing rental properties on behalf of private landlords. This leasing programme was an attempt to expand the stock of houses managed by the company while reducing its ownership of properties. The leasing programme added a couple of thousand rentals under management but did not compensate for the loss of stock arising from its sales programme.

The privatisation programme at this time was in line with international trends, particularly with the experience of Britain.[17] However, in contrast to the British experience, sales to sitting tenants, although encouraged, were limited. The sales programme was dominated by vacant sales to investors and only 25 per cent of sales were through a Home Buy scheme for tenants. Clearly, the overall objective of the sales programme was to maximise returns to the company and was less focused on expanding the 'housing choices' of tenants. Significantly, approximately 20 per cent of sales were in Auckland, the city with the highest national house prices and average rents, and also the city experiencing the most serious housing affordability issues.[18]

The reconfiguration programme not only reduced the size of HNZ's stock, but contributed to an ongoing process of socio-spatial polarisation. State houses in, or near, high-amenity areas were sold while at the same time the company consolidated its position in areas where it was already a dominant provider. The intensification of socio-spatial polarisation had the dual effect of altering the experiences of tenants and constraining the future development options of the sector.

In combination with its reconfiguration programme, HNZ introduced market rents. The shift to market rents was designed to remove the distinction between the private and public sectors. As market rents were phased in by HNZ, the government introduced an accommodation supplement for all low-income households (see below for details). For HNZ tenants, the new supplement provided less assistance than income-related rents. Moreover, the new rent structure was superimposed on an existing tenant profile that was characterised by high levels of need and created a new geography of housing costs within the sector. Similarly sized houses commanded different rents based on their location and as a consequence considerable intra-urban rent differentials emerged, particularly in Auckland the city with the largest concentration of state housing. In 1997, average rents for a three-bedroom state-sector house ranged from NZ\$198 per week in a peripheral housing area to NZ\$249 in central Auckland.[19]

The new rent regime placed considerable pressure on tenants to move either within, or out of, the state sector. HNZ rents doubled between 1992 and 1999, while rents in the private rental market increased by 23 per cent. By 1999, the sector was characterised by high tenant turnover and mobility, with 60 per cent of HNZ tenants having a total tenancy history of less than five years and 25 per cent of tenants having a total tenancy history of less than one year.[20] From a neoliberal perspective, the increased level of tenant turnover could be interpreted as a successful outcome of the reform process, as it suggests that the price mechanism encouraged tenants to make 'choices' regarding their housing options. However, increased 'tenant churn' points to increased social costs. As the distinction between the public and private sectors blurred, state housing tenants encountered increased financial pressures that forced them to move. From a community perspective, it is arguable that the increased levels of tenant mobility seriously undermined processes of community formation and cohesion.

The Accommodation Supplement in the 1990s

In tandem with its restructuring of state housing, the government introduced a demand-side cash subsidy to assist all low-income households with their housing costs. For households whose housing costs exceed an entry threshold, and whose income and cash assets are below target guidelines, the accommodation supplement pays up to 70 per cent of the above-entry threshold housing costs, subject to regionally defined maximum payments.

The shift to a demand-side subsidy was wholly consistent with neoliberal perspectives on the housing market. An accommodation supplement assists households with their housing costs, but distances the state from direct provision in the market. At a broader level, it was envisaged that an accommodation supplement would act to stimulate the private rental market and encourage new supply. However, from its inception the supplement was subject to critique from housing activists and academics. The supplement was viewed as insufficient to meet the needs of the poorest households and, in common with housing benefits elsewhere, was believed to encourage fiscal blowout (rising state expenditures in the face of increasing needs).

Between 1994 and 1999, the number of accommodation supplement recipients rose from 251,505 to 317,505, while total annual payments increased from NZ$352 million to NZ$868 million.[21] Reflective of some of the inherent contradictions within neoliberal policies, the accommodation supplement represented a significant fiscal stimulus to the housing market at a time when fiscal austerity was being implemented elsewhere in the economy.

In terms of its effects, the accommodation supplement had mixed outcomes. A Department of Social Welfare[22] review indicated that the supplement had assisted a large number of households with their housing costs and had significantly reduced the incidence of households paying in excess of 60 per cent of their incomes on housing costs. However, the report noted that over 30,000 households receiving the accommodation supplement had paid more than 50 per cent of their income on rent. Moreover, while the supplement assisted with housing costs, it did not ensure the adequacy of after-rent incomes. In the context of wider welfare 'reforms' in the 1990s, which resulted in real cuts in welfare payments, housing-related poverty became more evident.[23]

Resisting the 'Reforms'

The reforms were implemented in a compressed time-frame[24] and represented a radical reworking of the state's role in the housing market. Within the context of a wholesale transformation of the welfare system, the housing reforms generated limited public debate. Yet the reforms were resisted.

Tenants and tenant groups pursued several strategies to resist the introduction of market rents. A partial rent strike was implemented in Auckland but secured limited support and ultimately had little impact on the policy. Joan Lawson, a pensioner and Queen's Service Medal holder, took HNZ to court over her rent increases in a highly publicised case. While the judge empathised with Mrs Lawson, he found that the legal mandate of the new company required it to operate in a profit-driven manner and thus found no grounds on which to overturn the rent increases. Significantly, tenants did successfully challenge the legality of the initial notification of rent increases and on this basis tenant representatives sought to overturn the rent increases in court. However, the state responded to this challenge by introducing retrospective legislation that legitimated their action after the fact.[25] Thus the urgency and vigour with which the reforms were introduced, implemented and defended, acted to stifle long-term tenant resistance.

However, as the consequences of the reforms became evident, welfare advocacy groups and those working with the poor became significant critics of the housing reforms.[26] The Salvation Army in particular highlighted the role of increased housing costs in pushing poorer households to depend on food-banks.[27] The actions of these groups, combined with critical policy reviews from academics and an increasing official awareness of ongoing housing problems,[28] prompted opposition parties to advocate new housing policies. Significantly, during the 1990s, the electoral system in New Zealand changed to proportional representation, which resulted in the inclusion of minority parties into government. This political transformation facilitated a new era of policy development that was less 'ideologically pure' and more pragmatic in dealing with the needs of interest groups. In addition, after ten years of wholesale neoliberal reform, there was increasing public concern over rising inequality and poverty. In this context, the increasing political will to address housing issues reflected a wider societal concern for the conditions of the poor in society rather than a direct response to tenant advocacy.

In 1999, a new Labour-led coalition government was elected and quickly introduced a set of new housing policies. Two key pieces of legislation were introduced that repositioned the role of the state as an active provider of housing assistance. First, income-related rents were reintroduced into the state sector. However, the new policy still allowed for the possibility of market rents in state houses in situations where a tenant's income exceeded a certain threshold. Secondly, HNZ was replaced by a new multifunctional housing entity, Housing New Zealand Corporation (HNZC), that managed state rentals, administered government support for homeownership and provided policy advice to the government.

At a broad level, the post-2000 housing reforms represented a significant retreat from the neoliberal housing policies pursued in the 1990s. However, in many ways, the new policy environment constituted a continuation of key neoliberal ideas. The accommodation supplement, a central element of the 1990s programme, was retained as was the broader commitment to the private market and the residual role of state housing. The next section reviews some of the key developments that occurred in the market post-2000.

Dealing with the Market

The housing strategy[29] of the new Labour-led governments included a role for the state as a provider of rental accommodation but stressed a sector-wide approach to addressing housing needs. While providing for an expansion of state housing, the state reconfirmed its commitment to the expansion of homeownership and the private rental market. Significantly, the state's focus on supporting and assisting the commodified provision of housing, positions state housing as a residual sector, that is, a sector confined to meeting the needs of those unable to secure housing in the private market. This ongoing support for a residual state rental sector accords with Harloe's argument that social rented housing, both historically and internationally, has tended to move toward a residual model as governments have increasingly favoured commodified forms of housing provision.[30] A residual role for state housing necessarily means that state tenants exhibit considerable social needs and, in addition, the focus on providing housing for the most needy can result in the creation of homogenous and socially deprived communities. Aware of the possibility of creating social ghettos and promoting social exclusion, the housing strategy incorporates wider housing interventions designed to encourage other housing options for low-income households. In this context, policymakers have looked at the international experience, especially the housing association sector in Britain, and have tried to encourage the development of 'third-sector' or 'community' providers.

The new policies have been implemented within a housing context that was profoundly shaped by the neoliberal reforms of the 1990s. The shift to the market during this period changed the nature and character of homeownership and the private rental sector (see below). Indeed the recent policy commitment to 'affordable housing' (that is, supporting households in the lower 40 per cent of the income distribution whose housing costs exceed 25–30 per cent of their incomes) has coincided with a period of declining homeownership rates, dramatic house-price increases and a rising affordability crisis.

The neoliberal reforms of the 1990s altered the context in which economic agents in the housing market operated. Wider financial reforms, combined with the withdrawal of the state as a mortgage provider for low-income households, created a context in which the mortgage market became dominated by banks. Commercial mortgage-lending criteria, focusing on incomes and asset values, favours certain socio-economic groups and works against the interests of 'marginal' homeowners. In contrast to the international experience where the subprime lending market expanded, the New Zealand experience of financial deregulation resulted in a flow of funds for existing owners to trade up in the housing market and for small investors to purchase properties for the rental market. Indeed, under the prevailing tax system, investors were at a significant financial advantage over first-time buyers. Significantly, between 1991 and 2006, national homeownership levels declined from 74 per cent to 66 per cent, while Auckland's homeownership rate declined from 73 to 64.6 per cent.[31] This decline in homeownership coincided with a significant expansion of the private rental sector, which grew from 20 to 28 per cent of the housing stock.[32] The growth of the private rental sector, dominated by small-scale landlords, reflected changes in the perceptions of investors and growing problems relating to housing affordability in the homeownership market. These changes occurred within a monetary and fiscal regime that was established under neoliberal governance structures. Reviewing the fortunes of the homeownership and private rental markets since the early 1990s provides insights into the impacts of neoliberal policies but also the problems and limitations of current 'third-way' housing policy.

Housing Dynamics

Since 1991, real house prices have risen by more that 130 per cent. This rise in prices accelerated considerably after 2002, with real prices increasing by over 80 per cent between 2002 and 2007.[33] While following broader international trends, New Zealand's experience of house-price inflation has been above the OECD average. The rise in house prices coincided with a period of relatively low mortgage interest rates and an increasingly dynamic mortgage market that offered new mortgage products (fixed-interest mortgages, revolving credit mortgages, and so on). Continuous capital appreciation in the housing market had the effect of enhancing the investment potential of housing and, since the 1990s, household wealth in New Zealand has been dominated by housing. For existing homeowners, rising house prices had a significant wealth effect that facilitated a considerable consumer boom. Using equity in their existing property, households could avail themselves of lower interest rates and the increased income multiples applied by mortgage lenders, to trade up in the housing market. The ratio of house prices to disposable household income has risen from 3.5 to 6.5,[34] and is considerably higher in high-cost areas such as Auckland. As house prices and, more recently, interest rates have increased, housing affordability has deteriorated. Between 2000 and 2006, the proportion of renters that could afford to buy a lower-quartile-priced house in their local area declined from 59 per cent to 29 per cent. In Auckland 'only 6 per cent of renting couples' in 2006 'could afford a lower-quartile-priced house'.[35]

At the lower end of the market, prospective homeowners increasingly competed with property investors. Rising capital values and the favourable tax treatment of investment properties, combined with a deregulated credit environment, provided a stimulus for small investors to purchase rental properties. These small investors serviced a range of housing needs, including low-income renters, but their goal was not to offer a social service but rather to attain a capital gain.[36] Underpinning the low end of the private rental market was the availability of the accommodation supplement. Between 1991 and 2007, over NZ$9 billion dollars was paid out in this benefit. Significantly, since 2001, the accommodation supplement has been given solely to meet the needs of households in the private sector. The reintroduction of income-related rents in the state sector, and the reduction in unemployment in the economy at large, led to a significant reduction in the numbers receiving the benefit from 2001. However, there has been a notable increase in payments since 2004, reflecting increasing housing costs and needs. From a policy perspective, the rise in the cost of the accommodation supplement is significant since unemployment is at an historically low level. Should unemployment rise in the future the demand for the accommodation supplement should increase.

The impact of the accommodation supplement has been the subject of considerable debate. This benefit has been viewed as open to 'landlord capture', a process whereby the government is seen as supporting rent increases. However, official analysis shows little evidence of this process, as rents have not risen at a rate in excess of inflation. For renters, the supplement does offer assistance with their accommodation costs, but within the context of an unprecedented housing boom affordability issues are still evident. A study of Auckland's rental market showed that even with the accommodation supplement, the two lower-quartile income groups were paying between 40 and 54 per cent of their incomes on rents and 52,000 households paid in excess of 30 per cent of their income on rent, while 31,000 paid in excess of 40 per cent.[37]

As house prices and rental costs have increased, the nature of the private rental market has changed. Historically, the private rental market was viewed as a transitory tenure, housing people before they became homeowners. Now the sector is housing long-term renters consisting of an increasing number of people who are unable to afford to buy a house and are ineligible for state housing. This 'intermediate housing market' has grown considerably and is expected to continue to grow over the next five to ten years.[38] The prospect of life-long renters in the private sector raises several policy issues. In contrast to the security of tenure enjoyed by state housing tenants, long-term renters in the private market are usually involved with short-term leases. In addition, long-term renters are excluded from one of the key forms of household wealth creation in New Zealand, the housing market. The significance of owning a house is highlighted by the fact that 'wealth per capita doubled between 1980 and 2001 and doubled again from 2001 to 2006 as a result of the house price boom'.[39] In response to the long-term consequences of these processes, there is increasing advocacy within policy circles for the need to support a 'not-for-profit housing sector to complement the state housing sector'.[40] This advocacy reflects a continued political reluctance to expand the state's role as a direct provider and an emerging desire to encourage nascent third-sector providers that have not been encouraged or supported in the past.

The reliance on, and support of, market processes in housing has resulted in significant and complex problems. The dynamics of the housing market have exposed deep contradictions in the operation of neoliberal policies relating to both the management of the economy and the provision of housing assistance. The consumer boom triggered by the housing market has had serious implications for inflation. The Reserve Bank, legislatively required to contain inflation, has sought to contain the demand for housing by consistently raising interest rates since 2004 and as a consequence New Zealand has some of the highest interest rates in the OECD. High interest rates have strengthened the New Zealand dollar and had significant negative impacts on New Zealand's economy, especially its export sector. In addition, while neoliberalism eschews government intervention, and promotes fiscal restraint, housing policy since 1991 has involved substantial subventions to housing via the accommodation supplement. It is in this context of market-induced problems that the New Zealand Housing Strategy has sought to mobilise sector-wide responses to housing issues. Yet, notwithstanding the various interventions proposed to deal with affordability issues, the New Zealand experience highlights the ongoing need for a social and not-for-profit housing sector. In this context, the New Zealand housing experiment brings into focus the limitations of the neoliberal model. Reliance on the market does not meet the housing needs of economically disadvantaged households and under boom conditions market processes can create an affordability crisis that also affects the middle classes.

Since 2007, as a result of the fallout from the US subprime mortgage crisis and the consequent global credit crunch, the future dynamics of the New Zealand housing market have become more difficult to predict. The rate of house price inflation in New Zealand has been declining since 2004 and, significantly, the average house price declined by 6 per cent in 2008. Currently, the Reserve Bank estimates that by 2010 nominal house prices could decline by as much as 16 per cent from their peak in 2007. This drop in prices may make homeownership more affordable, but will result in substantial problems throughout the housing system. For example, if capital values fall, private landlords will be under pressure to increase the cashflows (rents) from their properties, and as a result tenants in the private sector may encounter increased housing stress. In addition, homeowners who purchased at the peak of the boom could face the prospect of negative equity and, if they are unable to maintain their mortgage payments, they may lose their homes. Interestingly, the prospect of a 'market correction' does not in itself constitute a solution to housing problems in New Zealand.

In November 2008, a new centre-right coalition government, led by the National Party, was elected to power. National's housing policy, for the most part, builds on existing policies (for example, retaining the accommodation supplement, renovating and upgrading existing social rented housing), but places greater emphasis on market mechanisms. Its policies include amending planning practices that are seen to restrict housing supply and continued support for small-scale private landlords. Significantly, the National Party has indicated that it will reintroduce a tenant purchase scheme in the state sector, to promote homeownership, and will seek to better manage the state housing stock. The new government's policy stance is likely to cement the residual character of the social rented sector. However, it is clear from the New Zealand experience that neoliberal housing policies that rely on the market to meet housing needs simply expose households to the traumas of property booms and slumps, and low-income households are least able to deal with these traumas.

Conclusions

Neoliberal ideas and policies have had a profound impact on the nature and character of housing markets in New Zealand. Reliance on the market to provide efficient and fair outcomes has had significant implications for state housing tenants and lower-income households more generally. While the reforms have altered the organisational character of the housing market and fundamentally reshaped the experience of housing for state tenants, issues of affordability and access continue to be a problem. The neoliberal vision of an effective market, functioning to provide for consumer needs, has become a reality of declining homeownership rates and rising housing costs. The accommodation supplement has moderated housing costs but a significant number of low-income households continue to pay in excess of 30 per cent of their income on rent.

During the 1990s, the New Zealand housing reforms represented a rather unique experiment, as the state sector became profit-oriented and introduced market rents. These reforms were implemented as part of a commitment to a broad set of neoliberal ideals. The reforms emphasised the commodity dimensions of housing and sought to 'liberate' exchange processes. In doing so, they marginalised, in a policy context, the broader socio-cultural dimensions of housing and downplayed the capacity of state/social housing to provide 'non-housing outcomes', or positive externalities (for example, providing stable communities and improving health and educational outcomes for low-income households).[41] Reliance on the market intensified residualisation processes within the social rented sector and increased tenant turnover. At a broader level, the operation of the accommodation supplement, combined with financial deregulation and a favourable tax environment, prompted an expansion of the private rental market. The new landlords are generally small scale with investment strategies centred on capital gains. As the reforms became embedded, the primacy of exchange values (house prices and rental returns) was asserted and the foundation for a house-price boom was established.

Since 2000, housing policy has recognised the broader social and economic impacts of housing. In line with the development of 'third-way' policies, state intervention increasingly involves engagement with stakeholders including house-builders, local authorities, social agencies, government departments and, significantly, tenants. Much of this engagement is discursive in nature and centred on the production of policy options. In this context, considerable attention has been directed towards research-informed policy development.[42] While policy development has occurred, actual, on the ground, developments have been limited and it is notable that the stock of state housing continues to be below the 1990 levels. More positively, HNZC has developed more tenant-focused management practices and tenant satisfaction has improved.

At a broader level, the new housing policies represent a form of 'soft' neoliberalism that differs from the extremes of the 1990s but continues to be market-oriented. Under this new regime, market provision is tempered by pragmatic and strategic housing interventions. The social dimensions of state housing have been reasserted but the sector's role continues to be residual. With a focus on housing affordability, rather than housing provision, and in the face of increasing house prices, the state has sought to mobilise sector-wide (community, local government and private capital) interests to deal with housing issues. Following overseas models, the state has sought to promote partnerships, announced a range of interventions including shared-equity schemes, and proposed an affordable housing bill that will allow local authorities to set affordable housing targets for private developers.[43] Notwithstanding these initiatives, the capacity of the state to effect broad changes in levels of housing affordability in the private sector is limited by the scale of market dynamics and a commitment to 'fiscal responsibility'. Significantly, the continued dominance of neoliberal thinking constrains the extent to which state housing is viewed as a possible alternative to market provision, or as a solution to housing needs.

The neoliberal reforms of the 1990s sought to remove the state from housing provision. However, the experience of housing change in New Zealand shows that there is a continuing need for social rented housing, although its form may change over time. During the 1990s, the reform agenda effectively marginalised the concerns of state tenants and those suffering from housing disadvantage. While the reforms were comprehensive and effective in containing tenant resistance, they were subject to critique. In the face of neoliberal hegemony, welfare and tenant advocacy groups highlighted the problems of the reforms and pushed for change. Since 2000, the social character of state housing has been reasserted, but state housing continues to be provided within a residual model. Compared to the 1990s, the current regime provides a better housing outcome for the HNZC's 198,000 tenants, but the sector remains vulnerable to political whim, and it is unclear how the sector will develop under a new National-led coalition government. In the absence of a strong commitment to social provision, third-way neoliberal housing policies will continue to struggle to address the housing needs of low-income groups in New Zealand.

Further Reading

HNZC (2005) *Building the Future: The New Zealand Housing Strategy* (Wellington: Housing New Zealand Corporation).

Murphy, L. (2003) 'Reasserting the "Social" in Social Rented Housing: Politics, Housing Policy and Housing Reforms in New Zealand, *International Journal of Urban and Regional Research* 27(1): 90–101.

Murphy, L. and R.A. Kearns (1994) 'Privatisation by Stealth: Housing New Zealand Ltd', *Environment and Planning* A(26): 623–37.

Thorns, D. (2006) 'The Remaking of Housing Policy: The New Zealand Housing Strategy for the 21st Century', *Housing Finance International* 20(4): 20–8.

Websites

Centre for Housing Research Aotearoa/New Zealand (CHRANZ) <http://www.chranz.co.nz>.

Department of Building and Housing – Key source of information for tenants which provides information on tenant rights and dispute resolution <http://www.dbh.govt.nz>.

Housing New Zealand Corporation (HNZC) – Key information on social rented housing <http://www.hnzc.co.nz>

Notes

1. Kelsey, J. (1995) *The New Zealand Experiment: A World Model for Structural Adjustment?* (Auckland: Auckland University Press and Bridget Williams Books).
2. Le Heron, R. and Pawson, E. (eds) (1996) *Changing Places: New Zealand in the Nineties* (Auckland: Longman Paul).
3. Peck, J. and Tickell, A. (2002) 'Neoliberalizing Space', *Antipode* 34(3): 380–404.
4. Ibid.
5. Luxton, J. (1991) *Housing and Accommodation: Accommodation Assistance* (Wellington: Government Printers).
6. Craig, D. and Cotterell, G. (2007) 'Periodising Neoliberalism?', *Policy and Politics* 35(3): 498.
7. Murphy, L. (2003a) 'To the Market and Back: Housing Policy and State Housing in New Zealand', *Geojournal* 59: 119.
8. Schrader, B. (2005) *We Call it Home: A History of State Housing in New Zealand* (Auckland: Reed Books).

9. Ferguson, G. (1994) *Building the New Zealand Dream* (Palmerston North, NZ: Dunmore Press Ltd).

10. Murphy, L. and R.A. Kearns (1994) 'Privatisation by Stealth: Housing New Zealand Ltd', *Environment and Planning* A(26): 623–37.

11. Thorns, D. (2006) 'The Remaking of Housing Policy: The New Zealand Housing Strategy for the 21st Century', *Housing Finance International* 20(4): 20–8.

12. Priemus, H. (1997) 'Growth and Stagnation in Social Rented Housing: What is "Social" in Social Rented Housing?', *Housing Studies* 12(4): 549–60.

13. Murphy and Kearns, 'Privatisation by Stealth'.

14. Ibid.

15. Thorns, D. (2000) 'Housing Policies in the 1990s: New Zealand a Decade of Change', *Housing Studies* 15(1): 129–38; Murphy, 'To the Market and Back'; Murphy, L. (2003b) 'Reasserting the "Social" in Social Rented Housing: Politics, Housing Policy and Housing Reforms in New Zealand', *International Journal of Urban and Regional Research* 27(1): 90–101.

16. Murphy, L. (2006) 'Counting the Costs: Reflections on the Impacts of the Privatisation of State Housing in New Zealand', *Housing Works* 4(1): 22–4.

17. Jones, C. and A. Murie (2006) *The Right to Buy: Analysis and Evaluation of a Housing Policy* (Oxford: Blackwell).

18. Murphy, 'Counting the Costs'.

19. Murphy, 'To the Market and Back'.

20. Ibid.

21. Murphy, 'Reasserting the Social'.

22. Department of Social Welfare (1999) *Social Environment Scan* (Wellington: Social Policy Agency, DSW).

23. Thorns, 'Housing Policies in the 1990s'.

24. Murphy and Kearns, 'Privatisation by Stealth'.

25. Murphy, 'To the Market and Back'.

26. Friendship House (1997) *The Impact of the Accommodation Supplement on South Auckland Housing Markets 1993–1997* (Manukau City, Auckland: Friendship House (PO Box 76-140)).

27. Gunby, J. (1996) *Housing the Hungry: The Third Report* (Wellington: New Zealand Council of Christian Social Services and the Salvation Army).

28. Department of Social Welfare (1999) *Social Environment Scan*.

29. HNZC (2005) *Building the Future: The New Zealand Housing Strategy* (Wellington: Housing New Zealand Corporation).

30. Harloe, M. (1995) *The People's Home?* (Oxford: Blackwell).

31. DTZ (2007) *The Future of Home Ownership and the Role of the Private Rental Market in the Auckland Region*, report prepared for the Centre for Housing Research, Aotearoa (New Zealand).

32. House Prices Unit (2008) *Final Report of the House Prices Unit: House Price Increases and Housing in New Zealand* (Wellington: Department of the Prime Minister and Cabinet).

33. House Prices Unit (2008) *Final Report of the House Prices Unit*.

34. Ibid.

35. Ibid., p. 73.

36. Ibid.; DTZ (2007) *The Future of Home Ownership*.

37. DTZ (2007) *The Future of Home Ownership*.

38. Ibid.; House Prices Unit (2008) *Final Report of the House Prices Unit*.

39. House Prices Unit (2008) *Final Report*, p. 80.

40. Ibid.

41. Cheer, T., R.A. Kearns and L. Murphy (2002) 'Housing Policy, Poverty and Culture: Discounting Decisions Among Pacific Peoples in Auckland, New Zealand', *Environment and Planning C: Government and Policy* 20: 497–516.

42. Thorns, 'The Remaking of Housing Policy'.

43. HNZC (2007) *Housing New Zealand Corporation Briefing to the Incoming Minister: Housing November 2007* (Wellington: Housing New Zealand Corporation).

9

GOING ONCE, GOING TWICE: A SHORT HISTORY OF PUBLIC HOUSING IN AUSTRALIA

Peter Phibbs and Peter Young

This chapter provides a short history of public housing in Australia, highlighting the recent trends of reduced stock, reduced funding and a reduced political commitment to public housing. Despite these negatives, recent Australian research has highlighted the positive impacts of public housing on the lives of public housing tenants. The research also reveals that tenants prefer public housing compared to other forms of housing assistance.

Public housing in Australia has a patchy history.[1] The earliest forms of public housing were built as small demonstration projects in a few Australian cities in the first half of the twentieth century. From these experiments, state governments began founding housing commissions, commencing with the South Australian Housing Trust in 1936.

Housing commissions in different states initially had different missions, such as slum clearance to remove threats to public health, or fostering economic development through the provision of workers' housing. However, a national programme for building public housing that commenced in 1945 under the first Commonwealth State Housing Agreement (CSHA)[2] contributed to a converging approach of developing new housing estates in suburbs and towns.

The early decades of the CSHA were the heydays for the supply of rental housing.[3] Under the first agreement (which operated until

1956), nearly 100,000 dwellings were built for allocation to those inadequately housed or on low income and to military service personal and their families. This approach was conceived primarily as a response to the housing shortage of the time (estimated at 300,000 dwellings) and to concerns with poor-quality housing.[4] Building accelerated in the 1950s and 1960s, with an average of over 15,000 dwellings being completed each year. However, under new arrangements in the 1956 CSHA that was negotiated by a Conservative national government, a high proportion of these homes were sold to tenants rather than being retained as public housing. Publicly subsidised building for homeownership under the CSHA continued until 1981, by which time it was estimated that 840,000 dwellings had been built by the state housing authorities. However, of these, only 120,000 had been retained for public rental housing, representing 5 per cent of the total dwelling stock at that time.[5]

From then until the mid-1990s, investment in public housing was sufficient only to maintain it at around 5 per cent of all dwellings nationally, although the level varied somewhat by state. As a result, the small public-housing sector came under enormous pressure in a context of growing need, driven by demographic trends, social changes (such as the rise of single-parent families), economic difficulties and policy shifts (for example, the move from institutions of many people with disabilities). The main housing policy response to housing-related poverty and acute demand was twofold. It involved a gradual but sustained move away from supply-side responses to more immediate responses to people in need (especially rent assistance, a cash payment to private tenants, but also emergency accommodation), and the introduction of policies designed to target the limited number of places in public housing to those with immediate unmet need and those having special needs that are not catered for in the private rental market (for example, housing linked to support or accessible housing). Public housing became repositioned as 'welfare' housing and, later, 'high-needs' housing, a safety net for those who were homeless or at risk of homelessness and lacking other immediate options. The impact of this approach on the profile of public housing tenants can be seen in a dramatically growing share of tenants who were eligible for a rent subsidy.[6] This rose from 20 per cent in 1976 to 65 per cent in 1985 and 88 per cent in 2005–06, as targeting policies were intensified.[7]

The extended period of privatisation followed by the repositioning of public housing as 'welfare' as described above has had far-reaching impacts on the sustainability of this tenure in Australia. Financial sustainability of public housing providers has been eroded by reductions in rent revenue that accompanied targeting to low-income households paying subsidised rents on the one hand, and rising service costs (linked to the higher cost of sustaining tenancies for the changing client profile, *inter alia*), on the other. The rising costs are also associated with an ageing asset base. In 1990–91, all State Housing Authorities (SHAs) bar two had a surplus in their operating accounts. By 2005–06, only two SHAs operated with a small surplus.[8]

Public housing is now seen by its critics to be socially unsustainable because it is associated strongly with neighbour-hoods of disadvantage and patterns of social exclusion. The marginalisation of public housing has contributed also to a decline in wider community support for this tenure and, consequently, political support. Thus, instead of being perceived as a necessary and desirable service, public housing is seen increasingly as a failure and a drain on government budgets[9] – as indicated by a decline in expenditure on CSHA assistance by 31 per cent in real terms between 1994–95 and 2003–04.[10]

The combined result of cumulative funding cuts and growing operating losses has been no growth in public housing. Moreover, as operating deficits deepen, the only option for SHAs is to sell assets to make ends meet. This is, of course, self-defeating as it decreases capacity in the system further (at a time of record levels of housing stress), yet does not resolve the structural insolvency of providers. Public tenants too have borne their share of pain with rent increases in the order of 25 per cent over the last decade and a disturbing trend of reductions in their security of tenure in some states,[11] with the aim of increasing turnover and, thereby, places for 'more needy' households.

The Benefits of Public Housing

While funding has been reduced and there has been decreasing political commitment to public housing, there is increasing evidence of the benefits of public housing. Benefits have been measured using a conceptual framework that acknowledges that housing can affect much more than shelter. In developing a framework for examining non-shelter impacts, it is useful to start with the characteristics of the *dwelling*. For example, a house that is cold and damp can have a direct impact on the health of its residents. A house that is not matched to the needs of the occupying household (for example, it is too small) can have dramatic impacts on factors such as educational outcomes for children living in the house.

The next step in the hierarchy relates to *locational* outcomes. These include the nature of the area in which the house is located. Some factors are immediately local (for example, the impact of traffic noise on sleep), whilst others are more regionally based (for example, access to good schools, tertiary education, or major hospitals). The next part of the framework highlights the impacts of neighbours on non-shelter outcomes. In extreme cases, it is clear that neighbours can have dramatic impacts on the health and well-being of residents. Given the magnitude of these impacts, it is considered worthwhile to identify them as a separate component of the framework. Further, since housing is usually the single most expensive outlay for low- to middle-income families, housing costs can affect a household's ability to purchase other goods and services. Finally, it is evident that characteristics of the *tenure* can have a significant impact on non-shelter impacts. For example, a major non-shelter impact relates to the insecurity of households operating in the private rental market (see Figures 9.1 and 9.2).

The authors attempted to examine the magnitude of the non-shelter benefits of public housing by interviewing new public housing tenants in an Australian city – Brisbane – just after they moved into public housing from the private rented sector, and between six and twelve months later.[12] The survey focused on changes in the lives of these tenants, particularly with regard to

Figure 9.1 Private rented housing in Brisbane (*photo: Peter Phibbs and Peter Young*).

Figure 9.2 New social rented housing in Brisbane (not all Australian social rented housing is of this quality) (*photo: Peter Phibbs and Peter Young*).

their health, employment and the education of their children. It explored how the different aspects of assistance provided through public housing affected these different aspects of their lives. As well as participating in interviews and completing a health and well-being survey, 80 per cent of the 178 participants in the study allowed access to their health records a year before and a year after they moved into public housing.[13]

A number of participants reported an improvement in their health as a result of entering public housing. They reported:

- eating better foods as a result of increased financial resources,
- an ability to prepare their own foods rather than being obliged to buy takeaway food, since they now had a functioning kitchen,
- improved conditions in their dwelling, such as less dust,
- increased self-esteem, often associated with independent living, meaning that people were now looking after themselves better,
- extra income enabling them to participate in illness-prevention programmes such as joining a gym and getting more exercise,
- more support from neighbours,
- reduced stress due to security of tenure and more income, and
- improved access to medical resources (from having a stable address).

Analysis of the participants' health records revealed some interesting trends. Overall, there was a small decrease in the use of Medicare services. The net cost outcome was a saving of $30 of average benefits per person per annum. However, there was a marked difference between previously light users of the Medicare system and heavier users. Light users tended to increase their levels of usage whilst heavier users reduced both the number and cost of services after they moved into public housing. It is possible that the reduction in stress levels and improved well-being of public housing tenants led to a reduction in visits to local doctors. On the other hand, the increased stability of some tenants might have provided improved access to local doctors for other households.

There were mixed findings in this study about what was happening to respondents' participation in the labour market. In some cases, households used the extra disposable income they had since entering public housing to reduce their employment. Sometimes, this enabled them to provide extra care for a household member, to spend more time with their children, or to give themselves a little more free time. Some households reduced their employment in order to undertake additional training. One man was able to give up his part-time job as a result of his extra disposable income and to work for a charity on a full-time basis. Households were often aware that a benefit of reducing their employment levels was that their rent would go down, since they were paying subsidised rents that were set at 25 per cent of their income. However, it was not clear that this was a primary financial consideration or that it influenced labour-force participation decisions. On the other side of the ledger, the increases in self-esteem and free time that some people reported meant that they wanted to work on their career: 'Well, I've got my housing organised; now it's time I got a good job organised.' Others reported that they had invested their financial savings into starting up small businesses.

The impact of public housing on education outcomes is possibly the clearest illustration in this study of the link between housing and non-shelter outcomes. About 50 per cent of respondents with school-aged children identified that their performance at school had improved after they moved into public housing, and only about 10 per cent identified that things got worse. When pressed on the issue of why their children's performance had improved, people cited three main factors. The first concerned the nature of the neighbourhood and school, and included issues such as the quality of teaching and also having a more motivated group of peers. The second concerned changes at home, which ranged from the increased happiness of the child now that they were living in a good-quality dwelling, to the reduced stress levels of their parents. The third factor was more pragmatic: improved performance occurred because children now had more space and could do their homework without being disturbed by, or fighting with, their siblings. It must be noted that for many participants their current housing was in marked contrast to a very mobile past that included a number of school changes. (Forty per cent of the children surveyed had attended three or more schools in the two years before they moved into public housing.) These results suggest that the positive changes for both children and parents associated with a move into (mostly) 'good' public housing may have significant educational benefits, in addition to the reported health benefits. Moreover, neighbourhood characteristics – the quality of schools and teachers, and how motivated the other children are at the local school – seem to be a significant factor for this sample of families. One teacher interviewed as part of the qualitative component of this study summed up the neighbourhood issue well when she described the phenomenon of a school having a 'critical mass of families who value education', and the positive impact that this dominant culture can have on children who come from families where education is not valued. As a number of parents interviewed in this study reported, it helps if your child's peer group is also motivated.

According to the survey results, public housing tenants who participated in the study perceive that the major benefits of their change in housing far exceed the immediate issue of shelter. That is, they value things that go beyond the provision of a dwelling, such as the increased security of tenure available in their public dwelling. They also acknowledge that, on the whole, they are less depressed and consider they have better emotional well-being. Their experiences in public housing contrast markedly to some of their experiences in the private rental market where the inherent insecurity of the tenure meant that they were often frequent movers, resulting in a number of associated problems including disjointed schooling for their children and a lack of engagement with the surrounding community. Put differently, it is clear that for many respondents in the surveys, there is a clear product distinction between receiving rent assistance as a private renter and living in public housing.

One compelling finding of the study involves the impact of the stress of inappropriate housing. For many respondents, the cumulative day-to-day stress in their lives seems to have been so great that they were having trouble functioning. This appears to be a particular issue when children are involved. Environmental psychologists[14] refer to a concept of 'environmental load': when someone is overloaded, their ability to undertake even straightforward tasks is inhibited. For many respondents, their improved housing seems to be reducing their environmental load to the point where they can start dealing with a number of other issues in their lives – including employment, health issues, and so on.

On the whole, the respondents were very positive about their public housing. About 80 per cent of respondents rated their new housing as at least 'better', with about 60 per cent of respondents indicating their new housing was 'a great deal better'. They reported positive changes in their life stemming from reductions in stress as a result of the increased security of tenure and their ability to feel more in control of their housing. Many reported improved emotional well-being, and a reduction in their depression levels, to be the most significant changes resulting from their move. They also felt their financial situation had improved.

However, the results must be qualified by a number of factors. The sample is small and there is no control group. Moreover, the time between gaining public housing and the final interview is relatively short. However, the findings of the research are consistent with other research. In particular, subsequent research by Khan confirmed the positive impact of public housing on the educational outcomes of children.[15] This research is described in detail below.

Public Housing and Education

Khan undertook a survey of public housing tenants with children in Brisbane, Australia. The tenants were selected so that they had children who had completed some compulsory educational testing before they had entered public housing and some further compulsory educational testing after they had entered public housing.[16] The 170 households who completed the survey reported that even after controlling for changes of schools and other issues, there was a clear improvement in educational outcomes after their children had entered public housing. More specifically, 52 per cent of respondents indicated that there had been an improvement, 45 per cent indicated that there had been no change, and about 3 per cent indicated that their children had declined in performance.[17]

The same study undertook a series of qualitative interviews with public housing tenants that clearly identified the triggers or mechanisms that led to these improved educational outcomes resulting from housing improvements. The mechanisms fit into the same categories as were identified earlier in this chapter. The impacts include:

- the impact of security of tenure,
- the role of the dwelling, or dwelling amenity,
- the role of the neighbourhood, and
- the impact of housing costs.

Some of these act directly on children, whilst, as Young points out, other impacts operate indirectly, that is, by impacting on the parent or carer.[18] Some examples of each of these mechanisms are described below.

Security of Tenure

A key issue for the parents of children was the reduction in stress and disruption associated with being able to have the security of tenure associated with public housing. Susan, a single mother with five children, described the situation:

> I've found it very good – just the stability part of it – this is the most stable I have been – the most I've been in one place. That's been a big improvement in our lifestyle and the kids' education.[19]

Nancy, also a single parent, highlighted how a reduction in stress had resulted in better education outcomes for one of her children:

> He has really improved ... gone from Bs and Cs up to As and Bs ... I attribute that to not having to worry, not having to move, not having to shift ... and I don't have to worry about that, I am stress free so I can give them the time and attention that they need and as a result they are doing better at school.

She also described how reductions in stress helped her health:

> I mentioned that before, my health is related to the stress as well ... it gets worse when I'm stressed. It's something that I am aware of ... it's something I need to manage ... Since I have moved in, the housing has been managed and my health has improved ... so then I can concentrate on the other things such as being a more effective parent.

The Dwelling

The size and quality of the dwelling can have impacts on educational outcomes. For example, Tina, who had a boy and a girl with an age gap of five years, commented:

> This house is better because my kids have their own bedroom now ... They are very happy – they were always fighting before ... she wants to study. He didn't leave her alone ... he wanted to play in the room ... they ended up fighting. But now they have their own rooms, so she can do her homework in her room ... .

Samantha described her previous house as a health risk, but was unable to find alternative private rental housing that she could afford. She considered that more space for her daughter had led to better outcomes: 'Susan has probably improved in school. Bigger space has helped in her studies, she has her own room and own desk. She can do work in her own room. The other place was so tiny it was difficult to do projects.'

The quality of the dwelling can also impact the educational outcomes for children indirectly, through its impact on health. Tina is an immigrant with two children. She lived in private rental accommodation before shifting to public housing. She now lives in a spacious detached dwelling, whereas her previous accommodation was an apartment. Tina feels her own sinus problem and her daughter's asthma problem have improved a great deal since moving into their current housing:

> Before, I was living in a unit and it had carpet. [Besides my daughter] it was giving me problems, even for myself – I was having allergies and trouble with my sinuses. I was allergic to dust … It was an old carpet and the owner didn't want to change it. He said if you want to change it, then change it by yourself. How am I going to change it? It is not my house … All of our health has improved [since moving into this housing].

Tina's poor health associated with her previous housing had direct implications for her children's schooling. When Tina became sick, she could not drive the kids to school and they missed class. In addition, her daughter was often sick with asthma. For health reasons, the children missed about four days per term in that period. Following the move to public housing, this dropped to about one day per term.

The Impact of Housing Costs

Nancy emphasised that limited resources affected not only her ability to purchase educational goods, but also her ability to parent:

> The rent was such a large proportion of the income it was harder to balance the budget so things like uniforms, text book and things like that … it was difficult to get those things … to give them the essentials so that they could concentrate on study … so that was a bit difficult in that they didn't have the resources for school … With that being a stress for me, that sort of affected my parenting of the children as well.

Samantha explained the increase in disposable income in this way:

More money in my pocket helped Susan's schoolwork – Excursions, even a project, even school books. I was not able to buy school books and teachers would ask 'why don't you have this book? Why don't you have that book?' I didn't have money to buy them. I had to write to the teacher to get off my back, get off Susan's back. But, now I can buy books a year before when they are on discount and I can afford that and she is ready for the next year. It is a huge difference. She can now go to excursions. Everything you do at school is going to cost.

Conclusion

The arrangements for public housing in Australia are unsustainable in their present form. Continuing funding and policy pressures have had a number of serious outcomes. First, there has been a dramatic decline in the availability of public housing at a time when many people are struggling under the burden of unaffordable rents in the private rental market. A recent major research review of housing affordability in Australia estimated that over 850,000 lower-income households were in housing stress in Australia, with the largest problem group being lower-income households stranded in the private rental market,[20] where they face ongoing unaffordable rents and have weak security of tenure.

Secondly, changes to allocation policies, which have reduced access to public housing for many lower-income families starting out on the housing ladder, along with changes to rents and security of tenure in that sector, have made the sector less attractive, although it still provides substantial benefits compared to the private rental sector.

Following the recent change in government at the national level and some positive statements by the Minister of Housing about the future of public housing, there is some optimism that the steady decline of public housing will cease and the sector will be able to rejuvenate with additional resources and to play its part in a comprehensive national housing policy. Unless this occurs, the housing futures of many Australian families will be uncertain and the positive non-shelter benefits of public housing will not be realised.

Further Reading

Australian Institute of Health and Welfare (AIHW) (2008) *Public Rental Housing 2006–07.*

Hall, J. and M. Berry (2007) 'Operating Deficits and Public Housing: Policy Options for Reversing the Trend: 2005/06 Update', Final Report (Melbourne : AHURI) <http://www.ahuri.edu.au>.

Hayward, D. (1996) 'The Reluctant Landlords? A History of Public Housing in Australia', *Urban Policy and Research* 14(1): 5–35.

Khan, A. (2007) 'Housing and Children's Education', unpublished PhD thesis, University of Sydney.

Phibbs, P. and Young, P. (2005) *Housing Assistance and Non-Shelter Outcomes* (Sydney: AHURI Sydney Research Centre, University of Sydney).

Notes

1. With thanks to Vivienne Milligan for her help with the history material in this chapter.
2. This is an administrative agreement between the Commonwealth and each of the eight state and territory governments that is negotiated periodically. The most recent agreement covers the period 2003/04 to 2007/08.
3. Hayward, D. (1996) 'The Reluctant Landlords? A History of Public Housing in Australia', *Urban Policy and Research* 14(1): 5–35.
4. Munro, A. (1998) 'Two Cheers for Public Housing: Commonwealth State Housing Agreement, 1945–1997, A History', unpublished ms., Department of Social Security, Canberra.
5. Public housing sales have continued after this period but at a much slower rate; see Jones, M.A. (1983) *The Australian Welfare State* (Sydney: Allen and Unwin).
6. State Housing Authorities charge market rent for all their properties. However, if the household has a low or moderate income, it can apply for a rent subsidy, reducing the rent tenants pay on their property to a fixed proportion of their income. Under this approach to rent-setting historically, the proportion of gross household income paid for rent in public housing was limited to around 18–20 per cent typically. Today, it is around 25 per cent for most tenants. See Young, P. (2002) 'Non-Shelter Outcomes of Housing: A Case Study of the Relationships Between Housing and Children's Schooling', unpublished M.Phil. thesis, University of Sydney, Sydney.
7. See Harmer, J. (1986) *The Funding of Rent Rebates: Issues and Responsibilities* (Melbourne: Council of Social Welfare Ministers

and Standing Committee of Social Welfare Administrators); FaCSIA (Department of Families Community Services and Indigenous Affairs) (2007) *Housing Assistance Act Annual Report 2005–06* (Canberra: Commonwealth of Australia), Table A5.

8. Hall, J. and Berry, M. (2007) 'Operating Deficits and Public Housing: Policy Options for Reversing the Trend: 2005/06 Update', Final Report (Melbourne: AHURI) <www.ahuri.edu.au>.

9. Dalton, T. (2004) 'Public Housing in Australia: A Political Problem', *HousingWORKS* 17(10): 10.

10. Australian Institute of Health and Welfare (AIHW) (2007) *Australia Welfare 2007* (Canberra: AIHW).

11. In some states, lifetime tenure in public housing has been replaced by renewable leases. If tenants' circumstances improve they may not be able to renew their lease.

12. Detailed study results are available in Phibbs, P. and P. Young (2005) *Housing Assistance and Non-Shelter Outcomes* (Sydney: AHURI Sydney Research Centre, University of Sydney).

13. This process was facilitated by Australia's universal health insurance programme, Medicare.

14. See, for example, Bell, P., T. Greene, J. Fisher and A. Baum (1996) *Environmental Psychology* (Fort Worth, TX: Harcourt, Brace College Publishers, 4th edn), pp. 118–20.

15. Khan, 'Housing and Children's Education'.

16. In Australia, primary-school children undergo compulsory educational testing. In Queensland, this occurs in Year 5 and Year 7. The survey respondents in the study had children who entered public housing after their children had completed the Year 5 test, but before they had undertaken the Year 7 test.

17. Note that these findings are consistent with the findings of Phibbs and Young, *Housing Assistance and Non-Shelter Outcomes*.

18. Young, 'Non-Shelter Outcomes of Housing'.

19. All these quotes are taken from Chapter 4 of Khan, 'Housing and Children's Education'.

20. Yates, J. and Gabriel, M. (2006) 'Housing affordability in Australia, National Research Venture 3: Housing Affordability for Lower Income Australians', Research Paper 3 (Melbourne: AHURI).

10

DESTROYED BY HOPE: PUBLIC HOUSING, NEOLIBERALISM AND PROGRESSIVE HOUSING ACTIVISM IN THE US

Jason Hackworth

Placing Public Housing in the US

As news rolls in daily about record-high foreclosure rates in various parts of the US, and as borrowers, lenders and other guarantors deal with the fall-out, it is easy to lose sight of a much deeper crisis in housing that has been afoot since the early 1970s – the destruction of subsidised rental housing. The victims of this destruction have very little political capital, and this story rarely makes it to the front page of any major newspaper. But it is arguably the most acute danger facing the sustainability of affordable housing in the US right now. Much, though not all, of this destruction has been prompted by the neoliberal desire to reduce government involvement and promote 'self-sufficiency' in housing. This chapter will focus on one part of this larger process – the destruction of public housing in the US.

Before proceeding with this discussion, it is perhaps important, especially for an international audience, first to place public housing within the spectrum of subsidised housing in the US. As of 2005, there were approximately 120,530,000 housing units in the US,[1] of which about 31.2 per cent (37,650,000 units) were rented or 'for rent'. The rest, roughly 70 per cent, are owner-occupied. It is difficult to overstate the significance of this figure statistically or politically. Extraordinary energy is spent on protecting the interests of homeowners and on expanding their ranks.[2] It also contributes to the belief that most housing in the US exists without the benefit of any government programme, the corollary being that any obvious investment like public housing is abnormal and un-American. Putting aside the fact that the *largest* (by far) federal housing programme – that is, tax-deductible mortgage interest, which is *only* available to resident homeowners – costs the federal government $76 billion a year,[3] and that the entire homeownership market is structured by federal laws, federal assistance to most borrowers,[4] and a federally created secondary mortgage market, this belief/delusion is politically very powerful. It contributes to a relative political marginalisation of rental housing in general, and the extreme marginalisation of public subsidised housing in particular. The latter includes public housing (the focus of this chapter), but also includes much more.

According to Schwartz, there are more than 6.9 million federally subsidised housing units, or about 5.7 per cent of the total,[5] but the nature and volume of what constitutes 'subsidy' varies widely. Twenty-six per cent of federally subsidised units are, for example, not actually 'units' at all, but rather vouchers that tenants can redeem with a participating landlord. Other units are subsidised initially by tax credits which are then sold for funds used to build housing and then turned over to local managers (sometimes private) who may have no formal connection with the federal government. Many others are financed by a patchwork of vouchers, tax credits and non-federal government programmes. Formal public housing – that is, units financed fully by the federal government and currently owned by a local Public Housing Authority (see below) – constitute about 1.22 million housing units, a small percentage by any comparison. Given its obvious marginality, it is appropriate to ask why the US public housing system would be a useful vehicle through which to understand the wider processes of neoliberalism. It is, however, precisely this marginality that makes US public housing a useful vehicle through which to observe the process of neoliberalism. Because it has never enjoyed a broad constituency, public housing has been historically more malleable in the face of ideological shifts than other parts of the welfare state in the US. As such, the impact of various ideological movements – including but not limited to neoliberalism – tends to be more exaggerated, and thus more readily observable in this sector than others.

A Short History of Public Housing in the US

The period between 1937 and 1973 gave rise to both the birth and apex of what might be called 'Keynesian public housing' (KPH) in the US. Major Acts in 1937, 1949 and 1968 (along with many smaller programmes and experiments) paved the way for an expansion of the public housing stock.[6] Though never reaching the level of provision in western Europe and always sensitive to the needs of real estate capital, the period can be deemed 'Keynesian' to the extent that it was justified on the grounds of redistribution, boosting effective demand, and increasing investment in the built environment. The first major piece of federal public housing legislation and the inauguration of KPH in the United States was the 1937 Housing Act. Successful lobbying by the US Chamber of Commerce and the US Savings and Loan Association kept the Act from being a central part of President Roosevelt's New Deal agenda.[7] Even Roosevelt was persuaded that public housing was 'too socialist' a solution to the existing scarcity of homes, and kept it out of the administration's agenda until the mid-1930s.[8] After a bitter, ideological debate in Congress, the Act was finally passed in 1937, but not without significant concessions to the private sector. Among the most important were requirements that public housing schemes include 'equivalent demolition' of housing in the surrounding community (and compensation to the owner) so that no new units were added to the overall stock.[9] Furthermore, nearly a third of the units authorised under the Act were reserved for military housing, and the remainder of 'proper' public housing units were reserved for the working poor, rather than the destitute.[10] The 1937 Act also established a decentralised system of delivery, composed of public housing authorities (PHAs). PHAs were established to receive direct subsidy from the federal government, and continue to be responsible for the day-to-day management of housing in cities across the US. The diffuse nature of public housing governance in the US would become one of its hallmarks.

None the less, public housing remained firmly 'socialist' within the minds of key Congressional leaders even during the later years of the Depression.[11] At the same time, many recognised that the US's severe housing shortage would inhibit its ability to build and enlarge military facilities – a key Congressional priority, as the prospect of war loomed in the late 1930s. The Lanham Act of 1940 was a response to this priority, enabling the construction of thousands of new housing units close to military bases and factories around the United States. But even the special circumstances of this Act would not inhibit the private sector from lobbying against 'unfair competition'. In response to the housing lobby, Congress mandated (and implemented) that all Lanham Act housing be transferred to the private sector, or demolished outright, upon the cessation of hostilities.[12] This was, of course, very unpopular in many parts of the country, such as Dallas, Texas, where thousands of units had been built to house defence industry workers and where, like many other parts of the US, affordable housing was in short supply following the Second World War.

Despite severe post-war housing shortages, the first major piece of housing legislation was not enacted until 1949. By this point, however, the private house-building lobby had achieved even more power than it had enjoyed during the 1930s, and became even more influential on the legislative process.[13] In addition to being overwhelmingly oriented toward private suburban house construction (which likely worsened the inner-city conditions necessitating public housing), the 1949 Housing Act's public housing measures were severely compromised by private interests.[14] Among other things, public housing rents could only be 20 per cent lower than the lowest comparable housing units in the neighbourhood;[15] eviction authorisation was legalised for families exceeding rigid income limits; design limitations were created to make public housing stand out from the average stock,[16] and operating budgets for PHAs were set at unsustainably low levels.[17] One result of this legislation was a dramatic shift in the tenantry of public housing, from the 'temporarily submerged middle class' in the 1930s, to only the most extreme poor by the early 1950s. It not only limited public housing access to all but the 'least profitable',[18] but it also substantially undermined the prospect of income diversity in individual housing complexes – a key theme in today's public housing policy discourse. From this point onward, public housing became an increasingly segregated environment for its tenants (see Figure 10.1).

Figure 10.1 Public housing in New York's Lower East Side (*photo: Joel Raskin*).

The 1949 Housing Act was the only major legislation affecting public housing until the late 1960s, but there were several demonstration programmes and limited changes to existing legislation that continued to be shaped by private interests. The next major act, the 1968 Housing and Urban Development Act (HUDA), instituted a number of important changes to public housing policy. The two most important were Sections 235 and 236 housing subsidies. Section 235 provided interest-rate subsidies to encourage public housing tenants to purchase housing of their own.[19] This served as an important precedent for the public housing homeownership policies of the 1980s, and also marked a turning-point wherein public housing tenants were seen as a potential market (rather than a threat to the market), if adequately subsidised by the federal government. Section 236 of the Act provided rent subsidies for developers of apartment housing,[20] which led to a dramatic surge in unit construction. The total number of housing starts subsidised by the federal government increased from 12 to 25 per cent between 1969 and 1970,[21] leading to production levels between 1968 and 1973 that nearly equalled the total output between 1949 and 1968.[22] KPH was at its productive apex during this period.

Despite the institutional limitations and relatively small size of KPH (compared to other industrialised countries), President Nixon (among others) decided that the programme was too expensive; he declared a moratorium on all new public housing in 1973, and formally dismantled the 1968 Act with the 1974 Housing and Community Development Act (HCDA) the following year. These actions initiated a period of what might be usefully understood as 'neoliberal public housing' (NPH) because it was justified by a discourse of reducing public outlays for welfare, and increasing 'local control' over such decisions. The 1974 Act shifted resources away from the physical stock – much of which became uninhabitable (and thus vacant) only a few years later. More abstractly, the Act initiated a period of 'roll-back' neoliberalism.[23] The basic roll-back of KPH continued through the 1980s and 1990s as HUD's budget was slashed more aggressively than any other federal-level domestic branch of the government.[24] This continued through the 1990s, when the most active source of public housing funding came in the form of grants to facilitate the demolition and privatisation of the housing stock.

But the neoliberalisation of public housing in the US since the early 1970s has involved much more than just the withdrawal of funding. The roll-back of KPH has been paralleled (and followed) by a roll-out of various neoliberal measures that promote 'self-sufficiency', entrepreneurialism and private governance. In arguably the most extensive measure of this sort, the federal government began foregrounding Section 8 vouchers as the preferred mode of public housing in the early 1970s. Section 8 vouchers are payments by the federal government to individual landlords to cover the gap that exists between 30 per cent of a tenant's income and the prevailing fair-market rent (determined by HUD). Though several demonstration programmes in the early 1960s experimented with such demand-side measures, it was not until the 1974 Housing Act that the Section 8 programme was officially authorised and expanded as a significant policy device. The programme has evolved from being a fairly marginal outlay by HUD to being one of its largest in the past 30 years. The federal government further institutionalised the belief that the market is a normatively superior way to allocate public housing by initiating the Low Income Housing Tax Credit (LIHTC) programme in 1986. The LIHTC programme involves the allocation of tax credits to qualifying low-income housing builders. The builders of such units sell the credits to corporations or individuals with high tax liability in exchange for a cash payment that can be used to develop the housing.[25] Central to the expansion of both programmes is the belief that the market will be able to allocate goods more efficiently and effectively than any federal government office could hope to do.

Another mechanism used to roll out a neoliberal public housing order has been the encouragement of homeownership as a way to generate 'self-sufficiency' amongst the existing public housing tenantry.[26] The first major effort to provide federal homeownership subsidies for low-income families (the Section 235 Program) was initiated in the 1968 Housing Act, but the programme faltered shortly thereafter because of management problems and the expense of upgrading the stock to saleable shape.[27] This was followed by a series of smaller demonstration programmes during the 1980s, including the Public Housing Demonstration Program (in 1985) and the Nehemiah Program (in 1987), but both folded for similar reasons.[28] The idea of promoting homeownership amongst public housing tenants resurfaced again in the 1990s, as a component of the HOPE VI programme (see below), but the same aversion to substantive and widespread federal expenditures for physical improvement remained a constraint.

A further set of roll-out programmes sought to link housing to individual work ethic. The idea was to wean the existing tenant base from the federal government by improving the work ethic and entrepreneurialism of said group.[29] One of the earliest programmes of this sort was the Reagan administration's 'Project Self-Sufficiency', which provided assistance for 10,000 single mothers within the public housing system to become 'economically independent'.[30] The (first) Bush administration continued these efforts with 'Operation Bootstrap', which included another 3,000 families in a similar programme in 1989. The programmes encouraged job training and included light incentives for working. The Clinton administration's Work and Responsibility Act in 1994 expanded these efforts by providing more incentives for employers to employ welfare recipients, but was thwarted by a more restrictive (to the recipients) Republican-led effort called the 'Personal Responsibility Act'. After several years of debate, an agreement was finally reached with the Quality Housing and Work Responsibility Act (QHWRA) of 1998. Among other things, the QHWRA mandated community service requirements and stricter screening for tenants, opened access to public housing for higher-income families, and allowed PHAs to evict tenants for a wider range of reasons. It has also allowed newly installed private managers of public housing to enforce such rules. The roll-out neoliberalisation of public housing was thus well underway by the early 1990s.

The HOPE VI programme, initiated by a federal commission on 'severely distressed' public housing, and the Cranston Gonzalez Affordable Housing Act of 1990, folded many of the initiatives discussed earlier (both roll-back and roll-out efforts) into a more or less coherent public housing programme.[31] The HOPE VI programme is an embodiment of both roll-back/destruction and roll-out/creation neoliberalism. On the one hand, its mandate is to demolish the country's most 'severely distressed' public housing units.[32] Individual PHAs are competitively awarded grants for this purpose and are no longer required, or even aim, to replace all of the units felled as part of a redevelopment plan. The data on exactly how many families will be displaced are murky, but even using HUD's very conservative estimates, we can literally see the roll-back of public housing occurring in the US. Approximately 92,740 public housing units were demolished or slated for demolition between 1993 and 2003. Only slightly more than half of the units to be built with HOPE VI dollars will be even nominally 'public', and only approximately 50.7 per cent of these 'public' units will actually be available to the residents whose homes were originally demolished. That translates into an actual unit reduction for the poorest residents in public housing of 63,487. Using HUD's conservative estimate of household size in HOPE VI communities (that is, 2.9 residents), this suggests that (as of 2003) approximately 184,112 tenants have been, or will be, removed from the physical public housing stock in the next several years. Some of these families will be given Section 8 vouchers to redeem with private landlords, but with so many families flooding such markets, many families will have to leave the metropolitan area or face a housing situation even more precarious than the one from which they were removed. Supply has already failed to keep up with demand in places such as Chicago and Washington, DC, where thousands of residents have recently been displaced. Now that many of the HOPE VI development processes are well under way, the negative numbers on the plight of tenants continue to trickle in. Susan Popkin of the Urban Institute found that 40 per cent of relocated tenants reported having problems paying rent at their new residence; 50 per cent were struggling to pay for food, and 13 per cent were now living with relatives and friends.[33] Of those given vouchers, Popkin and her research associates found that less than half of the original tenants were able to find housing with their Section 8 vouchers.[34] Many are forced into a situation that is much darker than their 'severely distressed' previous housing option: homelessness, 'doubling-up', and so on. One recent tracking study simply lost track of 17 per cent of their sample of HOPE VI relocatees because they no longer had an address.[35]

HOPE VI thus marks the single most significant roll-back of public housing outlays in US history, and has not even achieved the modest goals that were intended to be beneficial for tenants originally living on target sites. HOPE VI and QHWRA also represent a more transparent roll-out of neoliberal policy in practice. Housing benefits have been linked to workfare programmes and the language of economic 'self-sufficiency' is rife throughout the programme's promotional material.[36] Increasingly, tenants must behave in 'acceptable' ways to continue to receive their housing benefits. QHWRA requires that all public housing tenants who are not working full time, studying, disabled, or over 62 years of age, perform community service to retain their housing benefits.[37] Enormous latitude is given to local authorities on how to enforce this policy and many exceptions that would appear easily justified – childcare, part-time work, looking for work, caring for a relative – are framed as little more than excuses by conservative housing administrators. PHAs have also been given new powers to evict for behavioural or even economic reasons. In HUD's new 'One Strike and You're Out' programme, for example, PHAs are able to evict tenants for criminal activity committed by any member of a household on or off the public housing complex grounds. In a recent case brought before the US Supreme Court, the right of PHAs to evict tenants for criminal activity over which they have no direct control was unanimously upheld.[38] Work requirements and punitive 'One Strike' regulations are part of a more transparently interventionist set of roll-out neoliberal state practices.

In general, while US public housing has never been a comprehensive (or even completely 'public') system of provision, recent efforts to restructure have demonstrably worsened conditions for current tenants. This restructuring has sought broadly to neoliberalise the public housing system by emphasising 'individual responsibility' (for example, 'One Strike and You're Out' programme), the market as social provider (for example, Section 8 housing, LIHTC, and so on), and the overall reduction of government oversight (for example, demolition of existing stock, and inclusion of private management). The net effect of such programme changes has been an environment of shrinking housing opportunities paralleled by the expansion of penalty for residents.

Challenging the Onslaught of Neoliberal Public Housing

As any serious activist knows, there is no simple answer to challenging the destruction of public housing in the US. The sentiment against public housing is so incredibly strong that many minds will have to be changed. Moreover, even the most regressive public housing reforms are wrapped in ostensibly progressive discourses that are difficult to dismiss or challenge unequivocally. But there is a lot to learn from the experience of housing authorities and tenant activists over the past 15 years. Many of the lessons are depressing, but they all underscore two lessons that activists can take away from their experience. First, despite all of the claims to the contrary by neoliberal theorists, and public officials who have passively accepted their ideologies, neither the onslaught of neoliberalism, nor the policies that emanate from it are inevitable. Even the most emphatic federal government decrees can be challenged locally – both by housing authorities themselves and by tenant organisations. Secondly, public housing reforms are often cloaked in ostensibly progressive discourses that are difficult to contest, such as 'improving design', or 'economic integration'. These discourses are often very effective at dividing public housing supporters, both within housing authorities and amongst tenant activists. The efforts of PHAs and tenant activists underscore the importance of understanding the complexity of forces angling to destroy public housing.

There have been numerous battles to prevent or even reverse public housing policy changes (particularly the destruction of public housing) at individual locations throughout the United States, but thus far they have remained highly localised in their orientation. Such struggles are often initiated by tenant leaders (usually elected as part of a tenant council) and assisted by outside activists, particularly lawyers who donate their time to assist tenant groups. They also draw on the assistance of members of local groups such as the Seattle Displacement Coalition or national groups such as the Association of Organizations for Community Reform Now (ACORN) who help with (and participate in) rallies, alternative redevelopment proposals and tenant rights counselling. No firm numbers exist on the size of these individual struggles, but it is reasonable to state that the majority of tenants have been involved in either some aspect of formal participation in a local HOPE VI plan, or in an openly antagonistic movement to thwart (or modify) it externally. Interaction with the programme has thus been markedly widespread. Thus far, however, localised efforts have failed to coalesce into a wider movement for public housing, despite the national scale of the programme and efforts of groups such as ACORN to draw wider attention to the issue. Three broad reasons emerge for why a wider social movement amongst tenants has thus far been elusive.

The Virtual Life-chances Lottery

Within the HOPE VI policy framework, there is a conspicuous lack of regulation pertaining to how housing authorities choose tenants for redeveloped communities. This is no accident, as one *raison d'être* for the programme has been to return power to PHAs in the governance of their tenants.[39] One central consequence is that tenants often lack a clear understanding of how to receive a better housing unit once redevelopment is complete. In certain locations, the process resembles a lottery with a lucky few receiving such units, while in others it more closely resembles a competition based on a variety of factors including the tenant's credit history, past behaviour, and/or participation in any activism against the PHA. Those who lose this competition are often given Section 8 vouchers, or removed from the public housing system entirely. There are two pertinent consequences to the highly variable way that HOPE VI units are meted out. First, the competition ethos fostered by the process (of unit allocation) has made it difficult to enlist tenants in critical activism, because many feel that their chances of receiving a redeveloped unit will be significantly undermined by participating in such activity. Secondly, the dispersal of tenants through Section 8 makes it logistically more difficult for activists to organise tenants.

Most tenant groups dealing with HOPE VI have expressed some concern about displacement resulting from the implementation of the policy in individual complexes. In some cases, such as New York City, the fear of displacement was sufficient to organise tenants against the HOPE VI programme in the mid-1990s. Tenant groups were successful at limiting the PHA's efforts in this case. The New York City Housing Authority has pursued and won only two HOPE VI grants since the programme's inception, and in both cases has carried out a strategy of full unit retention. In most cases, however, tenant groups have neither the level of organisation nor the wider political support enjoyed by activists in New York, so their protests are less critical, and often less successful. More often, tenant groups protest an aspect of the HOPE VI process early on in the planning stages. These protests have taken many forms (rallies, litigation, and so on), but are often undermined by the very process they are contesting. That is, because a certain percentage will receive a redeveloped housing unit, tenants are often faced with the *de facto* choice of making an effort to receive such a unit, or fighting against the programme in general. The PHA typically offers tenants the opportunity to participate in the formal planning process,[40] and many realise that this could enhance their chances of receiving a redeveloped unit. Conversely, many also realise that participating in any activism that is antagonistic to the overall plan or the PHA could undermine their chances of receiving a redeveloped housing unit. In Miami's Carver Housing Complex, for example, tenants were initially unified in their opposition to the HOPE VI programme. But as the planning process continued and began to appear inevitable, self-interest started to cleave tenant organising. Families for whom it appeared that the PHA had no interest in housing remained active against the plan,[41] but many others began to do everything in their power to put themselves in a favourable light with the PHA.

The actual method of dispersal also has the effect of undermining activist efforts. Dispersing tenants through the device of Section 8 vouchers often does not produce the intended result of deconcentration or desegregation,[42] but it is the most common method of removing tenants from the original housing complex. Often, such tenants are forced to move into neighbourhoods as poor and segregated as the public housing complex from which they were displaced, and sometimes it can even translate into a *de facto* eviction from the city (because of a lack of Section 8 units citywide). Much of this is because landlords are not legally required to accept tenants with Section 8 vouchers, so tenants are not actually 'free to choose' any, or even most, housing in the private market. Some landlords who are willing to accept vouchers, contract with HUD for an extended period of time (usually 40 years) to have their entire development dominated or entirely composed of voucher recipients (project-based assistance). Such landowners typically have difficulty in siting complexes of this sort in all but poor neighbourhoods. Residents of more powerful neighbourhoods in the US have consistently and successfully resisted the siting of almost any form of public housing. Those that do not contract with HUD on such a formal basis are often either the owners of large multi-family developments or the owners of property in poor communities who derive some benefit from their participation. In many large cities, existing opportunities for Section 8 redemption had already largely been filled before HOPE VI was even implemented. In cities like Chicago, for example, as many as 30 per cent of the tenants given vouchers as part of the HOPE VI programme are forced to either return the voucher within a few years, or move to another city where such units do exist.[43] Allocating Section 8 vouchers as a method of dispersal is plagued with problems that are well documented.[44] This issue is revisited here only to bolster the point that Section 8 voucher recipients in HOPE VI plans are often not receiving a better, or even less segregated, residential environment. Because such tenants are removed from the actual public housing development site, the likelihood of their participation in activism regarding the development of that site decreases. Once displacement has taken place, it is much harder for tenants to organise because many of the most likely participants have already been removed. To be sure, 'vouchered out' tenants face an array of problems that are conducive to activism, but they are often different from those surrounding the HOPE VI development site itself.

The Quandaries of Litigation

Litigation and the filing of formal complaints by tenants' groups against PHAs and HUD has arguably been the most common form of protest against the HOPE VI programme.[45] The litigation approach has, however, been largely unsuccessful at broadening individual struggles, or even at achieving gains within the frame of the judiciary. Most court cases take enormous resources to pursue effectively and, more importantly, require tenant groups to atomise their grievance to a single, locationally specific issue. This section describes several examples of anti-HOPE VI litigation to illustrate the point. Three anti-HOPE VI litigation strategies have emerged: (1) highlighting the issue of displacement, (2) noting violations of due process, and (3) pointing out improprieties in the procurement of private developers for the complex.

Highlighting displacement has been one of the most frequently used strategies by anti-HOPE VI litigators. Litigation of this sort has focused on the unreasonable nature of tenant screening, 'broken promises' (or 'bad faith' negotiations) by the PHA, and civil rights violations made during the development process. The complaint that tenant screening has grown too punitive under the HOPE VI programme has been voiced by activists in Seattle, San Francisco, Miami and New Brunswick (New Jersey), among other places. Much of the criticism has focused on unreasonable credit screening, housekeeping checks and security procedures to which those who receive rehabilitated housing units are subjected. The sharpest criticism has been reserved for HUD's 'One Strike and You're Out' programme described earlier. Activists argue that the policy is being used as a way to 'weed out' many of the tenants waiting for better housing units.

Arguing a violation of due process is a another broad litigation strategy currently being employed by anti-HOPE VI activists. A number of tenant groups involved in a HOPE VI application process have asserted that PHAs have not properly included their participation. In one case, Octavia Anderson, the former president of the Scott Homes Resident Council in Miami, filed a suit against the Miami-Dade Housing Agency for refusing to recognise her as the tenants' representative after she made her disapproval of their HOPE VI plan evident.[46] She survived an effort by the PHA to remove her, but was unable to stop a highly market-rate-oriented HOPE VI plan, despite widespread tenant support for her, and against the plan. In another case, residents from Cincinnati's Lincoln Homes Complex complained that the PHA disregarded their input during a planning process that culminated in a $31.1 million HOPE VI award in 1998.[47] Former tenants filed suit against the Cincinnati Housing Authority in 1999, alleging that it had not properly followed HUD's participation requirements. The case was later dismissed by Judge Sandra Beckwith, who argued that there was no federal law requiring such consultation with tenants.[48]

The final legal strategy for disrupting the HOPE VI programme in individual cities has been to highlight improprieties in the procurement of developers for the housing complexes in question. In many cases, there have been serious conflicts of interests where, for example, the PHA director uses their influence to obtain a construction contract for a company on whose board of directors they sit. The aforementioned case of the New Orleans Desire Complex is one such example. Tenants there have argued that former PHA Director Michael Kelly improperly channelled a contract for development of the complex to a non-profit group, New Orleans Works, that he had previously established.[49] Though probably successful at embarrassing Kelly, their strategy was unsuccessful at derailing the HOPE VI implementation there. In another case, the Seattle Displacement Coalition (SDC) recently charged a local developer involved in the city's Holly Park HOPE VI Complex, Bruce Lorig, with violating HUD's conflict-of-interest rules.[50] Lorig, the chosen developer for the housing complex, allegedly used his position of influence to divert a $1.9 million contract to an architectural firm with which he had business ties. The allegation was serious enough to prompt an investigation by HUD. But while auditors ultimately agreed with the SDC's complaint, they only asked that the Seattle Housing Authority implement a better strategy for dealing with such complaints in the future.[51] The legal strategy neither slowed the development process nor impeded the involvement of the private developer in question.

In general, litigation against the HOPE VI programme has not been very successful for tenants' groups. Though legally successful on a few issues, litigation has thus far been unable to derail a single HOPE VI plan, or one of the policies supporting it. More importantly, the experience demonstrates that this approach, for all of its potential at remedying short-term conflicts, can atomise and decontextualise (whether intentionally or not) individual tenant grievances if pursued in isolation from a wider movement for change.

The Invocation of HOPE

The legal system is not the only means through which the conflict in public housing has been articulated. The official policy discourse of the HOPE VI programme, as it has been conveyed by the media, PHA officials, planners and housing scholars has effectively silenced dissent for the programme by generating a narrative that situates the programme as an 'inevitable', and even 'progressive', intervention by the state to 'empower' tenants. Displacement has been obscured in the prevailing narrative of HOPE VI, and with this, even tenant conceptions of the process have been altered. Though the discourse and justification of HOPE VI have a variety of intellectual and political sources, one of the recurrent themes of this discourse has been public housing's inferior physical design.

Improving the architectural design of public housing is a central justification for the HOPE VI programme. The programme mostly targets high-rise public housing 'projects', and encourages PHAs to replace such structures with garden apartments and townhouses, scattered throughout the city. The underlying discourse focuses on how the physical design of most public housing: (1) stigmatises tenants, by forcing them to live in dwellings that stand out from the rest of the housing stock, (2) makes crime prevention nearly impossible because of the site design, and (3) makes activities such as childcare all but impossible. The idea of pointing out the flaws and improving the architectural design of public housing has a long history in the field of urban studies and architecture. Oscar Newman and Jane Jacobs are two of the original scholars who argued this point.[52] Newman continues to be outspoken in this regard, suggesting that public housing's design fosters crime and discourages nearby real estate investment because it lacks 'defensible space' – that is, areas over which tenants feel a sense of ownership, and are able to surveil properly. The work of both thinkers has influenced ongoing academic literatures in geography, architecture and urban planning, which attempt, through various means, to evaluate how better-designed housing influences tenants' attitudes, their integration with the wider community, and their chances for social advancement.[53] The 'faulty design' argument has also been harshly criticised by a group of housing scholars who argue that the overwhelming focus on design obscures more important causes of failure, such as Congressional funding levels, federally imposed design restrictions, and pressure by the homebuilder's lobby to make public housing distinct.[54]

The point of mentioning this literature here is less to engage with the debate itself, than to note that only one side has been co-opted by the HOPE VI policy discourse. The notion that public housing problems are reducible to a series of design mistakes is now popular among many housing planners, PHA officials and, increasingly, tenants themselves. It is used not only to justify the current state intervention in public housing, but to frame such intervention as a progressive, self-correcting response to one of the 'most serious' problems of public housing. Obscured in this discourse is, of course, any mention of either the scholarship contesting this notion or the displacement that this intervention appears to be causing.

The language of 'defensible space' and 'faulty design' is rife throughout media accounts of both the HOPE VI programme and public housing in general. Policy designers at the federal level frequently deploy the discourse of 'faulty design' as well. Henry Cisneros, former HUD director and key promoter of the HOPE VI programme in the mid-1990s, very directly deployed the discourse on a number of occasions.[55] The theme of 'faulty design' continued to be central to the HOPE VI programme, even after Cisneros' departure. HUD, for example, sponsored three workshops in 2000 to educate HOPE VI recipients on better architectural design.[56] By deploying the language of design as such, policymakers are able to frame the federal government as a saviour of sorts, who has finally decided to improve the lives of tenants by improving the design of their dwellings. Situating the problem and solution as such, has the effect not only of obscuring the regressive impact of the state's intervention, but also of allowing for a 'solution' that is relatively easy for policymakers to achieve (unlike the more complicated solutions to urban poverty). Obscured are the very legitimate arguments that have countered (or repositioned) this discourse, and the reality of displacement following HOPE VI implementation. Tenant activists have more difficulty using the deleterious effects of HOPE VI to inspire a wider movement, not least because the prevailing discourse has so successfully obscured the fact that such effects even exist.

Reclaiming HOPE and Rejecting TINA

It is a complicated time to be an activist or scholar interested in retaining, much less expanding, access to public housing in the US. On the one hand, recent public housing reforms have been cloaked in a quasi-progressive discourse that is difficult to contest. 'Public housing is derelict', 'its tenants are massively unemployed', 'the life in the projects is hellish, dysfunctional, even apocalyptic' – these are all arguments that are difficult to contest, not least because they were largely derived from progressive activist positions on the state of public housing in the US virtually since its inception. By extension, it has become very difficult to contest the programmes, namely HOPE VI and QHWRA, that have ostensibly been established to address these problems after years of benign neglect. Yet in retrospect, it appears that all of these arguments were simply co-opted by a neoliberal right bent on destroying entitlement programmes including (perhaps especially) ones such as public housing. Most tenants 'saved' by HOPE VI and 'reformed' by QHWRA must now navigate the private housing market with Section 8 vouchers that the federal government is already talking about reducing.[57] Despite the 'offer' to train public housing tenants for meaningful work, the most significant effort by the government is a series of demeaning and unevenly applied work requirements for public housing tenants. Promises of work training, new housing units and a better life now seem like a distant, naïve memory for many public housing tenants and their advocates. I think that it is not hyperbolic to say that public housing policy during the past 15 years has represented little more than a punitive, almost vengeful, disciplining of labour by the state. I say this not because I believe that individual housing managers, or even national policymakers, are particularly vengeful people, but because the individual shifts seen in public housing policy can be seen as part of a neoliberalisation of state-managed social reproduction.

Contesting this is very challenging, but any strategy must revolve around a rejection of neoliberalism's ostensible inevitability, and quasi-progressive packaging. In this case, and many others, reformist housing programmes are situated either as something that cannot be avoided – something that Peter Marcuse calls the TINA ('there is no alternative') syndrome[58] – or as a progressive response to a problem that the left has been agitating against. The former needs to be rejected outright, and the latter needs to be more critically assessed by activist scholars, who can often help shape or justify public opinion by writing positively or ambivalently about such policies. In any case, there needs to be a challenge from scholars, activists and tenants. This challenge can and should happen on many levels – from books such as this, to the classroom, but most importantly from tenant groups who are directly affected by such programmes.

Further Reading

Manzo, L.C., R.G. Kleit and D. Couch (2008) '"Moving Three Times Is Like Having Your House on Fire Once": The Experience of Place and Impending Displacement among Public Housing Residents', *Urban Studies* 45(9): 1855–78.

Popkin, S.J., M.K. Cunningham and M. Burt (2005) 'Public Housing Transformation and the Hard to House', *Housing Policy Debate* 16(1): 1–24.

Schwartz, A. (2006) *Housing Policy in the United States* (New York: Routledge).

Vale, L. (2000) *From the Puritans to the Projects: Public Housing and Public Neighbors* (Cambridge, MA: Harvard University Press).

Wallace, L. (2008) 'First Came Katrina, Then Came HUD: Activists Battle to Save New Orleans Public Housing', *In These Times*, 16 January <http://www.inthesetimes.com/article/3504/first_came_katrina_then_came_hud/>.

Notes

1. American Housing Survey, 2005; this figure does include 11.66 million vacant units, but does not include the 3.85 million seasonal housing units that are not occupied for much of the year.
2. See, among others, Hackworth, J. and E. Wyly (2003) 'Social Polarization and the Politics of Low Income Mortgage Lending in the United States', *Geografiska Annaler* 85(3).
3. The vast majority of benefits of this programme have always gone to the wealthiest Americans whose mortgage interest payments are high enough to exceed the standardised deduction given to every tax-paying US citizen. The figure of $76 billion was from the year 2006.
4. This assistance includes mortgage insurance.
5. Schwartz, A. (2005) *Housing Policy in the US: An Introduction* (New York: Routledge).
6. Marcuse, Peter (1998) 'Mainstreaming Public Housing: A Proposal to a Comprehensive Approach to Housing Policy', in D. Varady, D.W. Preiser and F. Russell (eds) *New Directions in Urban Public Housing* (New Brunswick, NJ: Center for Urban Policy Research Press), pp. 23–44; Bratt, Rachel (1986) 'Public housing: The Controversy and Contribution', in R. Bratt, C. Hartman and A. Meyerson (eds)

Critical Perspectives on Housing (Philadelphia, PA: Temple University Press), pp. 335–61; Harloe, M. (1995) *The People's Home: Social Rented Housing in Europe and America* (London: Blackwell).

7. Marcuse, 'Mainstreaming Public Housing'.
8. Bratt, 'Public Housing: The Controversy'.
9. Marcuse, 'Mainstreaming Public Housing'; Bratt, 'Public Housing: The Controversy'.
10. Harloe, *The People's Home*.
11. Marcuse, 'Mainstreaming Public Housing'.
12. Ibid.
13. Checkoway, B. (2008) 'Large Builders, Federal Housing Programmes and Postwar Suburbanization', *International Journal of Urban and Regional Research* 4.
14. Bratt, 'Public Housing: The Controversy'.
15. Ibid.
16. Bristol, K.G. (1991) 'The Pruitt-Igoe Myth', *Journal of Architectural Education* 44; Bratt, R. (1990) 'Public Housing: Introduction', in W. van Vliet and J van Weesep (eds) *Government and Housing: Developments in Seven Countries* (Newbury Park, CA: Sage), pp. 115–22.
17. Kolodny, R. (1979) *Exploring New Strategies for Improving Public Housing Management* (Washington, DC: Government Printing Office).
18. Harloe, *The People's Home*.
19. Bratt, 'Public Housing: Introduction'.
20. Feldman, M. and R. Florida (1990) 'Economic Restructuring and the Changing Role of the State in US housing', in van Vliet and van Weesep, *Government and Housing*, pp. 31–46.
21. Lilley, W. (1980) 'The Homebuilders' Lobby', in J. Pynoos, R. Schafer and C.W. Hartman (eds) *Housing in Urban America* (New York: Aldine), pp. 32–50.
22. Bratt, 'Public Housing: The Controversy'.
23. Peck and Tickell were the first to use the language of 'roll-back' and 'roll-out' neoliberalism. Roll-back neoliberalism refers to efforts to destroy Keynesian interventions from the past; roll-out neoliberalism refers to subsequent efforts to initiate programmes that will reproduce a neoliberal order in the future. See Peck, J. and A. Tickell (2002) 'Neoliberalizing Space', *Antipode* 34.
24. Bratt, R. and W. Keating (1993) 'Federal Housing Policy and HUD: Past Problems and Future Prospects of a Beleaguered Bureaucracy', *Urban Affairs Quarterly* 29(1).
25. The bargain is worth it for individuals with a high tax liability because they can use the credits to exempt themselves from paying

taxes. For example, an individual might buy $1 of tax credit for 60 cents, thus effectively giving themselves a 40 per cent reduction in tax.

26. US Department of HUD (1995) 'Quality Housing and Work Reform Act Background Material' <http://www.hud.gov> [accessed July 2003].

27. Bratt, 'Public Housing: Introduction'.

28. Silver, H. (1990) 'Privatization Self-help and Public Housing Homeownership in the United States', in van Vliet and van Weesep, *Government and Housing*, pp. 123–40.

29. US Department of HUD, 'Quality Housing and Work Reform Act'.

30. Vale, L. (2000) *From the Puritans to the Projects: Public Housing and Public Neighbors* (Cambridge, MA: Harvard University Press).

31. Marcuse, 'Mainstreaming Public Housing'.

32. US Department of HUD, 'Quality Housing and Work Reform Act'.

33. Popkin, S. (2003) 'Testimony to US House of Representatives', Committee on Financial Services, 29 April.

34. Popkin, Susan, Diane Levy, Laura Harris, Jennifer Comey, Mary Cunningham and Larry Buron (2004) 'The HOPE VI Program: What about the Residents?', *Housing Policy Debate* 15(2).

35. Cunningham, M. (2004) 'An Improved Living Environment? Relocation Outcomes for HOPE VI Relocatees', September, Urban Institute website <http://www.urban.org/UploadedPDF/311058_Roof_2.pdf>.

36. US Department of HUD, 'Quality Housing and Work Reform Act'.

37. Chen, D. (2004) 'In Public Housing, it's Work, Volunteer, or Leave', *New York Times*, 15 April.

38. National Housing Law Project (n.d.) Unpublished memorandum <http://www.nhlp.org/html/pubhsg/onestrike.htm> [accessed 17 March 2000].

39. US Department of HUD, 'Quality Housing and Work Reform Act'.

40. For a critical description of this process, see Keating, L. (2000) 'Redeveloping Public Housing: Relearning Urban Renewal's Immutable Lessons', *Journal of the American Planning Association* 66.

41. Robinson, A. (2001) 'Confrontation and Lawsuit Fuel Debate on Housing Plan', *South Florida Community Development Coalition Newsletter* <http://www.floridacdc.org>.

42. Hartung, J. and J. Henig (1997) 'Housing Vouchers and Certificates as a Vehicle for Deconcentrating the Poor: Evidence from the Washington DC Metropolitan Area', *Urban Affairs Review* 323.

43. Fischer, P. (n.d.) 'Section 8 and the Public Housing Revolution: Where Will the Families Go?' <http://www.metroplanning.org/resources/101intro.asp>.

44. Hartung and Henig, 'Housing Vouchers and Certificates'.

45. This is not to deny the significance of activist litigation that was very much in line with the goals of HOPE VI in the early 1990s. Inequitable demolition plans in at least 13 US cities were the ironic result of settlements to well-intended lawsuits filed on behalf of tenants to deconcentrate urban poverty by demolishing public housing complexes. But as the implementation details of these settlements became clearer in the mid-1990s, the overwhelming emphasis of tenant litigation has been directed against the HOPE VI programme and its methods.

46. Housing Research Foundation, 'HOPE VI Press Clippings'; Robinson, 'Confrontation and Lawsuit'.

47. Housing Research Foundation, 'HOPE VI Press Clippings'.

48. Ibid.

49. DeVault, J. (2001) 'HOPE VI Suit Names Kelly', *The Common Denominator* <http://www.thecommondenominator.com>.

50. Bush, J. (1999) 'Prickly Holly: Activists Charge Conflict of Interest in the Most Expensive Housing Project in Seattle's History,' *Seattle Weekly* 11–17 March <http://www.seattleweekly.com>.

51. Baca, F. (n.d.) Unpublished memorandum <http://www.hud.gov>.

52. Newman, O. (1995) 'Defensible Space: A New Physical Planning Tool for Urban Revitalization', *Journal of the American Planning Association*, Spring; Newman, O. (1972) *Defensible Space* (New York: The Macmillan Company); Jacobs, J. (1961) *The Death and Life of Great American Cities* (London: Peregrine).

53. See, for examples, Coleman, A. (1985) *Utopia on Trial: Vision and Reality in Planned Housing* (London: Hillary Shipman); Schnee, D. (1998) 'An Evaluation of Robert Pitts Plaza: A Post Occupancy Evaluation of New Public Housing in San Francisco', in D. Varady, D. Preiser and F. Russell (eds) *New Directions in Urban Public Housing* (New Brunswick, NJ: Center for Urban Policy Research Press), pp. 104–18; Varady, D. and W. Preiser (2001) 'Scattered-site Public Housing and Housing Satisfaction: Implications for the New Public Housing Program', *Journal of the American Planning Association* 64.

54. Marcuse, 'Mainstreaming Public Housing'; Stockyard, J. (1998) 'Epilogue: Public Housing – The Next Sixty Years?', in Varady et al., *New Directions in Urban Public Housing*, pp. 237–64; Bristol, 'The Pruitt-Igoe myth'.

55. Cisneros, H. (1995) 'The Public Interest the Greater Good: How Government should Work', *Journal of Housing and Community Development* March/April; Cisneros, H. (1995) 'Defensible Space: Deterring Crime and Building Community' (Washington, DC: US Government Printing Office).
56. Housing Research Foundation, 'Press Clippings'.
57. Chen, D. (2004) 'US Seeks Cuts in Housing Aid to Urban Poor', *New York Times*, 22 September.
58. Marcuse, P. and R. van Kempen (2000) 'Conclusion: A Changed Spatial Order', in P. Marcuse and R. van Kempen (eds) *Globalizing Cities: A New Spatial Order?* (Oxford: Blackwell), pp. 249–75.

11

POLITICAL MARGINALISATION, MISGUIDED NATIONALISM AND THE DESTRUCTION OF CANADA'S SOCIAL HOUSING SYSTEMS

Jason Hackworth

Framing the Canadian Social Sector

> ... the distinctiveness of Canadian cities continues – Canadian cities are more public in their nature and US ones are more private ... The public city is more attuned to Canadian values, ideologies, and practices.
>
> K. England and J. Mercer, 2006[1]

It may seem curious to begin a discussion of Canadian social housing with a quote about the differences between US and Canadian urbanisation, but the quote is emblematic of perhaps the most prevalent theme within studies of the Canadian social sector: juxtaposition of the ostensibly socially democratic Canada against the neoliberal US.[2] To some extent, the juxtaposition is justified. Political culture in Canada is less openly hostile to government-based welfare in general, and public housing in particular, than in the US, and for much of the twentieth century Canada has had a higher rate of government-subsidised housing than its southern neighbour. But as the Canadian social sector has continued to fall victim to neoliberalism over the past two decades, the juxtaposition with the US is rapidly becoming empirically debatable, and politically regressive. Empirically, the emphasis on divergence between the social sectors masks or confuses the incredible deterioration of Canada's once-formidable social housing system, not to mention the attendant problems of rising homelessness and housing deterioration that are beginning to rival rates in the US.[3] Politically, the perception that the social housing system is 'at least not as bad as the US', and/or that the government (at any level) will automatically intervene in the near-future to 'solve' the crisis, softens activism and distracts from the brutal reality facing an increasing number of impoverished Canadian families (regardless of how many there are, relative to the US, or in absolute terms). This chapter will attempt to provide a more sober antidote to this trend within the Canadian social sector, and to highlight the efforts of one radical group – the Ontario Coalition Against Poverty – that has emerged as the most hopeful source of change in this environment.

Before beginning this story, though, it might be useful to provide a few background details on social housing in Canada. First, it is somewhat misleading to speak of the 'Canadian social housing system' *per se* because, to a large extent, none exists. In a mid-1990s desire to devolve responsibility to provincial governments, the Liberal federal government 'downloaded social housing to the provinces'.[4] This immediately triggered or intensified (depending on the location) the social housing crisis across the country as provinces scrambled to figure out how to pay for, and manage, the stock that had been given to them from above. Each province established a slightly different management and funding style but with one underlying commonality: reduced federal support for social housing. The focus of this chapter will be on Ontario, Canada's largest province and the one with arguably the most neoliberalised social housing system. When the aforementioned downloading occurred, Ontario was governed by Mike Harris, a self-described economic conservative (North American code for 'neoliberal'), who immediately followed the federal announcement with one of his own: to get the province 'out of the housing business'. His solution was to download the system even further, to municipalities who have very limited abilities to raise revenues. The resulting system is diffusely and incompetently managed, under-funded and reliant on the private sector. And most of these features are the result of neoliberal policy shifts that have occurred over the past 15 years.

A Brief History of the Canadian Social Housing System

While social housing enjoys more public support in Canada than in the US, the Canadian (and Ontarian) sector is numerically and politically marginal by almost any other international comparison. Of the roughly 4.2 million housing units in Ontario, 267,888, or 6.3 per cent are 'social' in the sense that they are physical units either originally or currently receiving direct subsidy from a governmental source.[5] The provincial rate is roughly equal to the 6 per cent rate for Canada as a whole, but belies the variation within Ontario itself.[6] Large cities, with expensive land, have greater percentages of social housing, while rural areas have lower rates. Toronto, for example, has a social housing rate of roughly 10.1 per cent while some rural areas in the province have rates in the 1–2 per cent range.[7] Among other things, these statistics demonstrate the level of political marginalisation *vis-à-vis* other countries: that is, Canadian social housing is less marginalised politically than the same sector in the US, but does not experience the level of support seen in Germany, France, the Netherlands, Scandinavia, or even Britain. In general, this has meant that it is more vulnerable to broad ideological interventions by government than social housing in other countries, or even other, more broadly supported sectors within Canada, such as the health system.

Putting aside efforts to house workers during the First World War and various piecemeal investments in local charitable organisations, Canada's formal experience in social housing dates back to the Dominion Housing Act of 1935. The overwhelming emphasis of the Dominion Act, however, was to provide subsidies for middle-class homeowners who were hit by the Great Depression, rather than lower-income rental tenants. This emphasis continued through the formation of the country's first major, comprehensive housing act, the 1946 National Housing Act (NHA) (see Figure 11.1).

The NHA was broad in purpose, establishing the institutions for housing administration at the federal level, but it did not create a 'social housing system' *per se*. It was not until a series of amendments to the NHA in 1949 that a formal public housing

Figure 11.1   Regent Park, Toronto – Canada's oldest and largest social housing project, begun in 1947. This picture was taken in 2004, before the start of the current redevelopment (*photo: Erik Twight*).

programme was created.[8] Unit production was low (about 850 units per year), but the experience set the institutional stage for the expansion of the sector in late 1960s. Initially, the sector enjoyed relatively wide public support as a way to ameliorate slum conditions and to control housing costs more generally. The public antipathy towards privately produced slums such as those in the near east end of Toronto was greater than any fear of socialised housing, so initial efforts to build iconic developments, such as the city's infamous Regent Park development,[9] were comparatively uncontroversial. But, as the sector began to expand in the late 1960s, so did public antipathy. As was the case throughout the world, Canadian social housing – almost regardless of its form, design, location and tenantry – became acutely stigmatised, and, by the early 1970s, pressure began to mount to modify the way that it was financed, built and managed. Out of this negative political energy grew a fairly progressive social housing form: co-operative housing. Though the buildings themselves are technically owned by the government – and thus not 'co-operatives' in a pure philosophical sense – they were managed locally and tend to be rather well-functioning communities. Co-op housing was initiated with the 1973 NHA amendments and became an increasingly common form of social housing for the next two decades. The co-operative model differed from traditional social housing in that it aimed for local tenant management, mixed incomes, and integration with the surrounding community. The sector was (and still is) seen by housing academics and activists as a success story, but public sentiment generally did not differentiate co-operatives from traditional public housing complexes and the entire social housing sector became even more politically marginalised during the 1970s and 1980s.

In addition to federal schemes, provinces and some cities developed their own social housing systems, starting in the 1960s, but they too struggled to withstand the political barrage against the philosophy of subsidised housing. By the early 1990s, the social housing system in Canada was regionally and insti-tutionally fragmented, consisting of four basic portfolios and multiple origins.[10] First, there was traditional public housing, which composed about a third of the social housing stock, and consisted of units built and, until 1993, owned and managed by the federal government. Secondly, there was co-operative housing – arguably the most successful portfolio in the housing stock – that was derived from changes to housing laws in the 1970s allowing more residential autonomy in non-market housing. Thirdly, there was private non-profit (PNP) housing, which was usually managed by a church, community group, or other non-governmental organisation (NGO), but which was funded almost entirely by provincial outlays. Finally, there was municipal non-profit (MNP) housing, consisting of units built with federal, provincial, or municipal money but managed by either a non-profit corporation owned by a city, or by a special administrative wing of municipal government. Despite the variation in success, management style, and cost of these portfolios, each has suffered marginalisation under the prevailing anti-social housing ethos of the past 30 years, particularly the last 15.

The election of a Liberal federal government in 1993 held great promise for activists in Ontario and beyond, who were worried about the continued rightward slide away from the social housing sector in the 1980s. But the Liberal government immediately established itself as one that was not sympathetic to this form of social redistribution, or just about any other for that matter. Deficit-obsessed Finance Minister Paul Martin immediately downloaded responsibility for social housing[11] to the provinces and removed almost all of the subsidies that had previously accompanied federal responsibility. Given that the federal government was the primary financier of social housing across the country, provinces were left in a serious political and fiscal bind by the announcement, with little room to manoeuvre.

In 1995, upon the election of Fraser Institute fellow Mike Harris, Ontario began privatising its social housing. Harris portrayed this as the 'Common-sense Revolution',[12] declared his intention to 'get Ontario out of the housing business', and immediately set about implementing this agenda.[13] Not only were subsidies cut for an estimated 17,000 planned new, affordable, housing units, but efforts to deregulate the private housing sector were pursued, primarily through reducing local land-development controls. The Harris government also began negotiations with cities about what to do with the existing stock of social housing in the province. The provincial government successfully angled to have responsibility for social housing be as diffuse and privately oriented as possible. These negotiations finally resulted in the Social Housing Reform Act (SHRA) in 2000. The SHRA downloaded responsibility for social housing to 47 'service managers' – provincially appointed local bureaucrats who would be responsible for regulating the portfolios in their region.[14] On-the-ground housing providers (municipal and private non-profits) were explicitly and implicitly encouraged to become more entrepreneurial, to ally more closely with the private building market, and to get used to working with their local service manager rather than a centralised authority.[15] If Harris' initial cuts represented the 'roll-back' of the previous order, the SHRA surely marked the 'roll-out' of a set of institutions that would reproduce neoliberalism in the sector long after the Harris government's exit.

Housing activists immediately decried both the cutbacks and the SHRA, as fundamentally antagonistic to the very idea of social housing.[16] But it was not until 2003 that voters in Ontario began *en masse* to agree enough with this sentiment (or with resentment against the parallel 'common-sense' reforms put forth in other sectors) to elect a non-Conservative provincial government. In October 2003, voters overwhelmingly elected Dalton McGuinty's Liberals in what was widely seen as a rejection of Harris' (and his successor Ernie Eves') 'Common-sense Revolution'. However, McGuinty has not fundamentally changed any of the structures put in place by the Harris-Eves social housing project. He ran on a promise of building 20,000 new, affordable, housing units, but as of 2008, only 8 per cent of this total had been generated or planned.[17] Moreover, social housing, as a political issue, has taken a back seat to health care, economic development, and federal-provincial funding relationships. In fact, some argue that McGuinty's disinclination to act definitively on this election promise, while at the same time giving ostensible support for social housing in general, has actually exacerbated the situation compared to the Harris-Eves regime. Much of this argument is rooted in frustration with recent inaction by the provincial government over utilising federal funds recently allocated to build social housing in the province.

The origin of these funds goes back to the autumn of 2005, when the federal New Democratic Party[18] negotiated a Canada-Ontario agreement that would send $2.2 billion to the province for social housing, in exchange for not allowing the Martin Liberal federal government to be toppled by a vote of no confidence. The Martin government eventually did fall, but Harper's Conservatives, elected in January 2006, promised to uphold the commitments made in the agreement. Thus far, $392 million has been allocated to Ontario by the federal government, but the province argues that this is $1 billion short of the agreement that was struck originally and is refusing to commit the funds received to social housing. Activists have decried the move as a cynical ploy by the McGuinty government to exploit a division between the provincial and federal government, while at least 122,000 households remain on provincial waiting lists for housing. Some providers and activists worry whether *any* funds will be forthcoming, as the province contemplates using the existing funds for other pressing issues that the federal government has neglected, such as health care and the environment.[19]

All of this might easily lead one to believe that there should be an uproar in the housing activist community. But activists, many of whom distinctly remember the brazen, unapologetically anti-social housing Tory government that ruled for nearly ten years, are caught in a political quandary. Because the Liberals are not openly hostile to social housing, and have actually made soft promises to improve the situation, they have generally refrained from unleashing their efforts on the current government. As the *Toronto Star* recently noted:

> ...because the [provincial] government has been seen as housing-friendly overall, advocates had held back so far on publicly embarrassing the Liberals over being nowhere near their election promise of creating 20,000 units of affordable housing.[20]

It has been over five years since the McGuinty Liberals were ushered into office with an electoral rejection of the Harris-Eves 'common-sense' project of social cutbacks and deregulation, but thus far little has changed at the structural level. Social housing providers, residents and those on provincial waiting lists are in a dire situation. Harris forced every social housing provider to behave like a business, and McGuinty has quietly acquiesced to the model. The big providers, such as Toronto Community Housing Corporation, are eking out an existence by selling land, letting out commercial space, and increasing their proportion of middle-class tenants who can be charged regular market rents, but most providers are struggling to cover their operating costs; and many rural social housing providers, who do not have the benefit of recently inflated land values, are worried about their basic survival in the coming years. The current system is unsustainable for them, and highly inadequate for everyone else.

For tenants, and potential tenants, the situation and its implications are even worse. Waiting lists have grown, along with the holes in the province's once-impressive social safety net. The provincial list now exceeds 122,000 families – over 60,000 of whom are waiting in Toronto alone.[21] Social housing is the lowest point in the formal housing provision for many families. The 'fall-back' options for these families are tenuous and inhumane – couch-surfing with friends or relatives, navigating the rooming-house world, enduring the emergency shelter system, or surviving the streets.

As activists struggle to work within the lesser-of-two-evils context of the liberal provincial government, housing managers and tenants are figuratively (and sometimes literally) struggling for their very survival. For the last two years, I have been conducting interviews with social housing managers throughout the province to gauge how they are coping with the demands of operating within such an anti-social-housing context. I've asked them how they are sustaining their current portfolios and whether they are able to expand upon them. The overwhelming majority of managers have conveyed to me a sense of desperation about the current situation. The 'successful' urban ones who own expensive real estate have been able to sell land, rent out commercial space, and attract more market-rate tenants, but only rarely have they been able to build more housing. It is hard to characterise this as a 'success' unless you do not want social housing to exist. The less fortunate ones – primarily, though not exclusively, located in rural areas of the province – are worried about their very survival in the coming years, as they struggle to manage more vulnerable populations with less financial support from the province.

What follows is a selective summary of the management environment in municipal non-profit housing as told by housing managers in a post-SHRA atmosphere. The prevailing finding amongst nearly all of the respondents was that while social housing has indeed been notionally placed more prominently and sympathetically in the public realm, virtually nothing has been done to roll back even the most punitive 'reforms' of the Harris-Eves period. The net effect has been a quieting (not a silencing) of dissent (compared to the Harris-Eves period) regarding social housing, as activists and providers cling to the hope emanating from a government that is not overtly hostile to the project of social housing. Obliterated by the effort to position for potential housing dollars is any serious consideration of rolling back the most obviously ineffective, punitive, or expensive of the reforms enacted. Agitating for the latter is viewed as politically foolish because it might jeopardise potential housing funds. In effect, then, the current Liberal government, which is ostensibly more sympathetic to social housing, is able to operate very similarly to the openly hostile (to social housing) Conservative governments, but without the dissent from housing activists. The 'common-sense' revolt against social housing under the Conservatives began as a brazen political assault, but has become an institutionalised way of life under the Liberals.

As mentioned earlier, the primary vehicle for codifying the Harris-Eves neoliberal order in social housing is the Social Housing Reform Act – a complicated, 184-page document that spells out the relationship between local providers and formal government in the province. The tone of the Act is fittingly technical, but the impetus was markedly political, and its effects on the sector have been pronounced. The overall effect has been to create pressures that force local providers to behave more like for-profit organisations. As one representative from a medium-sized MNP aptly summarised:

> Social housing providers are having to become more market-oriented. Under the old programme, there was less pressure for providers to increase market rents ... New benchmarks will mean that providers need to be more attentive to the market-place so that they don't place the corporation at financial risk/difficulty. It will be necessary that non-profit providers take the same market rent increases as [other for-profits providers] in the market-place.

The sentiment primarily reflects the changed ethos within the sector, but many MNPs (even those with officials sympathetic to SHRA) argue that the SHRA is illusory, and that it does not actually allow for a serious increase in entrepreneurialism or independence by providers. The narrow path of entrepreneurialism on which providers can trek ensures that they have little possibility of actually succeeding as independent quasi-private entities.

The Act also institutionalised a much more diffusely organised system than had existed in the past. Instead of one provincial agency responsible for all social housing matters, local providers must now deal with a local 'service provider' – there are 47 in the province. The ostensible goals of this diffusion were to make social housing less 'top down' and more entrepreneurial, and to enhance local autonomy, but most of the non-profits in my sample complain that the only 'autonomy' that has been downloaded to them has been in the form of responsibility – for more vulnerable populations; for expenses previously covered by the province – without any serious downloading of authority (to raise funds of their own, for example). As an official from a small MNP noted:

> SHRA has affected new development by placing costs for new development on municipal tax payers who are least able to afford social programmes. I feel that downloading/SHRA is a political statement in line with the Harris government. I don't feel the SHRA was set up to encourage increased local delivery, innovation, or to create a new relationship with the private market, but instead was set up to put the costs of social housing at the local level. This choice was made because local government is understood to be more cost-conscious, more hands-on, and having less money to waste. As a result, social programmes are hurt by devolution particularly in less affluent municipalities.

The Act clearly has generated scepticism at the delivery level about its true political intentions and fiscal implications, but it has also frustrated local officials, who argue that the current system is beset (perhaps by design) with inefficiencies and in some cases near-incompetence by provincial service managers. Where before, one provincial official (and their in-house legal staff) could handle inquiries from local providers about everything from eviction policy and waiting list procedures, to financing new construction, now 47 offices exist to deal with matters of this sort. As one official described it:

> Overall, SHRA has created 47 service managers who are struggling to learn how to develop/administer social housing. Movement from six regional offices to 47 offices makes portfolio management more expensive and challenging.

Another official at a small MNP concurred with this sentiment:

> The Act resulted in a huge learning curve in the rules that must be followed and this has taken a couple of years for service deliverers/administrators/tenants to understand what to do, how to do it, and why it must be done.

In essence, the current system does not lend itself to the accumulation or sharing of knowledge, but rather is more fragmented, uneven, and prone to turnover. Much of this is the result of the planned diffusion of the social housing system in the province, but it would be a mistake to assume that the system is composed of 47 equally talented, dedicated, pro-social housing service managers who will simply need a few years to learn the details of SHRA. There are, of course, huge differences in ability, experience and political affiliation of service managers, not to mention the nature of their clientele from place to place. Some have suggested that this feature of the system is deliberate. As an official from one medium-sized MNP noted:

> Downloading has made it easier for those who dislike social housing to complicate and negatively affect social housing administration. For example, a municipal politician has more ability to put a 'cap' on or prevent the development of new social housing.

Overall, the majority of my respondents indicated that whatever its original intention, the current SHRA-mandated system is confusing, legally contradictory and rarely conducive to an actual increase in autonomy. But while the cumbersome operational infrastructure created by the SHRA is a source of frustration for many providers, the looming omnipresence of the funding cutbacks that accompanied these changes is the greatest single source of worry for local providers. By far the most dominant theme of this survey was the very basic notion of fiscal cutbacks initiated by the initial neoliberal restructuring under Harris-Eves, and continued to the present day. Officials at virtually every MNP contacted for this project noted that their operating expenses were perilously close to breaching their operating income, and that the prospect of new social housing was not even on the table in most cases. Some MNPs, particularly smaller rural ones in the northern part of the province, even suggested that this breaching had already taken place, that their budgets were unsustainable, and that they were worried about their future as a provider.

The centrality of the austerity sentiment is hardly surprising given that Harris declared immediately that it was his intention to 'get Ontario out of the housing business', but the ways in which this austerity has been implemented are not as obvious. Though most officials complained of the basic reduction in finances from the province (either in the form of direct operating grants or RGI[22] supplement decreases), many others also noted that the most damaging cutbacks were more subtle – legal changes that require MNPs to take on more vulnerable populations without the requisite funds to care for them; inadequate increases in the inflation index that determines the level of funding that the province will provide for things such as utility expenses, and tax schemes that drain up to half of what even the most entrepreneurial MNPs can acquire through internal fund-raising efforts. For example, one provider in southern Ontario complained that the 'benchmarking' process had not been updated for a decade, thus effectively reducing the level of funding from the province in real dollars, and increasing their local exposure to swings in operating expenses. They lamented that

> The current funding model uses the 1995 operating expenses as a benchmark and applies a yearly inflationary factor to the 1995 amounts. The operating subsidies given to MNPs are based on this amount. However, although the province inflates these amounts by a certain percentage each year, the inflationary factor does not reflect [falls short of] the real increased costs in operating expenses.

The result is a basic reduction in funds that could be used for managing or even expanding their housing stock. To make fiscal matters worse, the SHRA mandates that MNPs take on more vulnerable populations without a concomitant increase in funding. As one exasperated official from a medium-sized MNP noted:

> Now MNPs house more vulnerable populations since they are given priority. However, these individuals do not receive any supportive resources and tend to have a high turnover rate. This increases the expenses for MNPs that house these individuals, especially given the short-term nature of their stay.

This subtle reduction of subsidy through benchmarking, combined with the subtle increase in expense through a mandated expansion of clientele, were worse, some officials argued, than the obvious reduction of subsidy that accompanied the original push by Harris to 'get out of the housing business'. The latter (cuts by Harris) were clearly framed as overt political moves to reduce the size of the sector, while the former (SHRA benchmark and population changes) are more often framed (unfairly) as technical budget matters that local MNPs are expected to solve – the implication being that those who cannot solve them are suffering from a lack of budgetary expertise, rather than a lack of funds. Many officials were willing to go along with the concept of local responsibility if there were meaningful opportunities for raising funds locally, but SHRA rules severely restrict this as well. In the rare instance that MNPs are able to find a way to raise funds locally within the system (for example, parking fees, laundry room, commercial space rents, and so on), they are required to turn over half their takings to the Social Housing Services Corporation (an entity established during the Harris-Eves years). The SHSC demands this money in return for a vague promise – 'replacement reserves' – to build a fund to help service and even build new housing for the future. As one frustrated official put it:

> Our organisation does not have autonomy over investment. We are making less money now with replacement reserves[23] than before the SHRA and SHSC. We are mandated to invest money through the SHSC, whereas before MNPs could invest wherever.

An official from a different MNP added:

> SHRA legislates that municipal non-profits cannot encumber the property without approval from the province, and the requirement of ministerial consent makes it difficult to do this. For example, if we have a property worth $10 million and only owe $2 million, we cannot finance a new building with equity out of the old building nor can we sell the current property and apply the $2 million toward new development. Private developers often leverage equity for new development; however, if an MNP has equity on an existing property, they cannot leverage this equity to place on a second mortgage.

These changes and others function as a form of shadow austerity that are presented to individual MNPs as technical matters for them to solve locally. They highlight the notion that cutbacks come in more subtle forms than the simple withdrawal of funding (to be sure, they come in that form as well), and also the fact that the McGuinty government has not shown any interest (or ability) in rolling back such subtle measures despite their importance to individual providers. Instead, the current government has left the SHRA and all of the measures that reproduce a neoliberal future virtually unscathed.

Fighting the Neoliberalisation of Canadian Social Housing

Ontario's social housing system – the largest in the country – has been fundamentally broken by neoliberalism. In place of a centralised administration that could bring economies of scale and accumulated competence, it is now organised around 47 service areas whose administrators have less understanding of the housing sector. In place of a continuous stream of funding 'from above', it is now incumbent upon social housing providers to develop new funding streams of their own. In place of a social safety net, the system now resembles a social safety lottery – for those who win, a relatively secure, relatively inexpensive form of housing awaits; those who do not win can look forward to an increasingly precarious existence in the private housing market.

Very few serious housing academics (or housing administrators) in Ontario would dispute these conclusions, yet the overwhelming trend in academic literature on the social sector is to minimise these realities by juxtaposing them with the realities of low-income housing in the US. Though I think it will take much more than a few academics deciding to come to terms with the brutal reality of social housing in the country to slow the creep of neoliberalism in the sector, it is counterproductive in a policy sense to continue promulgating the distracting view that 'at least it's not as bad as the US'. This view is increasingly empirically inaccurate, and is politically counterproductive to confronting and fighting neoliberalism as it exists in Canada.

Though academics are not irrelevant, their role in fighting neoliberalism is not nearly as important as activists and tenants in the social housing system. In Ontario, many officially recognised tenant boards exist to represent the tenants in an instrumental sense, but they have little power to contest decrees from above. When the province or federal government decides to demolish a housing complex such as Toronto's Regent Park, the expected role of tenants is to help with the details – the decision to demolish is not on the table. Serious resistance must be grass-roots, tenant-focused and organised, and it cannot be an instrumental extension of the local housing agency if it is to be fully effective at shifting the tide. One of the most interesting and direct groups aiming to provide a more militant vehicle for low-income people (both inside and out of social housing) is the Ontario Coalition Against Poverty (OCAP). I would like to end this chapter by briefly focusing on their strategy and positioning them as a viable way to fight neoliberalism.

The Ontario Coalition Against Poverty dates back to the late 1980s.[24] Their initial focus was on raising the unliveable welfare rates then being put in place by the Liberal provincial government. During the 1990s, they emerged as the most militant and active organisation in Ontario, fighting poverty, the neoliberalisation of welfare and the destruction of affordable housing. Their approach from the start has been direct, confrontational and controversial. They receive much of their funding from local unions and sympathetic individuals, but they are not beholden to their benefactors in strategy or purpose. The Canadian Autoworkers Union threatened in the late 1990s to pull their funding (which accounts for nearly a third of OCAP coffers) in criticism of tactics that include occupation of vacant buildings, vocal disruption of city council meetings, and marches that have been stopped by police violence (see Figures 11.2 and 11.3).

But while they are very controversial, and have engendered ambivalence amongst the centre-left Autoworkers, I would like to suggest that they offer a model that can be used to contest the spread of neoliberalism in housing policy in Ontario and the rest of Canada. First, they have oriented the debate around the brutality of welfare and housing policies, rather than entering into a contextual debate about how much worse it might be in other countries. Secondly, they have organised low-income people directly and have not stayed so focused on a particular set of policies as to lose sight of their *raison d'être*. In short, they are a coalition against *poverty* and have made that their focus. Thirdly, they are not blinkered by distracting arguments about

Figure 11.2   2004: OCAP on the march (*photo: John Bonnar*).

Figure 11.3   2003: OCAP at a protest squat (*photo: John Bonnar*).

improved design, and mixed income, that have split groups in the US and Canada who want to see social housing conditions improve. Fourthly, they have neither assumed that the state will automatically 'fix' the problem, nor have they let the state off the hook by falling into the neoliberal ethos of lower state intervention. They are not reliant on the support of one particular party and are willing to protest ostensibly left-leaning governments when they do not produce promised results.

Social housing did not organically develop in any country. It was the result of low-income people and their advocates fighting to show how the private market had failed. OCAP and organisations like it embody this spirit of highlighting injustice and advocating system change, rather than advocating soft reform and waiting for Canada's social democracy to solve the problem organically. If neoliberalism is going to be seriously contested in Canada, a strategy of confrontation rather than co-operation is surely the necessary condition.

Further Reading

Hulchanski, D. and M. Shapcott (eds) (2004) *Finding Room: Policy Options for a Canadian Rental Housing Strategy* (Toronto: University of Toronto Press).

Montgomery, B. (2002) *The Common (Non)sense Revolution: The Decline of Progress and Democracy in Ontario* (Creemore, ON: Mad River Publishing).

Skelton, I. (2006) 'Social Housing, Neighbourhood Revitalization and Community Economic Development', Canadian Centre for Policy Alternatives Report <https://www.policyalternatives.ca/Reports/2006/06/ReportsStudies1402/index.cfm?pa=6104ea04>.

Shapcott, M. (2008) 'Reverse the Housing Cuts: New Federal Affordable Housing Investment Required', Wellesley Institute Policy Statement <http://wellesleyinstitute.com/files/wifedpbc2008.pdf>.

Turner, S. (2007) 'Sustaining Ontario's Social Housing by Supporting Non-Profit Organizations', Ontario Social Housing Services Corporation Report <http://www.shscorp.ca/content/research/resources/DOCSCPRN_Sally_Turner_FinalReport.pdf>.

Notes

1. England, K. and J. Mercer (2006) 'Canadian Cities in Continental Context: Global and Continental Perspectives on Canadian Urban Development', in T. Bunting and P. Filion (eds) *Canadian Cities in Transition: Local Through Global Perspectives* (Toronto: Oxford University Press Canada), pp. 24–39.

2. Prominent academic examples include the aforementioned piece (built on a larger book) by England and Mercer (ibid.). A more popular example of this inclination is found in Adams, M. (2003) *Fire and Ice: The United States, Canada, and the Myth of Converging Values* (Toronto: Penguin).

3. In fact, Peressini and McDonald have argued that the rate of homelessness in Canada is actually *higher* than that in the US. Though this conclusion is debated by other authors and the data supporting a reliable estimate of homelessness in either country are shaky, their conclusion is at least persuasive enough to suggest that Canada does not occupy a moral or institutional 'high ground' when it comes to homelessness. (Peressini, T. and L. McDonald (2000) 'Urban Homelessness in Canada', in Bunting and Filion, *Canadian Cities in Transition*, pp. 525–43.)

4. The one exception to this pattern was 'on-reserve' housing for Native Canadians, which remained a federal programme.

5. Statistics here were derived from the Ontario Non Profit Housing Association website <http://www.onpha.ca>. These rates do not include subsidies for single-family private housing such as government-based mortgage insurance.

6. Doling, J. (1997) *Comparative Housing Policy: Government and Housing in Advanced Industrialized Countries* (New York: St Martin's Press).

7. Statistics here were derived from figures published on the city of Toronto website <http://www.toronto.ca>.

8. Hulchanski, J.D. (2004) 'How Did We Get Here? The Evolution of Canada's "Exclusionary" Housing System', in J.D. Hulchanski and M. Shapcott (eds) *Finding Room: Policy Options for a Canadian Rental Housing Strategy* (Toronto: University of Toronto Press), pp. 179–212.

9. Regent Park is a social housing complex located just east of downtown Toronto. It is Canada's oldest social housing development, and one of its largest. Its prominent location in Canada's most prominent city has made it a symbol, often a negative one, of the larger social housing system in the country. In 2005, a much-criticised effort to demolish and rebuild (a portion of) the complex commenced.

10. Smith, N. (1995) 'Challenges of Public Housing in the 1990s: The Case of Ontario, Canada', *Housing Policy Debate* 6; Sousa, J. and J. Quarter (2003) 'The Convergence of Nonequity Models in Canada: Changes to Housing Policy since 1990', *Housing Policy Debate* 14. These four sectors exclude on-reserve native housing which has experienced a very different history from other forms of social housing.

11. Bruce Porter makes the interesting point that Martin was warned in a confidential letter from the IMF against spending too much on social programmes in the mid-1990s – a warning that he and his ruling Liberal Party took very seriously by slashing all funding for public housing and significantly reducing it for other social programmes: Porter, B. (2003) 'The Right to Adequate Housing in Canada', in S. Leckie (ed.) *National Perspectives on Housing Rights* (New York: Martinus Nijhoff Publishers).

12. Keil, R. (2002) '"Common-sense" Neoliberalism: Progressive Conservative Urbanism in Toronto, Canada', *Antipode* 34.

13. Hackworth, J. (2005) 'Neoliberal Ideas and Social Housing Realities in Ontario', *Progressive Planning Magazine* 164.

14. Sousa and Quarter, 'The Convergence of Nonequity Models in Canada'.

15. Management of the co-op sector was also downloaded but individual developments thus far have not been very central to the SHRA

picture, and they continue to receive subsidies from municipalities and the province.

16. Shapcott, M. (2001) 'Made in Ontario Housing Crisis: Ontario Alternative Budget', Technical Paper #12 (Toronto: Canadian Centre for Policy Alternatives).

17. Goar, C. (2006) 'Province Starves Housing Sector', *Toronto Star*, 27 October.

18. The New Democratic Party (NDP) is a left-leaning democratic socialist party whose views are often quite similar to the left-wing of the Liberal Party (so pragmatic coalitions between the two parties are somewhat common).

19. Federal NDP leader Jack Layton – architect of the original agreement with the federal Liberals – has threatened to sue the provincial government in Ontario if the funds are used for non-housing purposes.

20. Gillespie, K. (2006) 'Plea for Housing Funds Unites Foes: Miller, Pitfield Rip Queen's Park, Feds Layton Says Legal Action may be Taken', *Toronto Star*, 27 October 27.

21. The best source for this information is the Ontario Non Profit Housing Association <http://www.onpha.org>.

22. RGI is an acronym that stands for 'rent geared to income'. It is a rental supplement cheque provided by the provincial government for families who qualify. Many social housing tenants receive an RGI supplement of some sort, and as such, social housing developments depend on this as a central source of subsidy.

23. Replacement reserves are capital accounts managed by the province to which individual MNPs are required to contribute. The idea – so far not materialised in a significant way – is to create a fund that will assist in developing more social housing in the province. Most MNPs – as this answer implies – find it to be a burden that does not specifically benefit their operations.

24. Information on the organisation can be garnered from their website <http://www.ocap.ca>.

Part III

The Way Forward: Strategy and Tactics

12

FIGHTING BACK: LESSONS FROM 100 YEARS OF HOUSING CAMPAIGNS

Sarah Glynn

Decent housing is a basic need: but that does not make it easy to fight for. Because it is so fundamental, campaigners are put under a lot of pressure not to do anything that may jeopardise the immediate situation of affected households. Nevertheless, there is an impressive history of housing struggle and some notable successes. This chapter will attempt to analyse some of those historic successes in the British context, drawing out the keys to, and the limits of, their achievements. It will then try to apply the lessons learnt to some current campaigns across a wider geography.

Just as new neoliberalism is an incarnation of old free-market capitalism, reviving past problems and attitudes, so past campaigns against some of the worst inherent injustices of that system can still have a lot to teach us. Of course, history never repeats itself exactly. Neoliberal globalisation has added new dimensions and new pressures, and we now have new tools in the form of the electronic media, but the idea that past history is not relevant today is another spin concocted by the Brave New neoliberal World.[1]

The Bigger Battle

Like other fights against the impacts of an economic system, housing campaigns are carried out at different levels; and they have had the greatest effect when these different levels have been combined. It is this combination that makes a movement – rather than isolated fights that can be picked off one by one. First, there is the everyday grass-roots work that helps ensure that existing legislation is complied with, that buildings are kept in decent repair, and that services are functioning. As well as bringing immediate benefits, this can also help to generate involvement and organisation and give campaigners confidence and credibility. Then there are single-issue-based campaigns, which might be fought against landlords – often over rent increases or poor conditions – or for legislative change. Besides what may be achieved around the immediate issue, these can develop new forms of organisation, involve new layers of people, and demonstrate the wider possibilities of fighting for change. Beyond this again are campaigns to change the underlying system, campaigns that apply a wider political analysis and build on the momentum – the mobilisation, organisation and impact – of more limited actions. Such systemic changes may only concern housing, but they may be linked to other issues and to the strengthening of involved political organisations. The broader linking of housing to other social issues can help force changes for housing itself – as with the introduction of state-subsidised housing following the First World War, which can be seen as a response to much wider political movements.

The risk of focusing on key moments, as histories tend to do, is that all the struggles in between may be forgotten. But it is these struggles that make the key moments possible, by building up organisation and knowledge, keeping alive the belief in a better alternative, and maintaining the pressure for change. Some did achieve their immediate objective, some resulted in a compromise, others in failure and disillusionment; but all are part of the bigger battle for decent housing, and many can still tell us something today. One message must be that the fight is never over. While each individual struggle may succeed in helping those immediately involved, any campaign for significant improvements in housing needs to be much bigger and sustained over a long period.

This was brought home to me when I was researching among the news clippings of Tower Hamlets library. I found reports that showed that the same mansion block, Grosvenor Buildings in Poplar, had rent strikes and protests in 1915, 1939 and 1963, before the London County Council was persuaded to serve a compulsory purchase order and redevelop the site under slum clearance in 1965. Another two cuttings show the Waterlow Estate in nearby Bethnal Green in 1962 and 1975. In the first, tenants are celebrating the local council's compulsory purchase of the building from its private owners after months of protests, including a refusal to pay a rent rise on the 'two-roomed, no-bath homes'. Thirteen years later, at the time of the second cutting, these tenants had been rehoused elsewhere and the buildings were boarded up awaiting demolition, when desperate squatters with no homes of their own were glad to break in and work hard to make them fit to live in again – if only temporarily.[2] The buildings were saved from the developers' ball and chain and are now smartly refurbished (complete with bathrooms); but with current sale prices (as of September 2008) of a quarter of a million pounds for a one-bedroom flat, these homes – originally built as semi-philanthropic model dwellings – are no longer of any benefit to those on low incomes.

Glasgow 1915

I want to begin by looking at the lessons of the rent strikes that took place on Clydeside, Glasgow in 1915, which played a part in the evolution of council housing outlined in Chapter 1. This story has been often told, but I will outline the main events. During the First World War, workers crowded into Glasgow to take up jobs in the munitions factories and the engineering and shipbuilding works. Housing was soon in short supply, and the landlords took advantage of the situation to raise the rents. This fell particularly harshly on the elderly and on the families of the soldiers and sailors who were away fighting. And if they could not pay, the factors (that is, the agents who manage rented housing in Scotland) were ready to evict them. The mounting anger at what was happening was organised through work-gate meetings and, crucially, through groups of women from the tenements, who rallied together to prevent evictions and protest their cause. Tenants went on rent strike, refusing to pay the increases, and they organised mass demonstrations. The government agreed to set up an inquiry, but the landlords, anticipating that they would be asked to compromise, got in first with notices of even bigger rent rises. Instead of more money, they got greater resistance from the tenants and strike threats from the munitions workers. When the landlords tried to force the issue by taking 18 tenants to the small debt court to get the rents deducted from their wages, a demonstration of thousands gathered outside the court-house, including all the men from five shipyards and an ordnance works. A deputation informed the sheriff that a decision in favour of the factors would result in a general strike, and the demonstrators telegraphed their resolve to the prime minister in London. The case was dropped, and eight days later, with a thousand men still on strike, the government brought forward a bill to freeze rents at pre-war levels.[3]

Putting the Campaign in Context

The events on the Clyde were the culmination of a wave of housing protests that had developed over the previous three years, not just in Glasgow, but across Britain. There were other rent strikes at the same time, including the Poplar strike mentioned above (where the local MP took an active part in the rent debates in Parliament). These actions, in turn, had built on previous battles from the start of the century and earlier, including mass riotous protests that, in 1869, resulted in what David Englander describes as 'the first major victory for collective tenant action'.[4] In 1867, rates, or local land taxes, had been made the responsibility of English tenants rather than landlords, but rents had not been dropped to compensate. The resulting protests forced the new Liberal government to make rates once again the landlords' responsibility.

Cumulative history has been important in generating organisation and inspiring later protesters. This was especially true of the experiences of the most recent years, which included rent strikes in Wolverhampton (in 1913) and Leeds (in 1914);

however, in places where big campaigns had previously ended in failure, further involvement might be discouraged for a period. The extent of the 1915 protests, and the sense that they were part of a growing movement, added enormously to their impact.

Protest did not stop with the 1915 Rent Act. Afterwards, across Britain, tenants were fighting evasions of the new legislation. Around crowded centres of war-work, tenants were fighting for more accommodation and greater security of tenure, and in new, government-built, war-workers' housing, tenants were fighting poor standards and high rents. Action ranged from detailed legal work to rent strikes and mass demonstrations, and all this helped to force appeasement of tenant unrest onto the government agenda.[5]

Besides considerable action in the major campaigns against rent rises and around other specific issues, housing activists had been getting increasingly involved in grass-roots work. This only increased when the government was persuaded to bring in emergency legislation, in 1914, to restrict evictions of families suffering hardship due to the war, and it was left to activists to try and ensure it was publicised and acted on.[6] Such bread-and-butter legal work helped generate organisation and understanding.

Scottish housing conditions were exceptionally bad, even for the period, and landlord tenant relations in Glasgow had been characterised by individual conflict, and increasingly by collective action. The extent of this conflict in the late nineteenth and early twentieth centuries is evidenced by the frequent recourse to sequestration of goods for non-payment of rent and the extraordinary number of court cases for summary ejectment (affecting on average 1 in 54 inhabitants of the city each year in the late 1880s[7]). In the pre-war years, individual Glasgow tenants, with the aid of grass-roots labour-movement activists, had been increasingly fighting their position in the courts.[8] At the same time, tenants were being mobilised collectively: first, through the prolonged campaign that finally, in 1912, brought a legal end to the system of year-long tenancies, and then in subsequent campaigns to prevent landlords using this as an excuse to raise rents. Tenants in Govan and Partick, at the core of the

1915 protests, had been further mobilised by the campaigns to stop their landlords pocketing the savings on rates when those areas became part of Glasgow. Glasgow tenants included seasoned campaigners and others well accustomed to the possibilities of organised tenant action, and landlords were well acquainted with the potential for co-ordinated protest.

Systemic Change

Although the Glasgow rent strikes arose from the immediate issue of profiteering rent rises, tenants were aware that this was just one battle in a longer war. If they were to avoid repeated conflicts with the landlords, then they needed to press for a change in the system that would free them from the landlords' monopoly. The solution lay in state-subsidised municipal housing.

Municipal housing had become an increasingly important demand in the labour movement and was a campaign issue for Glasgow tenants even before the turn of the century.[9] The Glasgow Labour Party, which was dominated by the ILP (Independent Labour Party), put housing reform at the centre of its campaigns and was especially prominent in promoting the issue of state-funded housing.[10] In 1915, the demand for municipal housing was spelled out on protesters' banners.

Government acceptance of the need for significant interference in the sanctity of the housing market through the introduction of state subsidies demonstrates an official acknowledgement of these demands. A market-based housing system might theoretically have been possible, but tenants had shown that they would not tolerate the conditions that this produced; subsidy also came to be seen as a consequence of the introduction of rent controls.

Key to the decision to subsidise municipal housing – and to subsidise it significantly – was the link between housing issues and unrest, which, as Chapter 1 has shown, was already widely acknowledged by 1917. The scale of both threat and response was new, but these were familiar ideas. The government was worried that Britain might follow a similar revolutionary path to Russia's and Germany's. They feared the eruption of demobilised rioters who would be better trained than the troops, and anyway, the loyalty of the troops could not be relied on. The answer had to lie in mass persuasion. Investment in housing, and importantly in housing of improved standards, 'would constitute visible proof of the irrelevance of revolution'.[11] The construction of these homes would also provide employment for returning soldiers. Discussing the 1919 housing bill in Cabinet, the prime minister, Lloyd George, argued, 'Even if it cost a hundred million pounds, what was that compared to the stability of the state?', and the Parliamentary Secretary to the Local Government Board told the House of Commons, 'the money we are going to spend on housing is an insurance against Bolshevism and revolution'.[12]

As this history demonstrates, fear of communism can push governments into reform if that fear is based on the existence of a significant strong left movement. However, it is interesting to contrast the situation in post-First World War Britain with that in 1950s America. In the latter case, the fear of communism, or even socialism, was so much in excess of any actual 'threat' that it could be manipulated by the real estate lobby to help stifle social-democratic housing reform. Don Parson has shown how opponents of public housing deliberately equated it with socialism, and attacked individual supporters as communists, in order to subvert developments at national and local levels.[13]

In Britain, economic slump and significant union defeats soon brought about a major decline in labour strength, and in 1920–21, the government responded to middle-class demands – backed by a powerful press – for cuts in public expenditure and taxes. As Mark Swenarton has observed, 'In 1919 these innovations in the provision and design of public housing were adopted as an insurance against revolution. Two years later the danger had disappeared and both were abandoned.'[14] However, as discussed in Chapter 1, this was not the end of state-funded housing.

Housing and the Labour Movement

The link between housing and other issues is crucial to political understanding and tactics. Labour activists, conservative employers and workers who had to find money from their wages to pay the rent all realised the importance of decent housing to what Marx termed the reproduction of labour power – the everyday subsistence of workers and their families that is essential for the continuation of capitalism. And improvements to the quality, cost and security of tenure of working-class homes was a key constituent to improving working-class life more generally.

The impact of housing tenure on the bargaining power of the working class was recognised early on by both sides of the political spectrum. In the nineteenth century, wealthier artisans attempted to escape the tyranny of the landlord through mutual aid societies dedicated to the self-help route of private ownership. This could provide a degree of independence from landlords, which was especially important in places where the landlord was also the employer;[15] however, as discussed in Chapter 2, the ties of property ownership can seriously restrict a worker's options, especially today when workers are often heavily indebted to a mortgage company.

In the course of a housing campaign, the wider labour movement can help housing activists through organisational support, including linking different campaigns across time and space, and through developing theoretical understanding that helps tenants to see the wider picture. In 1915 Glasgow – with its powerful trades council, strong ILP and active British Socialist Party – tenant groups were the driving force of the action, but they were supported in all these different ways.

The labour movement was also able to use its experience and contacts to lobby politicians and media. Even when such lobbying met a negative response – as in John Wheatley's attempts to prevent eviction of servicemen's families through town hall debate and an appeal to Kitchener,[16] and Andrew McBride's appeals for action to the national Labour Party[17] – these approaches were important in demonstrating the need for escalating protest, and were part of the process of building up pressure. The labour movement produced its own journals, and campaigners also attempted to win public support through judicious use of the wider media. Women and children fighting unpatriotic profiteering landlords ('the

Prussians of Partick' and the 'Hun at Home') made good copy, and – inevitably – campaigners' estimates for numbers involved in the strikes erred on the morale-boosting generous side.[18]

Individual tenants were able, too, to draw on their own experiences as trade unionists, which had taught them the importance of combination and organisation and of campaigning for the common good. Glasgow workers had been radicalised through active resistance to the 1915 Munitions Act and its attack on workers' rights,[19] and many had developed a socialist understanding through the Sunday afternoon classes and Sunday night meetings organised by John Maclean and the British Socialist Party.[20]

Importantly, the Glasgow campaign gained enormous strength from directly supportive industrial action, and, as already noted, the case for government intervention in housing more generally was heavily influenced by the climate of wider industrial unrest. The labour movement had achieved a new strength and radicalism in the years preceding the war and there was serious unrest during the war years; in 1919, the government was sufficiently afraid of revolution to send tanks into Glasgow's George Square. The organised working class had become a force to contend with. Although there was no revolution, there were major concessions to reform, including the widening of the franchise in 1918, which opened the gates to further changes.

Beyond the obvious rewards of better housing and a more comfortable and prosperous working class, housing campaigns contributed to the wider labour movement in their turn. They did this through the mobilisation of new layers – especially women, whose key role in the Glasgow strikes is well documented – and through strengthening wider working-class organisations such as the Glasgow ILP. Although the vital grass-roots networks of women were outwardly apolitical, socialists played an important part in their organisation and training. All those involved in the strikes learnt a quick lesson in radical politics and the possibility of forcing change.

For more revolutionary campaigners, a successful housing campaign was regarded as a possible first step to bigger mobilisations and more radical change. In December 1915, Maclean wrote:

> It should be noted that the rent strike on the Clyde is the first step towards the Political Strike, so frequently resorted to on the Continent in times past. We rest assured that our comrades in the various works will incessantly urge this aspect on their shop-mates, and so prepare the ground for the next great counter-move of our class in the raging class warfare ... .[21]

The Clydeside revolutionaries were to be disappointed, but, rather less dramatically, housing campaigners did manage to keep up pressure on government and landlords through the inter-war years, ensuring that the hard-won laws were complied with and that it was impossible to return to a system with no rent control. And it was not long before tenants of the new council houses began organising themselves to campaign for lower rents and better facilities on their often isolated estates, despite attempts by managers to divert them into less confrontational 'community associations' – as is still happening today.[22]

The Revisionist View

Revisionist historians have attempted to question the significance of these housing campaigns for working-class history. Central to their arguments is the pivotal role played by skilled workers, encouraging Quintin Bradley, of Leeds Tenants' Federation, to describe the 1914 rent strike in Leeds as skilled workers attempting to retain their distance from despised slum dwellers, and to use this to question the entire concept of a radical tenants' movement.[23] It is true, though hardly remarkable, that the Leeds strikers who were in better housing did not want to return to the slums and had a misplaced faith that their respectability would be enough to swing a court in their favour, but that is not the same as saying that their primary motives were fear of loss of status, and discrimination against the unskilled and unemployed. The Labour Party was quick to intervene in the Leeds strike and refocus it on a demand for municipal housing, though Bradley points out that this was to be unsubsidised homes for artisans.

Englander, in a rather more balanced account, gives several examples of pre-war tenant leaders stressing their respectability and their distance from the tenant who (even without a strike) 'would not pay his rent'.[24] And, as discussed in Chapter 1, many of the early housing activists could be described as coming from Engel's 'labour aristocracy'. But, while the Leeds strikers' demands failed to take account of the needs of the very poor, they did not actively discriminate against them; protection of existing gains by better-off workers need not be divisive. It is not possible to know what debates took place among the Leeds strike leaders, but it is probably fair to assume that any recorded statements and actions emerged through internal struggles paralleling those in the wider labour movement between those who favoured a careful reformist path and those who argued for more revolutionary action. Engels outlines a radicalising of the old labour aristocrats when their privileges became threatened,[25] and this chimes with Bradley's suggestion about the impact of the retribution meted out to the strike leaders. The strike as it played out became part of a radicalising process.

In a similar vein, but with rather less evidence, Alison Ravetz has attempted to explain that since the middle class also largely rented at that time, the Glasgow strike was 'as much a middle- as a working-class movement'.[26] In fact, war conditions and a strong radical labour movement were able to bring together the organised discipline of the skilled unionised workers and a powerful tradition of individual working-class resistance. Although the changes that finally emerged were more reforming than revolutionary – more in line with the model put forward by Ravetz's 'enlightened middle-class'[27] – the possibilities that had been demonstrated for the movement to take more radical directions were vital in giving both shape and force to the reformers' arguments.

Just as revisionist accounts of the labour movement focus on divisions within the working class, so Ravetz emphasises how housing can reinforce intra-class divisions, and argues that visions of a tenants' movement as an organised force for change are unrealistic.[28] At a time of labour-movement retreat, such arguments may seem to have the ring of truth, but history demonstrates that this view is as one-sided as the activist optimism it ridicules. Class unity of workers or tenants is not, of course, automatic, but it can be consciously and actively developed.

The Growth of a National Movement

The possibility of developing class unity is demonstrated by the next great surge in housing activism, which took off in the late 1930s and was cut across by the Second World War.[29] The importance of the housing campaigns of the 1930s was founded on their ability to co-ordinate activities at all the different levels – from grass-roots concerns to the wider political perspective – and to co-ordinate geographically across Britain. Local groups supported each other and combined together to form regional and then national structures. Vital to this was the role played by the organised left: the Communist Party and many Labour Party and trade union organisations. They were involved practically, in the development of strategy, tactics and co-ordination and, theoretically, in the development of overall analysis and alternative policies.

At an everyday level, there was sufficient organisation for campaigners to begin to take on issues proactively: as well as responding defensively to the actions of the landlords, activists went out to look for things that needed improving.[30] At a more conceptual, but also practical, level, professionals contributed their expertise. These included experts in property law and a radical group of architects around Berthold Lubetkin. The scale of the activity and its co-ordination meant that parallels can be drawn with the TUC. As in industrial action, tenants united behind campaigns even when they were not directly affected. This was exemplified by tenants who were paying controlled rents not just demanding that landlords respect those controls, but that they bring down all rents – controlled and uncontrolled – to more reasonable levels.[31]

The vigorous campaign in Stepney, in London's East End, has been described by Phil Piratin, who was elected Communist MP for Mile End in 1945. His somewhat airbrushed account, entitled *Our Flag Stays Red*, was written to serve as a handbook of grass-roots activism. Nevertheless, it manages to portray the essential events and nature of what happened. He explains how, as the movement grew and spread, more people realised what was possible through organisation, and how people gained confidence and organising skills. At one point, he describes tenants' committees 'acting as a kind of shop stewards' committee'. What was developing – until it was cut across by the war – was a sort of trade union for tenants.

Different struggles against high rents and poor conditions were being brought together with a political campaign for better housing that included the continuation of rent control and more investment in municipal housing. Actions included rent strikes against private landlords charging high rents for poor conditions, and a massive rent strike of council tenants in Birmingham, where the council was attempting to use a rise in other council rents to pay for subsidies to poorer means-tested tenants. (The strikers' argument was for greater investment, rather than taking money from those only slightly better-off, and against invasive means testing.) The housing movement even extended to new lower-middle-class homeowners, who went on mortgage strike, arguing that the building societies had enabled and encouraged the supply of substandard homes, and that they would only pay after essential repairs had been done. These mortgage protests, which had mixed success, had been prompted by the actions of Elsy Borders, a member of the Communist Party, who famously took her building society through the courts.[32]

The explosion of activity was made possible by more general growth of left forces and action, and it fed back into that growth. Again, housing issues were able to mobilise new layers, who were then helped to make the link to wider politics. Although outsiders might regard this as opportunism, communists and socialists argued that without a wholesale change in the social system, significant and lasting improvements to housing would not be possible. The well-organised Communist Party was a major beneficiary of this mobilisation, and so were many local Labour Parties. For political activists, housing campaigns were not just ends in themselves, but part of a wider campaign of politicisation. They were acknowledged to be an important way of recruiting women,[33] but it is worth recording that the Communist Party did not immediately recognise the full significance of the tenants' movement and the role it could play in the wider class struggle.[34]

In London's East End, housing campaigns were used as a strategic weapon in the fight against fascism. As is being increasingly recognised today, provision of more low-cost housing can cut across the racist scapegoating that results from competition for scant resources. As well as attacking the social and economic conditions on which fascism thrives, communist-dominated tenant campaigns in pre-war Stepney brought Jews and gentiles together to fight a united battle. Important tenants' campaigns were deliberately organised in the areas in which the fascists were recruiting so as to demonstrate the strength of working-class unity in action, and of the Communist Party as a force for change. The housing campaigns were seen by the Party as one front in a bigger interconnected battle.[35]

Britain has not since seen housing campaigns of this scale and intensity; none the less, despite major investment in council housing after the Second World War, there have always been more battles to be fought. There is no scope here to outline this history, but before examining some of the attempts to arrest the impact of today's neoliberal tide, I want to continue to look backwards briefly, in order to highlight examples of different forms of action: specifically squatting, film, and the protest by elected councillors exemplified by Clay Cross.

Squatters

Squatting can be seen as the ultimate example of individual self-help, but there have been times when co-ordinated groups of squatters have been able to effect wider change beyond their own homes. Squatting must be carefully planned if squatters are not to be accused of queue jumping and trying to put themselves ahead of others who may have greater needs. Squatters and legal occupants need to be able to make common cause, and avoid conflicting interests, which are easily exploited. Many squats have little or no impact on other households and can take pressure off immediate demand, while organised mass squats can provide an important source of pressure in campaigns to force government action and legislative change.

The most pervasive and persuasive squatting action in Britain arose as a result of appalling housing shortages following the Second World War, when it was clearly going to be a long time before the government's ambitious plans for municipal house-building had any effect. Then squatters were able to find and organise a temporary solution to at least part of the housing crisis, relieving immediate need but at the same time, as Paul Burnham explains, 'put[ing] pressure on government and councils to keep housing high on the policy agenda'.[36]

In 1946, mass direct action spread across the country as thousands of families without their own home moved into disused army camps, anti-aircraft gun sites and prisoner-of-war camps, mostly living in Nissen huts. Crucially, the squatters got themselves well organised, forming estate committees, and even paying rent into a collective fund ready for when they might be given official tenancy rights. In some of the camps, organisers were non-political, but others had a large Communist Party, and also Labour Party presence. In a post-war society used to making the most of limited resources, the squatters received widespread public support,[37] and an embarrassed government was forced to accept their position. The squatters were tolerated as a form of council tenant, though the government also sent troops into the camps that were not yet occupied – including demobilised Polish troops who did not want to return to Poland, which caused predictable tensions. In the following years, the squatters, and sympathetic supporters, were able to persuade local authorities that their best option was to make major improvements to these homes, so that they had proper bathrooms, cooking ranges and internal walls, and the government provided considerable sums to make this possible. Gradually, families were moved from the

Nissen huts into new council estates, but the last of the huts were only emptied in the 1960s.

Squatters in late-1960s London looked at this mass movement as a model. Small groups of activists worked together with families from the notorious homeless hostels and some of the worst slums, who were desperate for a decent place to live. Their squats were chosen with care: council-owned buildings that were lying empty and unused waiting redevelopment. Ron Bailey, one of the activists involved, has described their well-planned operations and judicious use of the law and the media.[38] Squats of this period were notorious for attracting 'outsiders', including students, who did not all share the aims or political canniness of Bailey's group. However, the majority of squatters were local people who had exhausted all other options and were able to win considerable sympathy for their position. The movement spread across London, with the first hard-won successes encouraging similar actions and quicker capitulation, and squatters were able to force councils all over the capital to accept the idea of using their empty housing stock as short-life accommodation.

The result was not only an immediate improvement of living standards for the many families involved in the campaign and for the many more who continued to benefit from the use of short-life housing, but also a powerful contribution to the pressures to improve homelessness legislation. These are no mean achievements, but what the movement of the 1960s and 1970s failed to do was make a link between the concerns of the squatters and those of the wider labour movement. It contributed to the growth of some independent housing associations, which managed the short-term housing, but it did not link with wider campaigns for more council housing, or make an active connection between housing and wider economic and political forces. This was partly a result of the aggressively negative role played by Labour councillors in the areas involved, but also of the anarchist sympathies of the leading activists, who saw themselves as creating an 'alternative housing force'.[39] Such links might have helped cut across the inevitable conflicts that arose through competition between homeless families and long-established residents for limited council housing. The squatting movement also missed the opportunity to follow pre-war example and use housing activism to bridge the new racial divisions that were emerging in London's East End. In fact, it helped concretise these divisions through the development of a separate Bengali squatters' organisation.[40]

'Cathy Come Home'

In 2006, a whole range of articles and television and radio programmes marked the fortieth anniversary of Ken Loach's television drama about a family destroyed through homelessness. *Cathy Come Home* was the modern equivalent of publications such as Andrew Mearns' 1883 pamphlet *The Bitter Cry of Outcast London*, or Arthur Morrison's 1896 novel, *A Child of the Jago*. The drama made a huge impact at a time when there were few television channels and a high proportion of homes tuned in to the BBC's Wednesday Play; the story it told shook the nation's complacency and it continued to be shown long afterwards. Indeed, I remember it as the one film we watched at school in the late 1970s. *Cathy Come Home* hit a nerve, and the film has been credited with generating a new understanding of homelessness and creating huge public support for Shelter, the homelessness charity that was launched two weeks after the programme was broadcast. However, as the fortieth-anniversary responses showed, homelessness is far from ended;[41] and as discussed in Chapter 2, Shelter has become increasingly compromised as it tries to work within the neoliberal system. (Ken Loach has even joined Shelter workers on the picket lines protesting against cuts in their pay and conditions.)

Councillors in Revolt

My last historic example has been chosen not so much for what it achieved but for what it showed might be possible. In 1972, the Conservatives' Housing Finance Act required all councils to bring the rents of their houses into line with those in the private sector. By that time, council rents were generally significantly lower, so this meant large rent rises as well as the loss of council control in rent-setting. There were widespread protests and over a hundred councils announced their intention not to implement the new system. However, the Labour Party's National Executive refused to back such illegal action, and one by one the councils fell away, until all that was left was a council in South Wales, where the government put in a commissioner, and Clay Cross in Derbyshire.[42] The eleven Clay Cross councillors were not only all Labour, but they had an established record of following an independent socialist programme that prioritised their council tenants.[43] They were prepared to fight the government to the end, which meant personal surcharges and being debarred from office, but also no rent rises until 17 months after the passing of the Act. Clay Cross demonstrates that councillors can resist unpopular legislation. If more had had the courage to carry their promised intentions through – and if, too, the different protest rent strikes had been able to co-ordinate into a national campaign – then the end result might have been different. As it was, the new rent system was withdrawn when Labour came back into government in 1974; however, subsequent legislation has put councils under increasing pressure and given them little (legal) choice but to raise rents.

The Battleground Today

As this book demonstrates, housing is under attack at many levels; and the battle for better housing, or even to preserve something of previous victories, has to be fought on many fronts. Housing activists hardly need to be reminded that the fight is never over.

The people in the front line of these battles are generally those who are the poorest, with the fewest resources and least political influence; especially when it comes to defending increasingly residualised public housing. The most capable of them may already be doing several jobs to make ends meet or have other cares and worries. They may find it hard to come to protest meetings – or even stay awake. In a finely balanced existence, problems such as illness in the family can quickly disrupt the best-made plans. Nevertheless, people can, and do, work together to make their case and push their demands, but what then if no one listens? High levels of dependence on housing benefit, and only a proportion of tenants paying full rent, rule out a rent strike. In fact, housing benefit acts to divide tenants, with some rendered oblivious to rent rises that affect their neighbours (a division that was predicted by both tenants and politicians[44]).

Those whose homes are threatened with demolition are often prepared to stay and fight their ground, but they face a long war of attrition, and they need some sense that they can win – the morale boost that comes from a victory, or, more crucially, the knowledge that they are not fighting alone. If people are to be expected to fight together to force a fundamental change in policy for the common good, they must have some hope of success. Otherwise, although a few individual families may hold on in decaying buildings in the hope of being made better housing offers for themselves, wider combined protest will be hard to sustain. History has demonstrated the importance of the involvement of the labour movement in co-ordinating and supporting housing struggles, but now, for the first time in over a hundred years, tenants feel isolated and abandoned: not so much cynical, as realistic in their lack of expectation. Parliamentary parties, such as Labour, have always been somewhat fickle friends, but the concerted attack on public housing by New Labour and other nominally socialist governments has left tenants stranded. In Britain, there has been some support from the unions – primarily passive, with some (largely financial) help for high-profile campaigns – but they have been generally emasculated by their uncertain relationship with Labour. They prefer to concentrate on more immediate employment issues – and a decreasing proportion of their membership is made up of council tenants. In Canada, the Autoworkers Union threatened to withdraw its funding when the Ontario Coalition Against Poverty adopted confrontational tactics.

The labour movement is fighting a rearguard action and every bit of ground lost lays it open to further attack. However, sometimes that ground seems to have been given up without a fight. Even some of those who express concern over the direction of modern politics are unwilling to challenge its rules, and instead limit themselves to seeking the least offensive way of carrying them out. As neoliberalism appears to take firmer and firmer hold, this approach is becoming more widespread – from politicians to academics, and trade unionists to housing activists. There have always been divisions between those who are pushing for different degrees of change, but, with the labour movement on the defensive, the divisions have shifted to separate those who are prepared to concede a degree of marketisation and those who are not. This type of retreat can break the link between individual campaigns and movements for wider change, and is exemplified by tenant groups who have persuaded themselves that privatisation or demolition cannot be fought, and all that is left is to get involved in the process and make sure tenants get the best deal out of it.

Central to any campaign is a well-argued position backed by evidence – and this needs to be publicly presented and gain sympathetic coverage in the media. But despite the plethora of alternative outlets, the ability for critical analysis to cross from these into the mainstream is becoming progressively more difficult as the terms of public debate are increasingly tuned to the business agenda.

The final part of this chapter will explore some of the ways that campaigners are attempting to overcome these difficulties, and discuss what more could be done.

A Broad, Sustained Campaign

The English organisation Defend Council Housing (DCH), set up in 1998 'to fight *against* the privatisation of council housing [through transfer to housing associations] and *for* direct investment to make council housing first class housing for all who need it',[45] has seen its ideas being more and more generally accepted – though not yet by the government. It has also demonstrated the potential of a sustained campaign that has been built up over several years and ties together different groups across the country (including links with campaigns in Scotland and Wales). The future of council housing is an important issue that affects large numbers of people, and DCH has provided campaigners with essential information and co-ordination. Despite Socialist Workers' Party domination of the central organisation, DCH has attracted wide support, including from trade unions and a large number of MPs and councillors (see Figure 12.1). This support is largely passive, but the unions have been able to help with the production and delivery of campaign material to the numerous council tenants affected by stock-transfer proposals; and sympathetic MPs, with union sponsorship, have co-ordinated a powerful report based on evidence from tenants, trade unionists, councillors and council officers.[46] Through its excellent website and other materials, DCH is able to pass on a library of background information and lessons learned from previous campaigns, as well as broadcast news of victories won. It provides an invaluable resource for any group of tenants and activists fighting off a proposed stock transfer, whether or not they are officially affiliated to the organisation.

Figure 12.1   January 2008: At the Defend Council Housing lobby of Parliament (*photo: Alan Walters*). The 'Fourth Option' demanded on the placards (an option that is never offered) is direct investment in council housing on the same terms given to housing associations.

Uniquely among privatisations, in stock transfer, those most affected – the tenants – are given a vote on whether transfer should go ahead: a right won through resistance to an earlier transfer scheme in 1988. Although the government and local authorities use all available tricks to weigh the odds heavily in favour of a 'yes' vote,[47] those opposed to privatisation have something they can campaign around – and in around a quarter of cases, they have won. The hugely significant 2 to 1 'no' vote that put a stop to the proposed transfer of Birmingham's 84,000 council homes in 2002 was a testimony to DCH's organisation and what it had learnt from previous campaigns. The long campaign involved hundreds of thousands of leaflets, thousands of posters, estate-based meetings, and active trade union support; by the end, campaigners had won the backing of two local MPs and several councillors. That Glasgow, with its history of militancy, should have voted 'yes' at the same time on the same issue has been blamed on a divided and less well-organised campaign and what seemed to be better proposals for investment and 'community' involvement.[48] It could also be a function of the city's historic and close ties to the Labour Party, with old loyalties still surviving a reversal of policy towards municipal housing that, as described in Chapter 2, was to some extent pioneered by Glasgow City Council. However, the actual *experience* of transfer in Glasgow was a significant factor in the later 'no' votes in Edinburgh, Stirling, Renfrewshire and the Highlands.

DCH has achieved a lot at a time when political organisation on the left has become progressively more difficult, but it is still very much a single-issue campaign. Even on the issue of privatisation, it can become sidelined as the successes of anti-transfer campaigns have encouraged the government to introduce new privatisation routes that do not require a ballot; and DCH has made few links with other housing questions, such as those around 'regeneration', let alone with other fights against neoliberalism. Of course, many of those involved – tenants as well as political activists – are well aware of how everything links up, but this is not reflected in the organisational structures, which have relied heavily on one dedicated national leader. The great mobilisations that have been achieved against stock transfer have not formed the basis for further organisation, and DCH can offer little for those who are not already council tenants. If DCH succeeds in changing the law to allow public investment in council housing on the same terms as given to housing associations (and we have seen some concessions), the next stage of the battle will be much more difficult.

Direct Action

As Chapter 6 has shown, French housing campaigners have made use of some high-profile and well co-ordinated direct action that has linked together different organisations and different places. The encampment of red tents neatly lined up along the banks of the Canal Saint-Martin in central Paris, where sympathisers were invited to experience a night on the street alongside the homeless, was not only a powerful symbol, but was timed to take advantage of the politically sensitive pre-election period.[49] This was co-ordinated with similar encampments in other cities. No politician dared ignore the issue, and the government was forced to bring in the new legislation giving everyone a right – defensible in law – to be housed. It was an impressive and important victory, but such legislation has no value unless there are enough good homes. Once the international journalists had gone, homeless people were still being forced to leave their donated tents without being given an alternative solution.[50] France's housing activists know they cannot afford to sit back and enjoy their victory. There are much more difficult campaigns ahead, and a much more unashamedly right-wing authoritarian government.

Well-focused direct action can form an important part of a housing campaign, but squatting of any kind is not something that can be easily undertaken. It certainly helps to have a sympathetic public climate, and a good knowledge of the law and how it might be interpreted. In Scotland, squatting is a criminal offence, though that is not the case south of the border. In the United States, the legal situation varies from place to place.

Direct action on a smaller scale can take the form of the occupation of housing authority offices, which not only secures media attention, but may also help force reluctant officials into negotiation. The last few years have seen the group Glasgow Save Our Homes occupy government offices as part of their successful campaign to protest at cuts in concierge services for tenants,[51] and then again to protest at crippling service charges of thousands of pounds being imposed on Glasgow residents who bought their homes under Right to Buy. They have organised lobbies and blockades of key streets; and some homeowning pensioners were manhandled out of the Scottish Parliament after unfurling a banner demanding immediate financial investigation of the Glasgow Housing Association (GHA), which is now their factor. Although housing benefit has made the rent strike obsolete, the Right to Buy owners have been using similar tactics when faced with bills for thousands of pounds worth of work to their flats. They question both the sums being charged and the demand that payments be made immediately: a family with a joint income of £20,000 can be asked to pay £7,000 within a year. Many people have been taken to court for withholding payment, and a lot of them have persuaded the authorities that they should be allowed to pay in instalments. Agreement is now being reached to extend the payment period for everyone to two years; at the same time, increasing numbers of Scottish politicians have been persuaded to support the demand for an independent investigation into how the GHA awarded the building contracts.[52]

Fighting Through the Courts

While campaigners may more often find themselves on the wrong side of the law, there are also examples (especially from the United States) of campaigns pursuing their causes through the courts. As Jason Hackworth points out in Chapter 10, this is not an easy strategy. Legal action not only has the potential to be hugely expensive, but in focusing on a single point of law, it necessarily ignores wider economic and political issues and can become disengaged from the community it is meant to serve. Even where cases are won, this may take so long that much of the damage has already been done, and because the legal arguments rarely take on the fundamental questions, a win is unlikely to serve as more than a delaying tactic. Developers have deep resources and a lot to win (or potentially lose), and are unlikely to give up after the first battle.

In spite of all this, it is worth looking at a couple of ongoing examples of litigation. The tenants of Lincoln Place in Venice, California, were unlucky enough to inhabit 38 beautiful green acres near the beach: in other words, some very valuable real estate. The 795 rent-controlled apartments, built around garden courtyards shortly after the Second World War, were home to people of a wide mix of ages and races and fostered an enviable community spirit. The buildings' new owner, AIMCO, the largest owner of apartment buildings in the country, planned to demolish them and redevelop the site. However, the tenants' association has won a court ruling that AIMCO were in breach of an agreement, made as part of the original redevelopment proposal, that 'no existing tenant would be involuntarily displaced from the site'.[53] By the time this ruling was made, almost all the tenants had been bullied out or evicted, many of them in a mass lockout of 52 households (see Figure 12.2). The only people now left are a dozen old and disabled tenants in a landscape of boarded-up flats. Tenants are now suing for the restoration of 450 illegally terminated tenancies and for damages to cover the higher rents people have had to pay elsewhere, as well as the destruction of lives and community.[54]

The second example is Elizabeth Pascoe's challenge to the compulsory purchase order (CPO) of her house in Kensington in Liverpool, the Housing Market Renewal area cited in Chapters 2 and 3. When the public inquiry into the proposed demolitions (initiated by residents' objections) ignored all the residents' arguments, Pascoe, who had played a leading role in opposing the development, challenged her CPO in the High Court. She explains that this was not a one-person campaign, but simply that, as a former architect on disability benefit, she had the skills and the time and was poor enough to qualify for legal aid, so it made sense to use her home as a test case. Although she has been working with others, this focus has put her under enormous strain,

Figure 12.2   December 2005: Mass lockout at Lincoln Place – a line of sheriffs' cars, and groups of protesting tenants (*photos: Hans Adamson*).

in addition to which she has been publicly accused of selfishly holding up development, and has been subjected to suspected criminal harassment. The Renewal partnership had claimed, using a law created for brownfield sites and not for residential areas, that the CPOs were justified because the area was 'predominantly under-used and unsightly' (a process that they had engineered by deliberately emptying the area's socially rented homes[55]). Pascoe's lawyer argued that it was not enough to say that the area was *predominantly* under-used, and the judge halted development. But he could not prevent the Renewal partnership starting the whole process again, forcing all but the most determined residents to move and ensuring that the area became thoroughly run-down, with only a sprinkling of people living among boarded-up homes. Pascoe succeeded in getting a court order to prevent demolitions being carried out before the second public inquiry, which also concluded by recommending the 'regeneration'. At the inquiry, she presented a detailed alternative scheme drawn up by herself and another architect resident, but this was dismissed by the government inspector because it did not have the official consents and full costings, and its authors lacked a 'track record'. (Pascoe estimates that to have compiled the full environmental impact assessment and traffic modelling required to submit it for planning consent would have cost in the region of £350,000.) Shortly after the inquiry closed – why were they not asked earlier? – the government's own Commission for Architecture and the Built Environment (CABE) produced a report that was highly critical of the Renewal partnership's scheme. Despite this, the Secretary of State backed her inspector and supported the demolitions. As of January 2009, Pascoe was again making a legal challenge to her CPO. This is based around two main arguments. First, the Secretary of State should have responded to the CABE report. Secondly, it should be assumed that a serious alternative scheme would be given the same level of support from the authorities as the Renewal partnership's proposal; otherwise, if we follow the inspector's argument, any alternative proposals put forward by local people will be simply dismissed out of hand (see Figure 12.3). Pascoe knows that her own community that she tried to save has gone, but she argues that it is important to prove that those instigating such developments cannot get away with deliberately running down an area and ignoring local people – or they will do it again and again.[56] In both these cases, victories can help set legal precedent.

Figure 12.3　Elizabeth Pascoe in her threatened home in Liverpool
(*photo: Christian Petersen*).

In other parts of Liverpool scheduled for 'Renewal', people are being encouraged to leave and neighbourhoods are being deliberately run down, but there have been no CPOs issued so there has been no possibility of a public inquiry or legal challenge. Residents of the 'Welsh Streets' have kept a photographic record of their homes during this process so that their 'before' and 'after' photographs can give the lie to the official propaganda, which is always illustrated by streets of boarded-up empty homes.[57] Residents of Cairns Street, off Granby Street, have gone a stage further to demonstrate the attractiveness and potential of their neighbourhood. Outside all the houses – lived-in or boarded-up – are plants of all kinds, including beans and strawberries (see Figure 12.4). Eleanor Lee, a local grandmother, has broken up and removed the concrete from front gardens, and containers of all sorts have been brought into use as plant pots – including the base of an old vacuum cleaner. The gardeners have even managed to get grant funding for their larger planters. All this work has helped build community spirit and residents have found that many people would now like to move into the street, if it were allowed.

Figure 12.4   Carol outside her house in 'Bloomin'
Cairns Street, July 2008 (*photo Sarah Glynn*).

In both Venice and Liverpool, conservationists have been outspoken against demolition. (Lincoln Place has been put on the State Historical Register, and the mass destruction of Victorian terraces across the north of England is the subject of a report by Save Britain's Heritage.) This can be important in broadening interest and media coverage, but risks drawing attention away from fundamental social and political issues, so allowing the impact on people and communities to continue to be sidelined. Conservationists are generally of little help to those in 1970s council blocks,[58] and wherever they do get involved, there is a danger that gentrification through demolition could be replaced by more old-fashioned gentrification through renovation.

Tenant Management and Tenant Organisation

The existence of public housing allows for an element of overall democratic control (and also for planning across a city or region and beyond the needs of current tenants), but there should also be scope, where tenants want it, for local tenant control in day-to-day management. And over and above this, there needs to be independent tenant-controlled organisation to make sure tenants can maintain their own voice, without ties to any official funding agencies. Tenant management and campaigning organisation are separate things and problems can occur if they become confused.

Tenant management can be important in making public housing work well and in a way that is responsive to tenants' needs.[59] There have been successful examples of tenant management, notably in Glasgow before the transfer to the GHA. As these showed, locally based and tenant-controlled management can prove especially effective and responsive in organising repairs and maintenance and in the sensitive handling of neighbourhood disputes. Tenants are clearly not in a position to take on all management functions themselves, and this sort of arrangement requires close co-ordination with the local authority or other landlord. More recently, tenants of the 'problem' Shiredale Estate in north Manchester persuaded the city council, through many lobbies and demonstrations, not to demolish their homes but to let them take over their management.[60] The demolition proposals were the council's response to anti-social behaviour and the consequent lack of demand for the houses, rather than to any sort of structural problems, and there has been no extra investment in the buildings. However, active involvement of local people has been able to improve the environment, provide a more sensitive response to behaviour problems and make the estate a place that people want to come and live in. The tenants employ a housing manager who is on secondment from the arm's-length company that now manages the city's council houses. He is clearly enthusiastic about what has been achieved, and argues that 'ordinary people know what's best for them and don't need other people who don't live in council housing to make decisions about them that will affect their lives'.[61] The problem is that the estate is small and the elderly management board has dwindled to six tenants. There are plans to incorporate an adjoining estate to bring in more members and a larger, more flexible budget.

Shiredale Housing Outraged and United Tenants, or SHOUT, is now SHOUT Tenant Management Organisation, working with the council. It is achieving what it set out to do; but if tenants want to be free to shout about problems that cannot be settled through negotiation, then, as this chapter demonstrates, they also need their own independent representative organisation. The need for tenant representation to be independent of the landlords can be compared to a union's need to be independent of employers. There is growing acceptance of the importance of tenant involvement, but official recognition has always gone hand-in-hand with a tendency to try and control the form that involvement takes, and never more so than today.

The general decline of the labour movement, increasing homeownership, the running-down of social housing, and new systems of registration and control have all taken their toll on independent tenant organisation; but, as this account shows, it does still exist. Some active organisations are listed at the end of this chapter.

The Activist Academic

Although it is undoubtedly true that research that is critically detached from neoliberal housing policy has been marginalised, there are still quite a lot of people out on those margins. There are researchers analysing what is happening, keeping alive and developing alternative ideas, and also getting actively involved in housing campaigns in what should be able to be a symbiotic relationship with those directly affected. Academics have the time and the tools to cut through official discourses and unwind the spin, and to explore what is actually happening. They may be less ready to go beyond commenting on events and suggest different approaches, but that should be part of the analysis. This could mean making the socio-economic case for more public housing, or it could mean something relatively simple, but none the less important, like ensuring that the term 'affordable housing' has a real meaning based on the same sort of calculations used to determine a living wage.[62] As activists, academics are contributing analytical and organisational skills and helping get different views heard; but even a well-argued case will not be listened to unless it is backed by action and wide support.

Making Links

Examples given here and in the previous chapters have shown campaigns linking together – such as the different fights against housing stock transfer in Britain, and the French campaigns against homelessness and against demolitions. The list below also includes international coalitions that help campaigners to share ideas and learn from each other's experiences. The internet provides an important tool for these geographical linkages, but it cannot replace hard work on the ground, and does not reach everyone. There are also connections being made with wider issues, for example through the Ontario Coalition Against Poverty. Housing campaigns now, as in the past, have been able to attract a coalition of supporters – including groups such as the Salvation Army and also the Church[63] – although some of these may be reluctant to be too critical of authority.

Most important, as this history shows, are links with the wider labour and trade union movement. With the decline of the left, these have become badly weakened. The benefits of such links run in both directions. Housing campaigns have brought more people into political activity, as well as playing an important part in improving working-class living standards. Many trade unionists are now homeowners rather than tenants, but in campaigning for an attractive social rented sector, unions can help narrow divisions between workers. More, and better, social rented housing would also allow fewer people to become effectively mortgage slaves, working long hours and not daring to do anything that might upset their employer and put their job at risk.

Unions have played a part in anti-stock-transfer campaigns, and a recent history of successful community organisation in Clydebank argues that this owes its independence and strength to its roots in and continued links with the trade union movement.[64] However, few organisations are so lucky. In fact, perhaps the greatest difficulty for housing campaigners today is the feeling of isolation and lack of wider support.

Looking to the Future

Things are happening in housing activism – they have to be, because so much that had begun to be taken for granted is now under attack – but there is still a long way to go until we can begin to see the sort of co-ordinated movement that history demonstrates is needed. There are the beginnings of geographical linkages, but other linkages are still very rudimentary, and most of what is happening consists of isolated single-issue campaigns. Those that are successful rely on grass-roots work, but this is rarely matched up with more day-to-day involvement in grass-roots problems. At the same time, new forms of partnership governance are being used to incorporate those organisations that are concerned with everyday problems into official structures, and so prevent them aligning with any protest movements.

On the wider level, different campaigns are not yet being combined together so as to form a concerted challenge to the neoliberal hegemony in housing or beyond. Homelessness, destruction of public housing, mortgage repossessions all connect, and connect too to the growing wealth gap, poor health, rising health costs and social exclusion. These issues cannot be addressed separately. For a start (as in the 1930s), the concerns of tenants need to be linked to those of lower-income homeowners, with whom they share many interests. The normalisation of homeownership should not make us forget the impact that this can have on the ability of the working class to organise and resist the demands of their employers. The ability to rent good-quality, secure and genuinely affordable homes is not just a housing issue. In the protection of working-class communities, the promotion of decent housing also needs to be tied to the promotion of decent jobs that consist of more than providing mundane service tasks for middle-class incomers. And (again as in the 1930s) we need to be aware how campaigning for more and better housing can help cut across racial and ethnic divisions, something that is likely to be of growing importance with high labour migration and a recession. Even a small number of migrants can have an effect on a tight housing supply – and a much greater *perceived* effect. Perhaps the most important lesson from this history is the importance of linking other issues into the wider labour movement, theoretically and practically, and the key role of housing within this.

The current crisis in neoliberal capitalism may make people readier to consider alternative approaches; however, it cannot be taken for granted that policies will move in a progressive direction. Certainly, economic forces will defeat some of the big regeneration schemes, and it should be easier for authorities to withdraw unpopular proposals in response to changing circumstances without seeming to do a U-turn. But, with so much up in the air, it becomes even more important to press on with campaigning and to raise the profile of critical analysis.

Some Campaigning Organisations

This list makes no pretence to be complete, but I hope that it is useful.

International

Habitat International Coalition <http://www.hic-net.org>
The International Union of Tenants <http://www.iut.nu>
International Alliance of Habitants <http://www.habitants.org>
World Tenant (with links to organisations round the world) <http://www.worldtenant.com>
Centre on Housing Rights and Evictions <http://www.cohre.org>

England

Defend Council Housing <http://www.defendcouncilhousing.org.uk>

Hands Off Our Homes! (Leeds) <http://handsoffourhomes.blogspot. com>

London Tenants Federation <http://www.londontenants.org>

Leeds Tenants Federation <http://www.leedstenants.org.uk>

Scotland

The Scottish Tenants Organisation <http://www.scottishtenants.org.uk>

France

Coordination anti-demolition des quartiers populaires (Anti-demolition Coalition of Working-class Neighbourhoods) <http://antidemolition. blogspot.com>

Droit au Logement (DAL) (Right to Housing organisation) <http://www. globenet.org/dal>

Les Enfants de Don Quichotte (The Children of Don Quixote) <http:// www.lesenfantsdedonquichotte.com>

Jeudi Noir <http://www.jeudi-noir.org>

Ministère de la Crise du Logement (Ministry of the Housing Crisis) <http://www.ministeredelacrisedulogement.org>

Sweden

Hyresgästföreningen (Swedish Union of Tenants) The website has a section in English <http://www.hyresgastforeningen.se>

Jagvillhabostad.nu (Network working for better youth housing) <http:// www.jagvillhabostad.nu>

Yimby (Yes-in-my-backyard) <http://www.yimby.se>

Wastedspace (Looking for spaces in Stockholm that can be reused, such as empty houses that can become houses) <http://www.wastedspace.se>

Makalösa Föräldrar (Remarkable Parents) (Working for single-parent families on housing, and other issues) <http://www.makalosa.org>

New Zealand

Child Poverty Action Group <http://www.cpag.org.nz> (includes material on housing as well as other issues)

Australia

National Shelter <http://www.shelter.org.au>
Tenants Union of Queensland <http://www.tuq.org.au>
Tenants Union of NSW <http://www.tenants.org.au >

United States of America

Right to the City (an alliance of campaign organisations, academics, lawyers and others, resisting gentrification and displacement) <http://www.righttothecity.org>
National Housing Law Project <http://www.nhlp.org>
National Alliance of HUD Tenants <http://www.saveourhomes.org>
New York State Tenants and Neighbors Coalition <http://www.tenantsandneighbors.org>
New York City Public Housing Resident Alliance <http://www.tvotb.com/nyc_public_housing_resident_alli.htm>
Coalition on Homelessness San Francisco <http://www.cohsf.org/eng>

Canada

Ontario Tenants Rights <http://www.ontariotenants.ca>
Ontario Coalition Against Poverty <http://www.ocap.ca>

Notes

1. See Greg Neale on politicians and history in the *New Statesman*, 19 December 2005.
2. See *East End News*, 30 November 1915; *East End News*, 5 May 1939; *East London Advertiser*, 8 February 1963; *Daily Telegraph*, 23 September 1963; *Daily Herald*, 2 August 1962, and *East London Advertiser*, 14 March 1975.
3. Englander, David (1983) *Landlord and Tenant in Urban Britain 1838–1918* (Oxford: Clarendon); Milton, Nan (1979) *John Maclean* (London: Pluto Press); Melling, Joseph (1989) 'Clydeside Rent Struggles and the Making of Labour Politics in Scotland, 1900–39', in Richard Rodger, *Scottish Housing in the Twentieth Century* (Leicester: Leicester University Press).
4. Englander, *Landlord and Tenant*, p. 86.
5. Ibid.
6. Ibid., pp. 96–7.
7. Rodger, *Scottish Housing in the Twentieth Century*, p. 42.

8. Melling, 'Clydeside Rent Struggles', p. 60.
9. Englander, *Landlord and Tenant*, p. 172.
10. Melling, 'Clydeside Rent Struggles', p. 62, Englander, *Landlord and Tenant*, p. 164, Grayson, John (1996) *Opening the Window* (Salford: TPAS and Northern College), p. 20. The ILP – Independent Labour Party – was one of the groups that co-founded the British Labour Party.
11. Swenarton, Mark (1981) 'An "Insurance against Revolution": Ideological Objectives of the Provision and Design of Public Housing in Britain after the First World War', *Historical Research* 54(129): 89.
12. Ibid., p. 94.
13. Parson, Don (2007) 'The Decline of Public Housing and the Politics of the Red Scare: The Significance of the Los Angeles Public Housing War', *Journal of Urban History* 33(3): 400–17.
14. Swenarton, 'An "Insurance against Revolution"', p. 99.
15. Forrest, Ray, Alan Murie and Peter Williams (1990) *Home Ownership: Differentiation and Fragmentation* (London: Unwin Hyman), p. 58.
16. Englander, *Landlord and Tenant*, p. 219.
17. Milton, *John Maclean*, pp. 88–9.
18. Englander, *Landlord and Tenant*, pp. 223, 225.
19. Milton, *John Maclean*, p. 91; Melling, 'Clydeside Rent Struggles', p. 67.
20. Milton, *John Maclean*.
21. Quoted in ibid., p. 104.
22. Grayson, *Opening the Window*, pp. 24–8.
23. Bradley, Quintin (1997) 'The Leeds Rent Strike of 1914: A Reappraisal of the Radical History of the Tenants Movement' <http://freespace. virgin.net/labwise.history6/rentrick.htm>.
24. Englander, *Landlord and Tenant*, p. 186.
25. Engels, Friedrich (1987) 'Preface to the English Edition' (1892) of *The Condition of the Working Class in England* (Harmondsworth: Penguin), pp. 44–5.
26. Ravetz, Alison (2001) *Council Housing and Culture: The History of a Social Experiment* (London: Routledge), p. 33.
27. Ibid., p. 29.
28. Ibid., pp. 154, 170.
29. Glynn, Sarah (2005) 'East End Immigrants and the Battle for Housing: A Comparative Study of Political Mobilisation in the Jewish and Bengali Communities', *Journal of Historical Geography* 31: 528–45.

30. Piratin, Phil (1978, 1st edn 1948) *Our Flag Stays Red* (London: Lawrence and Wishart), p. 36.
31. Graves, B. (1938) *Quinn Square Tenants' Rent Strike Victory* (London).
32. Branson, Noreen and Margot Heinemann (1971) *Britain in the Nineteen Thirties* (London: Weidenfeld and Nicolson), pp. 186–9.
33. *Daily Worker*, 6 October 1934.
34. Glynn, 'East End Immigrants', pp. 530–2; Jacobs, Joe (1978) *Out of the Ghetto: My Youth in the East End. Communism and Fascism 1913–1939* (London: Janet Simon), p. 282.
35. Glynn, 'East End Immigrants'.
36. Burnham, Paul (2004) 'The Squatters of 1946: A Local Study in National Context', *Socialist History 25: Old Social Movements?*, p. 41.
37. Grayson, *Opening the Window*, p. 36.
38. Bailey, Ron (1973) *The Squatters* (Harmondsworth: Penguin).
39. Bailey, Ron (1997) 'DIY for the Homeless', in John Goodwin and Carol Grant (eds) *Built to Last? Reflections on British Housing Policy* (London: ROOF, 2nd edn), p. 89.
40. Glynn, 'East End Immigrants'.
41. See, especially, the powerful documentary *Evicted*, directed by Brian Woods and shown on BBC1 on 29 November 2006.
42. Peter Malpass, 'The Road from Clay Cross', in Goodwin and Grant, *Built to Last?*
43. Mitchell, Austin (1974) 'Clay Cross', *Political Quarterly* 45(2): 165–78.
44. Grayson, *Opening the Window*, p. 50.
45. DCH affiliation form <http://www.defendcouncilhousing.org.uk>.
46. House of Commons Council Housing Group (n.d.) *Support for the 'Fourth Option' for Council Housing: Report of the Enquiry into the Future Funding of Council Housing 2004–2005* <http://www.support4councilhousing.org.uk/report/resources/HoCCHG_report.pdf> [accessed 17 September 2008].
47. Ibid.
48. Daly, Guy, Gerry Mooney, Lynne Poole and Howard Davis (2005) 'Housing Stock Transfer in Birmingham and Glasgow: The Contrasting Experiences of Two UK Cities', *European Journal of Housing Policy* 5(3): 327–41.
49. <http://www.lesenfantsdedonquichotte.com>; *Liberation*, 19 December 2006.
50. Médecins du Monde press release, 15 June 2007.
51. This campaign was carried out alongside the GMB, the concierges' trade union.

52. <http://www.gsohc.co.uk> [accessed 19 September 2008]; discussions with Sean Clerkin, chairperson of Glasgow Save Our Homes.
53. Quoted in the court decision of 19 September 2007, p. 4.
54. <http://www.lincolnplace.net> [accessed 18 September 2008].
55. Pascoe points out that at the time the CPOs were made, 131 out of the 400 homes were empty, but 127 were social housing units, where tenants had been moved out, so this was hardly 'market failure'.
56. This description is based on discussion with Elizabeth Pascoe (3 April 2008), her presentation at the Liverpool University conference 'Capital Culture and Power' (3 July 2008), an article by Ciara Leeming in the *Big Issue*, 26 June 2008, and Pascoe's Appeal against her second CPO.
57. The importance of this form of propaganda is highlighted by Lee Crookes in his ongoing PhD research.
58. In early 2008, *Building Design* ran a high-profile campaign to preserve a 'landmark housing estate' in Poplar designed by the Smithsons and completed in 1972, but there was little attention given to the social issues.
59. Scott, S. (2000) 'The People's Republic of Yoker: A Case Study of Tenant Management in Scotland', *Journal of Co-operative Studies* 33(1): 15–38; Glynn, Sarah (2007) 'But We Already Have Community Ownership – Making Council Housing Work', in Andy Cumbers and Geoff Whittam (eds) *Reclaiming the Economy: Alternatives to Market Fundamentalism* (Glasgow: Scottish Left Review Press).
60. <http://www.shouttmo.org.uk>; *North and East Manchester Advertiser*, 3 December 2004.
61. Telephone conversation with Nigel Rolland, 19 September 2008. Before the management organisation was established, Rolland worked directly for the council.
62. See Peter Ambrose in *ROOF*, October 2008.
63. Father Groser was an important figure in the Stepney campaigns in the 1930s.
64. Collins, Chik (2008) *The Right to Exist: The Story of the Clydebank Independent Resource Centre* (Glasgow: Clydebank Independent Resource Centre and Oxfam).

13

HOMES FOR TODAY AND TOMORROW[1]

Sarah Glynn

With the property bubble burst and dragging us into global recession, it might seem obvious that governments should try and restrain the drive to regard houses primarily as investments, and base their housing policy on the need for good homes. But while growing housing waiting-lists and rising repossessions are putting discussions about public housing back on the agenda, government ministers are still talking about restoring the housing market and creating new routes into ownership for those who cannot really afford it; and the chair of one of Britain's biggest housing associations does not consider it inappropriate to question publicly whether social housing should exist at all.[2] The only thing that seems to be commonly agreed upon is that housing is fundamentally important. Those who cling doggedly to a neoliberal vision like to portray anything else as naïve and simplistic – unlike the idea that house prices would go on rising for ever and that it is possible to have capitalistic boom without bust. In criticising neoliberalism, it is important to demonstrate that other approaches can be both practical and effective. We know from experience that the prophets of neoliberalism will never bother to engage with the arguments, but others will – especially if they must face the consequences of the failure of neoliberal economics. And one thing we can learn from the history of neoliberalism is that ideas can move in from the margins.

Greater equality in housing cannot be separated from greater equality in other areas, but it could be improved by reducing the incentives to use housing as an investment. Recent events have encouraged debate about whether a fall in house prices is really a bad thing. Few would argue that it would not be better to have lower house prices compared to income, but the process of getting there can be very messy – especially for people who have been persuaded to order their lives around a heavy mortgage and who face the spectre of negative equity (that is, owing more than they could recover by selling their home). With high levels of homeownership, no government would deliberately bring down house prices, but rather than try and reinflate the price bubble, governments should be ensuring that such disproportionate price rises do not happen again. At the same time, they should try and help those who are in a difficult situation as a result of previous policies, being careful that any help given to homeowners is not at the expense of renters.

Rather than bemoaning the end of the 100+ per cent (or 'suicide') mortgage, governments should be actively restricting high-risk and inflationary mortgage products. And rather than encouraging a growing reliance on private landlords, and increasing inequality through a rentier economy and property speculation, governments should be cracking down on the tax benefits currently awarded to those who 'buy to let'.[3] Other fiscal measures that would reduce this gambling with people's homes could include taxing homes left empty; taxing (or even forbidding) second homes;[4] more use of capital gains and inheritance taxes; and the introduction of a land-value tax to prevent land speculation, capture any increased land values for the public good, and encourage development.[5] Dependence on housing as investment would also be reduced by the resurrection of a properly financed state pension scheme. The result of all this would be a much more stable economic system.

It will be argued that many of these changes would act to stifle investment in the needed new housing, but this is only a problem if we rely on most building being done by profit-making developers – who have not succeeded in meeting housing need in the past. Reliance on the market also creates pressure to relax important democratic and strategic controls afforded by the planning system, such as those preventing suburban sprawl. Public housing, however, does not have to make a profit for the developer, and it provides the vital key to achieving a much more fundamental solution to the housing problem. It can also provide an important and steady source of employment for those in the building trades; the current crisis has already forced the British government to recognise the importance of the construction of social housing in 'helping the house building industry weather tough times'.[6]

The type of fiscal measures outlined above could hold down prices and make house purchase a possibility for more households, but this is never going to be the answer for everyone, nor need it be. There will always be people whose financial circumstances or lifestyles make this not an option, and there is no reason why they should be penalised by an economy based on real estate. As we saw in Chapter 1, far from being a 'natural' desire, preference for homeownership has been carefully cultivated by government policy, and there have been many times and places when people who could afford to buy have chosen to rent. There is no reason why renting cannot be as attractive as ownership – even an arrangement that people would deliberately choose. In fact, this would be a significant step towards breaking down the mechanisms of social exclusion and creating a more equal society.

For renting to be as attractive as ownership, rented homes must be of good quality, rental agreements must be both secure and flexible, and rents must be genuinely affordable and significantly less than the cost of paying off a mortgage. As was found in the past, this can only be achieved through the use of subsidised social housing; which, for best value for money, as well as democratic control, should be publicly owned. (The growing tendency to rely on the private rental market clearly will not help, as the laws and demands of the market tend to reduce quality and security and increase rents, and if rents are controlled then that will suffocate supply.)

Another way of helping some of the people trapped by the present crisis would be to extend the mortgage-to-rent scheme that operates in Scotland and has just been launched in England. Unlike most of the current English schemes – which have often proved an opportunity for more speculation at the expense of the most vulnerable – these are publicly run programmes. They allow some of those who find they can no longer afford to pay their mortgage, and would otherwise be forced to leave their home, to sell it at market rates to a social landlord and become their tenant.[7] There are firm restrictions on eligibility, consistent with the general policy of keeping social renting to a minimum; but if the tenure were to be developed more generally, such schemes could become a more frequently used and more attractive option.

More public housing may sound like an expensive option from a government point of view, but it is necessary to look at the wider picture. First, there are the direct savings. Current plans for 'regeneration' that involve major reductions in social housing are dependent on government subsidies and cost much more than upgrading existing buildings. In Britain, large savings (both one-off and running costs) could also be made by ending the drive towards stock transfer and investing directly in council housing. More tenants paying low social rents means less housing benefit subsidising private landlords. But much more important than all of this, though impossible to measure, are the savings that result from better housing, better health and life chances, and greater social cohesion – which all have financial as well as social implications.

Good-quality, good-value rented housing plays a crucial role in decoupling housing from investment and returning it to its primary purpose as homes. It breaks down the social divisions between those on the housing ladder and those unable to reach it, and removes some of the massive financial burden of personal debt. (While politicians may like to portray Britain as a nation of homeowners, it is in reality a nation of debtors.[8])

Investment in expanding as well as improving public housing is also the best way to end the residualisation of the tenure that has resulted from years of under-investment and privatisation. Concerns over concentrations of poverty have led planners to adopt the mantra of 'mixed-tenure' development, despite lack of evidence of the benefits of having a homeowner next door. The main result of these policies has been the sale of publicly owned sites in city centres and more desirable districts to private developers, with social housing becoming increasingly marginalised. But if public housing were allowed to expand, then so would the social base of its tenants, generating much more stable communities.

The first step in creating an attractive rental sector is to discard assumptions that social housing should only be made available as a last resort for those who cannot find anything else. That means scrapping ill-conceived arguments about social housing need and demand, and ending large-scale demolitions (except where there really are serious structural problems). It also means no more privatisation and sell-off of the best homes. Instead, long-term tenants could be rewarded with rent holidays (which would be transferred to the new tenancy should they move), retaining their home in public ownership for future use.[9]

Next, we need investment in new public housing and in upgrading existing homes and estates. Homes that are less popular can usually be improved rather than demolished, and it is important that each place is properly analysed and understood so that any plans can tackle genuine problems: so that, for example, buildings are not demolished because one of the residents has started to deal in drugs, or even because there is a damp problem that could be resolved by over-cladding.

Improving public housing is not just about architecture and layout, though that is important; it is also about the spaces between the buildings, good local services and transport links, good maintenance, and responsive local management (that could be tenant controlled). There are plenty of examples of well-designed public housing, and this is increasingly employing green technology (in fact, despite financial constraints, British social housing must comply with higher environmental and space standards than private housing is required to follow). There are also examples of tenant management and well-used local services. However, none of this gets written about very much (outwith uncritical promotional blurbs) and there has been little attempt to research with tenants to analyse the ingredients of a successful neighbourhood. There are awards for best practice, of course, but their donors do not tend to consult much with those who live in the buildings. More needs to be done to highlight what is genuinely good as well as what is bad. And to ensure that all this works in the interests of those for whom it is built, we need to promote thriving independent tenants' organisations.

For this to become reality, governments would have to make a major shift of emphasis and look beyond the urgent demands of the market. But we have seen what happens when they don't. The proposals outlined here are not simply for better housing. They would also help improve economic stability and would result in a healthier, more equal society, which would feed back into the management and maintenance of homes and neighbourhoods in a virtuous circle.

Notes

1. This was the title of a report setting out minimum standards for new British housing that was drawn up by Parker Morris in 1961. The standards were made mandatory for all new council housing in 1969, but were abandoned in 1980.
2. Speech by the chair of Places for People to the Liberal Democrat Conference, reported by *Inside Housing*, 17 September 2008.
3. Such as the ability to offset mortgage interest against rental income when calculating tax.
4. Despite recent changes, British second homes still pay a bit less tax than first homes, rather than more. Limited restrictions on second homes are already a reality in some places. In some rural areas of Britain that are under particular pressure, local laws restrict the building of new houses for sale (and resale) as second homes or to those who are not long-term residents. Most of these laws are recent, but the area around Loch Lomond has had restrictions of this kind for over 30 years. In the summer of 2008, a government-commissioned review on the rural economy, carried out by the Liberal MP Matthew Taylor, argued that in some places, to protect the sustainability of rural communities, 'there is a case to be made for controlling (through the planning system) further conversion of full time homes into second homes and holiday lets'. ('Living Working Countryside: The Taylor Review of Rural Economy and Affordable Housing', p. 117 <http://www.communities.gov.uk/documents/planningandbuilding/pdf/livingworkingcountryside.pdf> [accessed 12 October 2008]).
5. Land Value Tax (unlike property tax) is a tax on the rental value of the land alone. This value takes account of the potential of the land,

so that changes in planning law or infrastructural developments that increase its value, bring revenue back to the wider community, and owners are encouraged to realise that potential. It is a curious tax in that it is promoted by both the political left and right (including Milton Friedman), but the difference is that the right see it as an alternative to other taxes. (This difference was the basis of Marx's criticism of Henry George's proposals too: see <http://www.marxists.org/archive/marx/works/1881/letters/81_06_20.htm>.) The suggestion here is not, of course, for an alternative to a progressive tax on income. The idea is being put forward as part of a bigger package. Land tax, like community land trusts, can reduce speculation in land, but not in houses – as this would stop development. There have been several botched attempts to introduce such a tax in Britain, but it has been argued that these have confused it with development tax; see Blundell, V.H. (1993) *Essays in Land Economics* (London: Economic and Social Science Research Association).

6. Communities Secretary Hazel Blears announcing that investment in social housing would be brought forward (though not increased), September 2008 <http://www.communities.gov.uk/news/corporate/950558> [accessed 13 October 2008].

7. See the Shelter websites for Scotland and England <http://scotland.shelter.org.uk/> and <http://england.shelter.org.uk/>; also *ROOF*, September/October 2008 for problems with private schemes. Owners in negative equity are still left in debt, but should be in a better position to be able to pay it off. The English 'mortgage rescue scheme', launched in January 2009, includes a shared ownership option and could only help 'up to 6,000 households' across the country; see *Inside Housing*, 16 January 2009.

8. In 2007, 56 per cent of English owner-occupiers had a mortgage, with less that 12 per cent of owner-occupier couples with dependent children owning their home outright <http://www.communities.gov.uk/documents/housing/doc/housingsurveysbulletin2.doc> [accessed January 2009].

9. A scheme along these lines was put forward by the Scottish Socialist Party, before it split into two.

ABOUT THE AUTHORS

Eric Clark is Professor of Human Geography and head of the Department of Social and Economic Geography at Lund University. He is editor of *Geografiska Annaler B* (Blackwell) and a Fellow of the Royal Society of Letters at Lund. He has published extensively on gentrification.
eric.clark@keg.lu.se

Sarah Glynn is a practising architect who has also been a Lecturer in Human Geography at the University of Edinburgh and has an honorary research fellowship at the University of Strathclyde. She has taught and published on housing issues, and her recent publications have included work on multiculturalism, Islamism and immigrant political mobilisation. Her academic interest in housing issues evolved out of practical involvement with tenants' organisations in Dundee, where she lives, and in other parts of Scotland.
SarahRGlynn@hotmail.com

Jason Hackworth is Associate Professor of Urban Planning and Geography at the University of Toronto. He writes about neoliberalism, social housing, and urban geographical issues. His recent book, *The Neoliberal City*, was published in 2007 by Cornell University Press.
jason.hackworth@utoronto.ca

Stuart Hodkinson is an activist researcher and private tenant, based in Leeds. He campaigns with other tenants, leaseholders and freeholders for the end to neoliberal housing policies and provides frontline action research support to all those facing the loss of their homes under privatisation, Compulsory Purchase Orders and demolitions. He also teaches and researches at the School of Geography, University of Leeds.
s.n.hodkinson@leeds.ac.uk

Karin Johnson is a PhD candidate in the Department of Social and Economic Geography at Lund University. Her research is mainly focused on gentrification in Swedish cities.
karin.johnson@humangeo.su.se

Laurence Murphy is Professor of Property at the University of Auckland Business School. He has published a number of articles in international

journals that address housing issues in New Zealand, and was part of an advisory group to the New Zealand government that led to the establishment of the Centre for Housing Research Aotearoa/New Zealand (CHRANZ).
l.murphy@auckland.ac.nz

Corinne Nativel is a Lecturer at the University of Franche-Comté in Besançon, France, where she teaches English and Economic Geography. She conducts her research within the Centre d'Études Urbaines dans le Monde Anglophone, or CEUMA (Centre for Urban Research in the Anglophone World), at the University of Paris-Sorbonne. This focuses on the relationship between urban, labour and welfare restructuring. She has authored and edited several books, including a comparative book on housing problems and policies in France and the United Kingdom, co-edited with David Fée (*Crises et politiques du logement en France et au Royaume-Uni*, Presses Sorbonne Nouvelle, 2008).
Corinne@nativel.org

Peter Phibbs is the co-ordinator of academic programmes at the Urban Research Centre, University of Western Sydney. Prior to that he was a faculty member in the Urban and Regional Planning program at the University of Sydney. He is also a researcher in the Australian Housing and Urban Research Institute network. His main research interests are the link between housing and other life outcomes and the development of affordable housing.
P.Phibbs@uws.edu.au

Peter Young is the manager of Care Housing, a not-for-profit social housing provider in the state of Queensland. Prior to that, he was the inaugural Child Safety Director, and the Director of Housing Policy and Research, at the Queensland Department of Housing. When he worked in the Department of Housing, his interests in better understanding the ways in which aspects of housing (such as security of tenure, housing quality and location) affect other aspects of people's lives (such as health, employment and education) was instrumental in this theme becoming prominent on the Australian housing research agenda.
p_g_young@yahoo.com.au

INDEX